Proceedings of the International Symposium on
Human Aspects of Information Security & Assurance (HAISA 2007)

Plymouth, United Kingdom
10 July 2007

Editors

Steven Furnell
Nathan Clarke

Information Security & Network Research Group
University of Plymouth

ISBN: 978-1-84102-174-4

Preface

It is increasingly recognised that security requirements cannot be addressed by technical means alone, and that a significant aspect of protection comes down to the attitudes, awareness, behaviour and capabilities of the people involved. Unfortunately, while people can potentially represent a key asset in achieving security, factors such as lack of awareness and understanding, combined with unreasonable demands from security technologies, can dramatically impede their ability to do so. Ensuring appropriate attention and support for the needs of users should therefore be seen as a vital element of a successful security strategy. People at all levels (i.e. from organisations to domestic environments; from system administrators to end-users) need to understand security concepts, how the issues may apply to them, and how to use the available technology to protect their systems. In addition, the technology itself can make a contribution by reducing the demands upon users, simplifying protection measures, and automating a variety of safeguards.

With the above in mind, the Human Aspects of Information Security and Assurance (HAISA) symposium specifically addresses information security issues that relate to people. It concerns the methods that inform and guide users' understanding of security, and the technologies that can benefit and support them in achieving protection.

This book represents the proceedings from the 2007 event, which was held in Plymouth, UK. A total of 14 papers are included, spanning a range of topics including the communication of risks to end-users, user-centred security in system development, and technology impacts upon personal privacy. All of the papers were subject to double-blind peer review, with each being reviewed by three members of the international programme committee.

We would like to thank the authors for submitting their work and sharing their findings, and the international programme committee for their efforts in reviewing the submissions and ensuring the quality of the resulting event and proceedings. Thanks are also due to the British Computer Society, Emerald (publishers of the sponsoring journal, *Information Management & Computer Security*), and Symantec, as the co-sponsors of the event.

Steven Furnell & Nathan Clarke
Conference Chairs, HAISA 2007

Plymouth, July 2007

About the Information Security & Network Research Group

The HAISA series is organised by the Information Security & Network Research Group (formerly the Network Research Group) at the University of Plymouth.

The Information Security & Network Research Group (ISNRG) is a specialist technology and networking research facility at the University of Plymouth. Originally established in 1985, the ISNRG conducts research in the areas of IT Security, Internet & WWW technologies and Mobility. The group has a proven pedigree including projects conducted for, and in collaboration with, commercial companies, as well as participation in European research initiatives. Over the years, our research activities have led to numerous successful projects, along with associated publications and patents.

At the time of writing, the ISNRG has eight affiliated full-time academic staff and twenty-six research degree projects (at PhD and MPhil levels). The group also supports Masters programmes in Information Systems Security, Web Technologies & Security, Network Systems Engineering, and eCommerce, and hosts a significant number of research-related projects from these programmes.

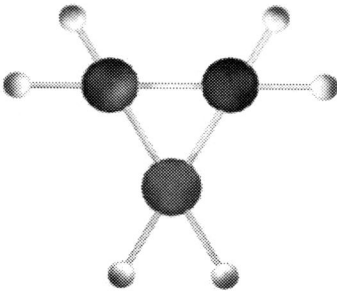

Address	Information Security & Network Research Group University of Plymouth Drake Circus Plymouth PL4 8AA United Kingdom
Telephone	+44 (0) 1752 232621
Fax	+44 (0) 1752 233520
Email	info@network-research-group.org
URL	www.network-research-group.org

International Programme Committee

Helen Armstrong	Curtin University	Australia
William Buchanan	Napier University	United Kingdom
Nathan Clarke	University of Plymouth	United Kingdom
Jeff Crume	IBM	United States
Dorothy Denning	Naval Postgraduate School	United States
Ronald Dodge	United States Military Academy	United States
Paul Dowland	University of Plymouth	United Kingdom
Jan Eloff	University of Pretoria	South Africa
Simone Fischer-Huebner	Karlstad University	Sweden
Kevin Fitzgerald	Fitzgerald InfoSec	Australia
Steven Furnell	University of Plymouth	United Kingdom
Ed Gibson	Microsoft	United Kingdom
Sarah Gordon	Symantec	United States
Dimitris Gritzalis	Athens University of Economics & Business	Greece
Stefanos Gritzalis	University of the Aegean	Greece
John Howie	Microsoft	United States
William Hutchinson	Edith Cowan University	Australia
Murray Jennex	San Diego State University	United States
Andy Jones	British Telecom	United Kingdom
	Edith Cowan University	Australia
Jorma Kajava	University of Lapland	Finland
Vasilios Katos	University of Portsmouth	United Kingdom
Sokratis Katsikas	University of the Aegean	Greece
David Lacey	David Lacey Consulting	United Kingdom
Costas Lambrinoudakis	University of the Aegean	Greece
Michael Lavine	John Hopkins University	United States
Javier Lopez	University of Malaga	Spain
Martin Olivier	University of Pretoria	South Africa
Maria Papadaki	University of Plymouth	United Kingdom
Malcolm Pattinson	University of South Australia	Australia
Andy Phippen	University of Plymouth	United Kingdom
Paul Reynolds	Orange	United Kingdom
Corey Schou	Idaho State University	United States
Rossouw von Solms	Nelson Mandela Metropolitan University	South Africa
Jeffrey Stanton	Syracuse University	United States
Kim Vu	California State University	United States
Jeremy Ward	Symantec EMEA	United Kingdom
Merrill Warkentin	Mississippi State University	United States
Matthew Warren	Deakin University	Australia
Chris Wills	Kingston University	United Kingdom
Louise Yngstrom	Stockholm University	Sweden
Mary Ellen Zurko	IBM	United States

Contents

An Information Security Reporting Architecture for Information Security Visibility

M. Viljoen[1], R. von Solms[2] and M. Gerber[3]

Centre for Information Security Studies, Nelson Mandela Metropolitan University,
Port Elizabeth, South Africa

[1]s20310694@nmmu.ac.za, [2]rossouw@nmmu.ac.za, [3]Mariana.Gerber@nmmu.ac.za

Abstract

The importance of information in business today has made the need to properly secure this asset evident. Information security has become a responsibility for all managers of an organization. To better support more efficient management of information security (IS), timely IS information should be made available to all managers. This paper discusses an Information Security Reporting System Architecture that aims to improve the visibility and contribute to better management of IS throughout an organization by enabling the provision of summarized, comprehensive IS information to all managers.

Keywords

Information security, information security reporting architecture, information security visibility, information security management.

1. Introduction

Information has and will continue to be seen as an extremely important asset in today's business environment (Business Link, 2006; Ernest & Young, 2006). It is, therefore, important that an organization recognizes the critical need to properly protect and secure their information like they would any other valuable asset, for example, their financial assets (Business Link, 2006; ISO, 2006). It is also important that every member of the organization recognize that they play a role and share responsibility for the organizations information security (IS). This is especially true of managers who are responsible for directing and controlling the assets they are answerable for (Whitman and Mattord, 2004). If every member of an organization is to be able to have a share in information security it follows that every person, and especially managers in the organization, should have access to relevant information about the organization's IS. It is therefore important that the appropriate IS reports are available to people at all levels of an organization.

Today there are dozens of tools that can be used to gather and report on IS information (Insecure.org, 2006). Each of these tools have there different strengths and weakness but no single tool is able to completely report on all information security concerns to all levels of the organization. It is, therefore, often difficult for management to see the 'big picture' with regard to information security (B. Robison, 2005).

The objective of this article is to describe and motivate an architecture that makes use of existing network monitoring and reporting tools to enable reporting of IS information to all levels of an organization. This architecture should enable the organizations to have available a customizable, summarized and comprehensive overview of information security. It should enhance the visibility of information security in the organization and should assist managers at different levels of the organization to direct and control appropriate information security concerns more effectively. A prototype has been developed, based on the recommended architecture, as a proof of concept. The prototype system is called the Information Security Reporting System (ISRS). The recommended architecture is referred to as the ISRS architecture.

Before beginning with the description of the architecture, some desirable characteristics for an ISRS architecture that supports efficient information security management will briefly be discussed.

2. Desirable characteristics for ISRF

Managers have the responsibility for directing and controlling the individuals and assets under them in an organization. They will direct (let people know what they have to do) and control (make adjustments as it becomes necessary) these assets in a way that will enable the organization to meet its objectives (Marchewka, 2003). One of the important objectives of an organization should be information security (Whitman and Mattord, 2004). Information security is such an important concern that in many countries a failure to demonstrate due diligence may lead to legal liability (Frazer, 2005; Whitman and Mattord, 2004). Managers should therefore accept responsibility for directing and controlling information security concerns under there sphere of influence. As mentioned above, this is true for managers at all levels of the organization. This includes: staff like CIO, CISO, network and system administrators who work directly with information technology or information security; members of the board and board committees that are responsible for the governance of the organization and managers of other departments of the organization (Corporate Governance Task Force, 2004). The corporate governance task force recommends that there should be a manager in each organizational unit responsible for information security concerns under the control of that organizational unit. They contend that management responsibilities include conducting risk assessments for their units, implementing policies and procedures and testing that information security controls and techniques are being implemented properly for their unit (Corporate Governance Task Force, 2004). If managers are going to have these responsibilities it follows that they should be equipped with IS information. An architecture that effectively facilitates the reporting of this information will include some of the desirable characteristics mentioned below.

A good reporting system should be configurable to meet the needs of the different managers. Different managers will have different responsibilities and amounts of influence when it comes to information security. For example a manager in the human resource department, a manager in the information technology department and the CEO of an organization are all going to have different responsibilities, amounts of influence and interest in information security. It is therefore important that each manager receives appropriate IS information that pertains to that manager.

Furthermore, it would be of great value if the relevant information for a particular user is presented in a manner that is easy to understand and shows the state of IS as a whole or the state of a particular IS concern at a glance. This will contribute to enabling managers to take corrective actions as they see that things are going wrong.

An ISRS architecture will also be of value if it assists managers to measure how well they comply with internationally accepted IS standards. Standards and policies are essential for the proper management of information security (Whitman and Mattord, 2004; Purser, 2004). Security standards, such as ISO/IEC 17799, prove invaluable in helping managers at the governance level to define information security goals, organizational information security standards and effective management practices (ISO, 2005). It is also valuable for information security policy development.

It would, moreover, be desirable if the ISRS is highly extensible and flexible in that it allow for different tools to be easily integrated with the system. Although security standards, such as ISO/IEC 17799, will provide general guidance, each organization is different, and will make use of different tools and technologies to implement their information security controls. The amount of money that an organization has to spend on information security alone will cause different organizations to have tools and systems that differ widely. Today there are dozens of tools that can be used to gather and report on IS information (Insecure.org, 2006). Insecure.org mentions some of these such as SNORT, Nessus, NetStumbler, Nmap, MBSA. As mentioned before, each of these tools have there different strengths and weakness but no single tool is able to completely report on all information security concerns to all levels of the organization. This often makes it difficult for management to see the 'big picture' with regard to information security. Advances in technology will also undoubtedly lead to the development of new and improved monitoring and reporting tools that make new IS information available. There are also organizations that have IS tools that have been custom written for them. The challenge is therefore to develop architecture that easily interfaces with different tools and modules as the need arises to gather information form these different tools and to present it in a useful manner.

It would be beneficial to have an architecture that is scalable and supports large or small heterogeneous distributed environments. Many organizations today have IT infrastructures that incorporate different platforms. For example it is not uncommon

3

for one organization to run Windows and UNIX operating systems. There is also a lot of work been done in the area of distributed computing. An architecture that allows for interfacing across platforms to gather and report on IS information would therefore be of great value.

Another desirable characteristic of an ISRS is that it will facilitate new ways of correlating and analyzing data. It would be useful to pool information gathered by different tools with different file formats and application programming interfaces such as SNORT, Nessus, NetStumbler, Nmap, MBSA in such a way that allows one to find new relationships between the information form each tool, show the history of the specific information gathered, do new forms of analysis on the combined information etcetera.

In summary it can be said that the desirable characteristics for ISRS architecture should include that it will be standards based, highly extensible, distributable and show the overall, summarized state of information security at a glance.

In the following section an ISRS architecture will be described as an envisioned solution that includes these desirable features.

3. ISRS Architecture

An ISRS architecture has been designed to incorporate the desirable features described above. A prototype system based on this architecture has been developed to test and demonstrate the feasibility of an ISRS that integrates information from different toolsets, and makes it visible to managers at different levels of an organization.

In developing the ISRS architecture the assumption was made that the best approach for an organization would be to link all their information security initiatives to controls specified by best practice standards such as ISO/IEC 17799 or CobiT. Every control is linked to a set of key performance indicators that are used to indicate the measure of compliance with that control. The ISRS accomplishes this by means of a survey component that is based on the SANS Audit Checklist compiled by the SANS institute (Thiagarajan, 2006). The checklist is based on the ISO/IEC 17799:2005 standard. This checklist consists of 11 main categories. These categories are used as security areas or controls in the current prototype implementation of the ISRS architecture. The key performance indicators can be grouped into the following categories: survey results, the progress of tasks or activities, and metrics.

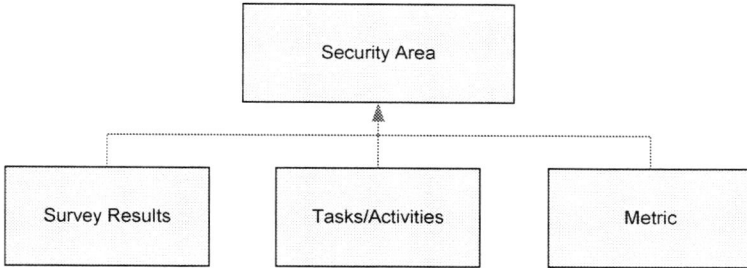

Figure 1: Categories of key performance indicators that are linked to security areas in the current prototype implementation of the ISRS architecture.

Each security area has a number of questions (based on the SANS audit checklist) related to it. In the ISRS system each of these questions can be assigned a weighting to indicate the level of importance that the company assigns to that question. The question also has three other important attributes associated with it. These are: The *"min acceptable"* value. This value indicates the minimum percentage of compliance that is accepted by that company for that specific question. The *"desired value"* to indicate to what level the company would like to have compliance with the question. The "actual value" which indicates to what extent the company is complying with the question.

Besides the questions a security area can also have a number of tasks related to it. With the ISRS system users can be assigned tasks that are related to one or more security areas. The task progress is updated by users to reflect whether the tasks progress is *acceptable, good* or *unacceptable*. A task is also assigned as critical or not.

A security area can also have security metrics associated with it. A metric can be gathered by means of available tools, modules or by audit/survey components. To illustrate a metric could be percentage of updates completely installed on machines in an organization. The information for this metric can be collected from tools like MBSA and Nessus by means of web service based modules. A metric could also be percentage compliance with the organizations physical security policy and information for this metric could simply be collected from a completed electronic questionnaire. Like the questions from the SANS audit checklist, a metric has "min acceptable", "desirable" and "actual values" associated with it.

The overall health of a security area is determined by using the weights and values associated with the questions, tasks and metrics associated with that area. The benefit of this approach is that it provides the managers of the organization with a standards-based way to look at IS and enables the level of compliance with controls to be displayed simply. By means of portal software and an operational database it is possible to link specific users to key performance areas and/or to specific metrics. This contributes to making it possible to display the relevant information to different individuals.

Another desirable characteristic of an ISRS is that it will facilitate new ways of correlating and analyzing data. To meet this objective the ISRS architecture makes use of a data warehouse to store the IS information gathered. Within the data warehouse there is a general purpose star schema that can be used to store the general information about metrics. If this general purpose schema does not meet the needs of the metric and information that has to be stored in relation to it another star schema will have to be added to the warehouse. Data warehouses are designed especially so that this type of analysis and can be done efficiently and easily to improve decision support (Kimball and Ross, 2002).

Yet another desirable characteristic of a good ISRS would be that it be extensible and distributable. The ISRS architecture allows for a system that would accomplish this by making use of a service oriented architecture approach. Figure 1.2 depicts the components of the ISRS architecture as described below. Briefly ISRF makes use of web services to interface with and retrieve certain information from existing monitoring and reporting tools. A Data Access web service is used to write the information to a data warehouse and to access information from the warehouse and operational database. A scheduler is a program that queries the operational database for a list of jobs (web service functions) that it must run and information pertaining to the running of these jobs and then makes the necessary calls to the web services that encapsulate the monitoring and reporting tools. Web service interfaces to various visualization tools can be plugged in to facilitate the visualization of the information stored in the data warehouse. The use of web services to encapsulate existing tools makes sense for a number of reasons. Different organizations may for many reasons have a wide array of monitoring tools that collect information security information running in their systems. With this framework, when a new tool becomes available it is easy to retrieve the information it exposes by writing a new web service that can interface with the tool or make use of an existing web service. Which web service should be called, how often this should be done and other information to do with the invocation of this service must then simple be added to the operational database from where the scheduler will retrieve it and invoke the service. The service will in turn have the responsibility of interfacing with the data access web service to store the data in the appropriate place in the data warehouse. As can be seen this approach to gathering information is very extensible because new tools and the metric associated with these tools can easily be integrated into the system as the need arises. Web services are commonly used to provide a standard way of remotely invoking functionality across different platforms (Kalani and Kalani, 2003, p 288-290). This makes the framework highly scalable and flexible since it means that the different tools and web services used can either all be located on a single machine, or they can exist on different virtual machines one a single physical machine (which allows for a box that can be plugged into a machine and with a bit of configuration can be used as a tool to provide information security reports for an organization), or they can be distributed across the infrastructure of an organization.

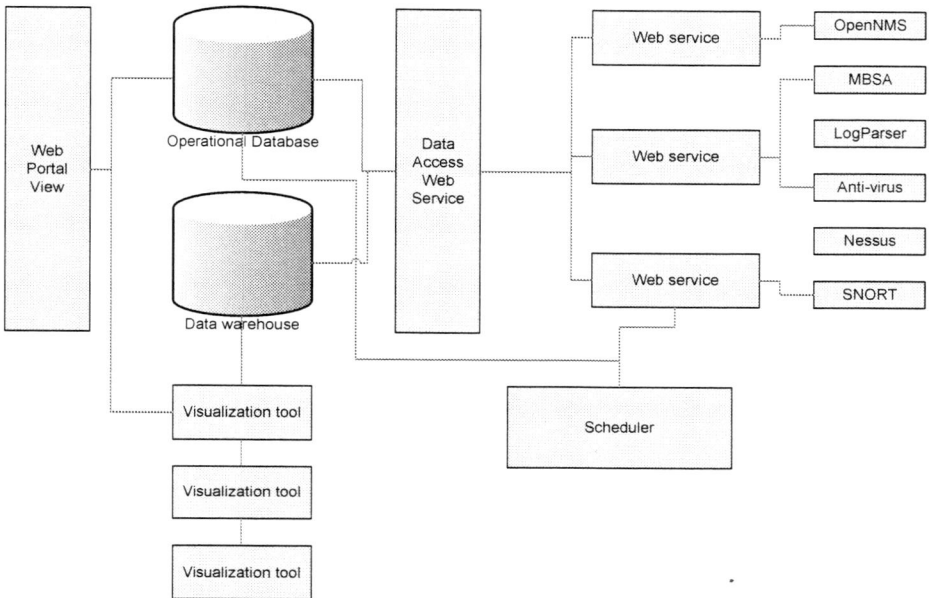

Figure 2: Components of an ISRS architecture.

The following illustrates how this architecture could be used practically. The ISO 17799 control number 6, Communications and Operations Management requires that there are controls implemented to detect, prevent and recover from malicious code. A member of the board may want to know what initiatives and controls are in place to protect the organization against malicious software and to what extent have the controls been implemented. The board may also wish to see evidence that the situation with regard to malicious software is improving over time. Suitable metrics to measure performance in this area might be the percentage of systems with up to date anti-virus patterns installed. The ISRS system should be able to gather information from the anti-virus system (possibly though a web based management interface used by the AV system or maybe from log files created by the AV system). The ISRS system will likely store the information in a data warehouse, and make it visible through a visualization subsystem.

4. Conclusion

The ISRS architecture has several features that make it a desirable approach to follow when implementing an ISRS to improve visibility of information security in the organization and to use as a means to aid in better management of information security throughout an organization.

By following a standards-based approach and making use of technologies such as web services, data warehouses, operational databases and visualization tools the architecture should be able to be used to enhance the visibility of information security in the organization. It should also allow for a customizable, summarized and comprehensive overview of IS concerns to managers. This should in turn help managers to direct and control IS concerns more efficiently. The principles of service oriented architecture applied in the design of the architecture also make the ISRS extensible, flexible and distributable.

References

Business Link. (2006). Information security best Practice [Online]. URL http://www.businesslink.gov.uk/bdotg/action/printguide?r.l1=1073861197&r.l3=1075406921 &topicId=1075406921&r.t=RESOURCES&r.i=1075406928&r.l2=1075408323&r.s=pg

Cisco systems. (2006). Simple network management protocol. [Online] http://www.cisco.com/univercd/cc/td/doc/cisintwk/ito_doc/snmp.htm

Corporate Governance Task Force. (2004). Information security governance: a call to action [Online]. URL http://www.cyberpartnership.org/ InfoSecGov4 04.pdf

Ernst & Young. (2006). Achieving Success in a Globalized World: Is Your Way Secure? Global Information Security Survey 2006 [online]. URL http://www.ey.com/global/content.nsf/International/Assurance_&_Advisory_- _Technology_and_Security_Risk__Global_Information_Security_Survey_2006

Frazer, A. (2005). Sarbanes-Oxley Compliance Journal. Due Diligence risks in network security. [Online] URL http://www.s-ox.com/Feature/detail.cfm?articleID=1148

Insecure.org (2006). Top 100 network security tools. [Online] URL http://sectools.org/

ISO. (2006). ISO/IEC 17799:2005 Information technology - Security techniques - Code of practice for information security management [Online]. URL http://www.iso.org/iso/en/prods- services/popstds/informationsecurity.html

Kalani, A., Kalani, P. (2003). MCAD/MCSD Developing XML Web Services and Server Components with Visual C# .NET amd Microsoft .NET Framework. USA:Que Publishing.

Marchewka, J.T. (2003). Information technology project management. Providing Measurable Organizational value. USA:John Wiley & Sons.

Purser, S. (2004). A practical guide to managing information security. [Online] URL http://books.google.co.za/books?id=mczgkqHSIXUC&dq=why+are+information+security+sta ndards+so+important&pg=PA147&ots=uY2Zws5uD4&sig=--T3VZUI0Fg4fir6vsc- 9MmsztU&prev=http://www.google.co.za/search%3Fhl%3Den%26q%3Dwhy%2Bare%2Binf ormation%2Bsecurity%2Bstandards%2Bso%2Bimportant%26meta%3D&sa=X&oi=print&ct =result&cd=2#PPR9,M1

Robison, B. (2005). Security dashboard - Are high-level views the answer to getting managers the cybersecurity status information they need to make decisions? [Online] URL http://www.fcw.com/article91327-11-07-05-Print#related

Swanson, D. (n.d.). IT compliance Institute. Ask the Auditor: Who is responsible for information security [Online]. URL http://www.itcinstitute.com/display.aspx?id=1823.

Thiagarajan, V. (2006). SANS Audit Checklist. [Online] URL http://www.sans.org/score/checklists/ISO_17799_2005.pdf?portal=f36013c72bc89932f16f84f4f89245dc

van den Bogaerdt, A. (2006). rrdtutorial. [Online] URL http://oss.oetiker.ch/rrdtool/tut/rrdtutorial.en.html

Whitman, M.E., Mattord, H.J. (2004). Management of information security. Canada:Thomson course technology.

Proceedings of the International Symposium on
Human Aspects of Information Security & Assurance (HAISA 2007)

Institutionalising Information Security Culture in Australian SMEs: Framework and Key Issues

S. Dojkovski, S. Lichtenstein and M.J. Warren

School of Information Systems,
Deakin University, Australia.

sneza.dojkovski@deakin.edu.au; sharman.lichtenstein@deakin.edu.au;
matthew.warren@deakin.edu.au

Abstract

Many companies would prefer employees to follow information security practices naturally rather than by management directives and enforcement. The paper reports some of the main findings from a large interpretive research project involving a literature review, three case studies and two focus groups, conducted in Australia. Findings include a framework for fostering information security culture in Australian SMEs and a discussion of key issues. The paper highlights the criticality of both the SME owner role and the national context in fostering information security culture in SMEs. Implications for theory and practice are discussed.

Keywords

Information security culture, small and medium-size enterprises.

1. Introduction

One of the most important areas for information security management is employee misuse and abuse of information assets, also known as the "insider threat" (Furnell et al., 2000). According to recent reports, employee misuse and abuse of internet services comprise 20 - 50 per cent of internet incidents (AusCERT, 2006; CSI/FBI, 2006). Whether employees are inclined to behave securely in their use of company information systems can be viewed socio-culturally. The socio-technical perspective may best reflect employee behaviour with information security technologies. This new approach to managing the insider threat is the institutionalisation of information security practices as an *information security culture*. The potential effectiveness of adopting a socio-cultural approach is highlighted by recent findings from Galletta and Polak (2003) that peer and supervisory culture may strongly influence internal internet abuse.

However currently there is very little guidance available for small and medium size enterprises (SMEs) in the development of an information security culture and the issues to be faced along the way. SMEs typically have different managerial concerns to large enterprises - for example, they may possess fewer resources and may lack internal information technology expertise. In addition, existing conceptual frameworks for the development of information security culture are mainly aimed at large organisations. Often, such frameworks centre only on managerial directives such as policies and procedures to perform the task of enculturation. New conceptual frameworks are needed that integrate the complexities of behaviour modification and cultural change with managerial directives, and that accommodate the special characteristics of SMEs operating in a unique national context such as Australia – the context for this research. Such frameworks should be based not only on existing theory but on the real world experiences of SMEs and the IT professionals who provide them with services.

This paper reports some of the main findings from a recent research project that explored this topic. The project involved a literature review, three case studies and two focus groups. Early results from the project were reported in Dojkovski et al., (2005, 2006). This paper provides the final framework, and presents a discussion of key issues of interest arising from the study.

The rest of the paper is structured as follows. Following this section, the paper provides a theoretical background for the research. It then overviews the research design for the study. A section then provides a conceptual framework for developing and maintaining information security culture in SMEs, developed from the study. Next, key findings are discussed, and finally, conclusions are drawn.

2. Theoretical Review

This section synthesises representative contemporary literature on information security culture and reviews the unique challenges of SMEs concerning information security culture.

2.1 Information Security Culture

As mentioned earlier, recent research aims to better manage the insider threat by developing an information security culture (OECD, 2002). Experts have previously proposed conceptual frameworks for information security management that include information security cultural development based on management initiatives of policy, awareness, training, and education (for example Lichtenstein and Swatman, 2001). However, such frameworks may be better suited to medium and large size organisations due to their significant infrastructure, stability and resources requirements. In recent years, dedicated frameworks for information security culture have been developed, as reviewed below.

Several frameworks have focused on organisational culture and the measurement of information security culture. Schlienger & Teufel (2000; 2003) describe a framework concentrating on a socio-cultural approach that is based on trust and partnership, accompanied by appropriate security technologies and employee security awareness.

To address weaknesses in information security, Siponen (2000) constructs a conceptual foundation for organisational security awareness based on prescriptive persuasion based on behavioural principles. The model consists of motivation principles, theory of planned behaviour and a technological acceptance model.

Also addressing awareness, Von Solms discussed the stages of information security awareness maturity (von Solms, 2000) culminating in an institutional stage, which involves cultivating an information security culture through standardisation, certification and paying attention to the human aspect of information security. An emphasis is placed on the continuous measurement of information security for proper management.

In another framework, Chia and colleagues (2002) argue that an information security culture has not yet been clearly defined. They identified the following important dimensions for measuring the effectiveness of information security culture: a belief in the importance of information security; balancing of long- and short term goals, policies, procedures and processes; continuous improvement; cooperation and collaboration; attention to objectives; and audit compliance. However, this list was recently criticised by Helokunnas and Kuusisto (2003) for de-emphasising the human aspects of information security.

A structured framework for information security culture was developed by Martins and Eloff (2002). Their framework is comprised of individual, group and organisational levels of information security enculturation. Issues that promote adequate information security culture were identified in each group. The effect of change agents on these issues will transform the organisational culture to an effective information security culture.

Helokunnas & Iivonen (2003) provide a framework based on shared values. The research looked at the values that a group of Finnish SMEs in the Tampere Region held in relation to security and developed a security framework based upon their beliefs and values.

Van Niekerk and von Solms (2003) examine the role that education plays in the establishment of information security culture. Their approach centres on the concept of an outcomes-based education forming the basis of cultural change, and they show how such an approach can play a positive role in creating a culture of information security.

A conceptual checklist of information security culture consisting of a compilation of information security and organisation culture concepts was proposed by Zakaria and Gani (2003). The model consists of three levels with analytical dimensions such as surface manifestations (artefacts, ceremonial, course, hero, language, motto, myth, norm, physical layout, rite, ritual, slogan, story and symbol), values (confidentiality, integrity, availability, authentication non-repudiation and legitimate use of information) and basic assumptions (mission and strategy, goals, means, measurement and remedial strategies) relevant to information security identified for each level.

A socio-technical perspective was proposed by (Stanton et al., 2004). In their framework they focus on the human actions that influence the confidentiality, integrity and availability of information systems. They suggest that security-oriented end-user behaviours are derived from a combination of relevant situational and personal factors and improving information security culture is done by examining the motivational antecedents of employees, such as situational and personal factors combined with a variety of interventions.

A framework based on informal methods was proposed by Vroom and von Solms, (2004) whereby the behaviour and culture of an organisation at all levels is examined in an informal fashion. They suggest that studying organisational behaviour and how employees are influenced would prove useful in improving the security culture of an organisation. They suggest behaviour be separated into three groups of: the individual, the group and the formal organisation. Each level needs to be examined simultaneously with how it impacts the culture of the organisation.

A framework based on personnel capabilities was proposed by Furnell and Clarke (2005) who suggest security awareness, training and education as important elements in establishing an information security culture. Management addressing the security risks and what awareness, training and education could do to combat these risks. They also suggest that a 'one size fits all' approach will not work, and that a company must determine which approaches will work in a given context.

While the above frameworks are clearly valuable, they portray a fragmented theoretical field and lack integration across the different areas of focus. Further, they do not address the unique challenges faced by SMEs operating in a national context.

2.2 Information Security Culture and SMEs

SMEs suffer special disadvantages compared with large organisations in pursuing an information security culture. First, SMEs generally possess a weak understanding of information security, security technologies and control measures (Dimopoulos et al., 2004). Second, they lack the funds, time and specialised knowledge needed to coordinate information security or offer effective information security awareness, training and education (Furnell et al., 2000; Dimopoulos et al., 2004). Third, SMEs are unlikely to have yet reached the stage of policy, procedure and responsibility definition (Helokunnas & Iivonen, 2003) let alone addressed the cultural issues. Fourth, they are susceptible to peculiar national influences such as the collapse of Australian information security coordination programs for businesses arising from the recent demise of the National Organisation for the Information Economy (NOIE)

(Warren, 2003). Fifth, recent studies highlight various SME concerns regarding the difficulties of developing an information security culture (Taylor & Murphy, 2004).

3. Research Design

This section overviews the conduct of the research study, which was an interpretivist study. A literature review was first conducted and an initial conceptual framework for fostering information security culture in Australian SMEs developed as a result (Dojkovski et al., 2005). The review also helped to develop questions for an exploratory focus group ("Focus group 1") held in November 2005 with four participants (representatives of SME IT service providers in the Geelong region of Australia). A focus group transcript analysis resulted in a revised conceptual model (Dojkovski et al., 2006).

Next, three in-depth interpretivist case studies explored the key issues and framework in greater detail. Three SMEs from technical industries in regional Geelong, Australia, were studied. Seven semi-structured one hour interviews were conducted with a total of seven participants in 2006. Interview questions were drawn from literature and participants were also asked about each element of the conceptual framework. Case study findings were used to further refine the framework.

To validate this framework, a final validation focus group with four participants was conducted. Three participants were from technically-oriented SMEs in the Geelong region and one was a national expert in IT security. The focus group validated each element of the framework and suggested several final enhancements resulting in a final version of the framework, described next. A transcript analysis also revealed other important findings, some of which will be reported later in this paper.

4. Conceptual Framework for Fostering Information Security Culture for SMEs

Figure 1 provides an issue-based conceptual framework for developing information security culture in SMEs in a national context, derived from the study. The framework is divided into three groups of elements: Organisational, External and Outputs. It is overviewed below and, due to paper size constraints, will be discussed in more detail in future publications.

4.1 Organisational Elements

Leadership/Corporate Governance: Corporate governance is concerned with managing the business operation of an organisation and administering the optimal utilisation of its resources. IT security governance is a subset of corporate governance and can be extended to address the issues and implications to business of security responsibilities.

Organisational Culture: Organisations already have their own values and cultures established. By working together, the interaction of these values and cultures can promote effective information security in organisations.

Managerial: There are many managerial activities and initiatives that might attempt to develop information security culture in SMEs.

- Risk Analysis/Asset Loss Protection: An asset loss protection process provides an approach to risk analysis that may motivate SME owners to focus on information security management and issues.
- Budget: A budget is needed for information security, especially in SMEs where resourcing may easily be overlooked. This will enable cultural initiatives such as training to be resourced.
- Policies and Procedures: information security policies and procedures are required to direct required and acceptable employee information security behaviour.
- Response: Procedures to respond quickly and satisfactorily to new information security issues (for example breaches) as they arise will also be beneficial in stressing the importance of information security to employees.
- Self Assessment: Every element of the management program should be regularly self-assessed seeking continuous improvement.
- Employment Contract/Handbook. During the induction of new employees it is important to use an employment contract or company handbook outlining what management regards as important information security information, policies and procedures and place restrictions and/or offer incentives.
- Management: As managers are responsible for information security and are role models for employees, they must model excellent information security behaviour.
- Assessment: Periodic assessment of each managerial element allows for continuous improvement.

Individual and Organisational Learning: For smaller organisations, a process of organisational learning from individual to an organisational level is needed. In SMEs there is likely to be a variation in, e-learning, training and education needs for individual employees.

Organisational Security Awareness: Informal awareness activities such as brown bag lunches are needed Marketing of these activities is needed.

Framework for Establishing an Information Security Culture
in Australian Small and Medium Size Enterprises

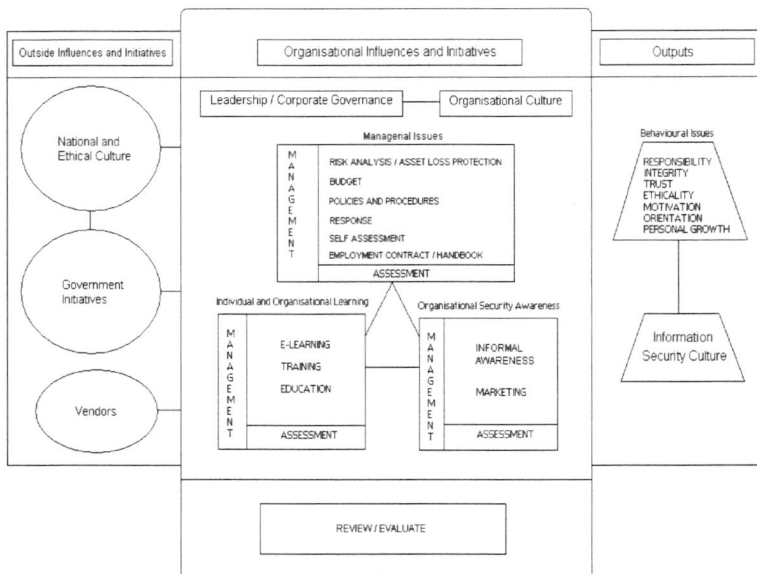

| Outside Influences and Initiatives | Organisational Influences and Initiatives | Outputs |

Leadership / Corporate Governance — Organisational Culture

National and Ethical Culture

Managerial Issues

MANAGEMENT
RISK ANALYSIS / ASSET LOSS PROTECTION
BUDGET
POLICIES AND PROCEDURES
RESPONSE
SELF ASSESSMENT
EMPLOYMENT CONTRACT / HANDBOOK
ASSESSMENT

Behavioural Issues
RESPONSIBILITY
INTEGRITY
TRUST
ETHICALITY
MOTIVATION
ORIENTATION
PERSONAL GROWTH

Government Initiatives

Individual and Organisational Learning

MANAGEMENT
E-LEARNING
TRAINING
EDUCATION
ASSESSMENT

Organisational Security Awareness

MANAGEMENT
INFORMAL AWARENESS
MARKETING
ASSESSMENT

Information Security Culture

Vendors

REVIEW / EVALUATE

Figure 1: Conceptual framework for fostering information security culture in SMEs in a national context.

4.2 External Influences and Initiatives

National and Ethical Culture: Different nations may have their own values and cultures which will impact the development of culture and must be considered by government and IT vendors, as summarised below.

Government Initiatives: In the Australian context, the national government (federal and state) can provide benchmarking, tax break incentives for implementing security procedures and technologies, training and education programs and implementation information, among other initiatives.

IT *vendors* have an important role to play to raise information security awareness for SMEs.

4.3 Outputs

Behavioural Issues: External and internal measures should develop the behavioural traits (in employees) needed for an effective information security culture. These traits are identified below.

Responsibility refers to employees needing to understand rules and responsibilities. *Integrity* refers to an employee feeling part of the company and thus identifying with its norms and morals and handling information with due integrity. Employees and management must *trust* one another. Finally, employees should behave *ethically*.

Employee motivation, orientation and *personal growth* are also important to consider when developing organisational culture. Such behavioural issues will influence the effectiveness of information security culture in SMEs. When employees are motivated, aligned to the organisation's objectives, and learning and improving their skills and knowledge, the information security culture will be strengthened.

Review/Evaluate: SME's should periodically review their information security measures in order to use lessons learned to continuously improve the information security culture.

5. Discussion

This section summarises information security at the three case organisations (a greater description is not possible due to paper size constraints), followed by a discussion of a range of issues that arose throughout the project. As this is qualitative interpretivist research, the voices of participants are provided to better highlight the issues.

5.1 Case Study Analysis: Information Security Culture at Organisations A, B and C

Organisation A is a small company specialising in engineering consulting with fifteen employees. Organisation B is a small IT consultancy company with three employees. Organisation C is also a small IT consultancy with two employees. Thus, it would be expected that at least some of the employees would possess some technical skills and be able to follow information security practices.

However, of the organisations interviewed, only organisation A had an information security policy and procedures in the organisation, although only a few of the employees were aware of the policy and knew that it should be implemented. Information security was not a priority in any of the organisations and very little effort was put into managing and implementing it effectively. Management in all of the organisations was of the opinion that information security was not a priority. However there was still a high expectation from employees regarding information security behaviour. Both employees and management were uncertain whether the level of security in the organisation was adequate, and believed that information security was not yet enculturated in their firms.

The broader findings from the overall project involving two focus groups and three case studies are now examined

5.2 Information Security Awareness, Budget and Risk analysis in Australian SMEs

According to focus group (1 and 2) participants, information security risks for Australian SMEs have increased as a result of greater internet access however the level of information security awareness in SMEs has not kept apace and remains low. A lack of awareness is a contributing factor to many Australian SME owners not having recognised the existence of an information security problem in their organisation, and thus their unwillingness to allocate a budget to this area. For example, one case study participant noted:

Employees and management don't have an awareness of security issues and the consequences of such issues. [SME owner, Organisation B]

According to focus group participants, very few Australian SMEs allocate a budget to information security. This was thought to be because SME owners must first clearly see the risks involved before they would acknowledge the need for a budget (and time) for information security.

...[budget is] probably the biggest obstacle. [It is] hard to get smaller companies to set a budget for information security. [SME owner, Organisation A]

In order for SME owners to acknowledge the risks, focus group participants argued that a risk analysis was essential. However, convincing SME owners to conduct a risk analysis currently presents a challenge. According to IT consultants in the initial exploratory focus group (focus group 1), clients do not trust IT vendors and consultants and do not wish to pay for a risk analysis which they feel is aimed at selling them IT security products. Organisations B and C expressed the view that their companies were too small to conduct a risk analysis. Participants in the validation focus group (focus group 2) suggested that the Australian government provide sample security risk scenarios derived from sources such as the SANS Institute in the US. Such scenarios would emphasise asset loss protection in order to attract the interest of SMEs. As one participant conceptualised it:

So federal government does their thing - you know, handing out templates - and then you have the state government ... roll it out to businesses who are [just] commencing (starting up). [SME Owner, Focus Group 2]

Further to the issue of awareness, it was noted in one of the focus groups that as SMEs generally do not have an IT department, they do not have internal knowledge of security issues and risks, unlike large organisations with dedicated in-house staff and budgets allocated to IT security. It was thought to follow on that SME owners would have the belief that information security is only a significant concern for large businesses.

Three case study participants also suggested that another challenge to being security conscious in SMEs was because management was preoccupied with the running of day-to-day business operations and was only reactive concerning security matters. For example, in one case organisation it was remarked that:

It is very hard to raise awareness as owners are generally too busy with other business issues to worry about security. [SME owner, Organisation B]

It was also suggested by focus group participants that IT vendors can play a key role in raising security awareness within SMEs. However it was noted that before they can provide information security information, they must (somehow) prove themselves trustworthy as SMEs can feel they are being marketed IT security technologies. In the past, IT vendors had issued numerous security warnings of viruses and other risks that never eventuated. As one participant recalled:

… there was a lot of hoo-ha (fuss) about the Year 2000 bug and, you know, we all sat down expecting our whole computer society to crash - and it didn't! [SME owner, Focus group 1]

5.3 Behavioural Issues

Commenting on the behavioural issues, participants in the focus groups and case studies supported the need for such behavioural traits in employees. They believed it would be very difficult to change a person's sense of responsibility, trust, ethicality and personal growth and that it is almost impossible to change a person's sense of integrity, values, orientation and motivation. For example:

I see that as a core value that comes from childhood. Ethics, values, trust and integrity - they're all core values that are very, very difficult to change. Almost impossible! [SME owner, Focus group 1]

It was also noted that workers often refuse to be held responsible for information security breaches and that personal behaviour is not easily changed by a policy document. It was suggested that it was better to hire the "right" person than to attempt to shape a worker into the "right" person.

5.4 Management Initiatives

Participants agreed that appropriate management initiatives can help shape employee information security behaviour. They suggested that policies and procedures should be marketed to employees with the timing and manner of such marketing deemed important. Many participants felt that policies were generally too long and often not easy to understand. Thus, employees find it difficult to follow them.

Don't make policies very long. Make them well structured and easy to read.
[SME owner, Organisation A]
It was also noted that SMEs do not understand the concept of benchmarking and why it would be considered important. They have no knowledge in how to benchmark against other organisations. They felt that this was an area in which the national

government should assist SMEs by providing more information on how to go about benchmarking and the benefits of such action.

[benchmarking] is a good idea however it will be difficult to do as SMEs don't know who or what they should be comparing against [SME owner, Organisation B]

Focus group participants also suggested that information security awareness could be integrated with the employee induction process so that employees understand, from the very beginning, the importance of information security to the organisation. However, it was pointed out by some that SMEs are often informally organised and so may lack a formal induction process. Focus group participants noted that this could be remedied by including the security induction within the employment contract/company handbook. Participants also mentioned the importance of explaining the business ramifications of information security breaches to employees – for example, by mentioning the potential disclosure of corporate strategic information. Showing the employees "What's in it for me?" in such meaningful ways would help "sell" the policy.

After employment, a build up to presenting policies could encourage employees to attend and become involved. Brown bag lunches were suggested as an example of an informal enjoyable environment in which to present and discuss security policies.

5.5 Individual and Organisational Learning

Participants noted that because of their size, there is generally good communication in SMEs which eliminates the need for extensive training and education.

You don't need a lot of education and training in a small business. Because it's a very closed environment there's a lot of communication, and once people know what they're meant to be doing they'll continue to do it and especially if they see everyone else doing it.
[SME owner, Organisation B]

It would be difficult for SME owners to measure whether employees are gaining much knowledge from any form of learning if they are left to do it in their own time or if they were to implement a learning program. They were unaware of any available programs for small organisations.

…at the moment, if I wanted to conduct training I would make up my own course because I'm not aware of any courses for employees except for large organisations.
[SME owner, Organisation B]

The question of whether SME owners would permit employees the time to engage in e-learning and online communities was raised by focus group participants:

Perhaps the smaller places wouldn't be able to afford the time for their employees to be able to become involved in that? And I wonder if the employees would take the

time on their own clock to become part of those sorts of experiences and those sorts of communities?
[SME owner, Focus group 1]

It was also mentioned that some types of employees may not be interested in such activities:
Some people go to work so they can show up at 8:45am and leave at 4:35pm, and earn their wage. And those people perhaps may not take as much out of it [e-learning] as somebody who's really interested in furthering their career. [SME owner, Focus group 1]

It was suggested that learning may be better accepted by employees if offered by an independent neutral business body such as a regional Chamber of Commerce, or academia, rather than an IT professional firm:

If it's a governing body or a body that's respected within the context of a society, where there's a means of interacting and benchmarking because you meet many peer businesses, then that's good for enculturation at the owner/manager level. [SME owner, Focus group 1]

5.6 Australian Governmental and Cultural Context

It was noted in the Australian SMEs interviewed that they often have a relaxed, unconcerned approach to security issues. Participants also criticised the lack of government initiatives in helping SMEs with security risks and issues. Suggestions were made by participants for a government (either Federal or State) marketing campaign raising security awareness; a brochure that includes a variety of case studies that would spark interest among SMEs; templates for risk analysis; and information security standards for SMEs.

In addition, it was agreed that different countries exhibit unique values and cultures. According to many participants, the Australian culture can be characterised by the catchcry "She'll be right, mate!" and, as such, is a barrier to information security culture development in Australian SMEs.

Well, you look at national culture and what to change, well, when it comes to computer security, the old Aussie saying of "She'll be right, mate!" [characterises the culture].
[SME owner, Focus group 1]

6. Conclusion

This paper has provided a theoretical perspective on information security culture and has presented an issue-based socio-cultural framework for developing and maintaining information security culture in Australian SMEs (figure 1). The paper also provided key findings from three interpretive case studies of Australian SMEs and two focus groups that explored the framework in the Australian context. Key issues hindering the development of an information security culture in Australian SMEs were highlighted by the case study and focus group findings.

The framework has highlighted that internally, SME owners have the greatest responsibility and role in ensuring a more security conscious organisation. They should perform an information asset protection process (that is, risk analysis) that helps them to identify the need for a range of measures including policies and procedures (supported by enabling technologies). However the effectiveness of these measures relies on an organisational security awareness program of informal activities to increase the awareness of SME employees. Awareness, training and education form the backbone of organisational initiatives to influence employee security behaviour.

Australian SMEs should also be given greater external support for developing an information security culture by federal and state governments. Many initiatives were proposed in this study, including a national SME information security awareness campaign, benchmarking of information security culture in Australian SMEs, a brochure, tax incentives, formal training and education programs, and opportunities for business collaboration.

In conclusion, this research has highlighted the criticality of a proactive SME owner role and the need to consider the national context in order to institutionalise information security culture in SMEs in a national setting.

References

AusCERT (2006) 2006 Australian Computer Crime and Security Survey, AusCERT, Retrieved 26 September, 2006, from: http://www.auscert.org.au/render.html?it=6311

Chia, PA, Maynard, SB & Ruighaver, AB 2002, "Exploring Organisational Security Culture: Developing A Comprehensive Research Model", Proceedings of IS ONE World Conference, Las Vegas, 2002.

CSI/FBI 2006, "2006 CSI/FBI Computer Crime and Security Survey", Computer Security Institute, Retrieved 26 September 2006 from:
https://event.on24.com/eventRegistration/EventLobbyServlet?target=registration.jsp&eventid
=27372&sessionid=1&key=42F39B89EE0B30BA951711A5E7A98EDD&partnerref=Netsem
inar&sourcepage=register

Dimopoulos, V, Furnell, SM, Jennex, M & Kritharas, I 2004, "Approaches to IT Security in Small and Medium Enterprises" Proceedings of the 2nd Australian IS Management Conference 2004, Perth, Australia.

Dojkovski, S, Warren, M & Lichtenstein, S 2005, "Information Security Culture in Small and Medium Sized Enterprises: a Socio-cultural Framework", Proceedings of the 6th Australian Conference on Information Warfare and Security, 24-25 November 2005, Deakin University, Geelong, Australia

Proceedings of the International Symposium on
Human Aspects of Information Security & Assurance (HAISA 2007)

Dojkovski, S., Lichtenstein, S. & Warren, M.J, 2006 "Challenges in Fostering an Information Security Culture in Australian Small and Medium Sized Enterprises", in Proceedings of 5th European Conference on Information Warfare and Security, 1-2 June, 2006, National Defence College, Helsinki, Finland.

Furnell, SM & Clarke, NL 2005, "Organisational Security Culture: Embedding Security Awareness, Education and Training", Proceedings of the 4th World Conference on IS Education WISE 2005, 18-20 May, Moscow, Russia, 2005.

Furnell, SM, Gennatou, M & Dowland, PS 2000, "Promoting Security Awareness and Training within Small Organisations" Proceedings of the 1st Australian IS Management (AISM) Workshop, Geelong, Australia, 2000.

Galletta, DF & Polak, P 2003, "An Empirical Investigation of Antecedents of Internet Abuse in the Workplace", Proceedings of the 2nd Annual Workshop on HCI Research in MIS, Seattle, WA, December 12-13, 2003

Helokunnas, T & Iivonen, I 2003, "Information Security Culture in Small and Medium Size Enterprises", Seminar Presentation, Institute of Business Information Management, Tampere University of Technology, Finland. Available: http://www.ebrc.info/kuvat/helokunnas_iivonen.pdf

Lichtenstein, S & Swatman, PMC 2001, "Effective Management and Policy in e-Business Security", Proceedings of 14th Bled Electronic Commerce Conference, Bled, Slovenia, 2001.

Martins, A & Eloff, JHP 2002, "Assessing Information Security Culture", Proceedings of the 2nd Information Security for South Africa Conference (ISSA 2002), 10-12 July 2002, Gauteng. South Africa.

OECD 2002, "OECD Guidelines for the Security of Information Systems and Networks: Towards a Culture of Security", Organisation for Economic Co-operation and Development, 2002.

Schlienger, T & Teufel, S 2000, "Information Security Culture: The Socio-cultural Dimension in Information Security Management", Proceedings of the IFIP TC11 International Conference on Information Security (SEC 2002), Cairo, Egypt.

Schlienger, T & Teufel, S 2003, "Analysing Information Security Culture: Increasing Trust by an Appropriate Information Security Culture", Proceedings of 14th International Conference on Database and Expert Systems Applications (DEXA 2003), IEEE Computer Society.

Schultz, E 2005, "The Human Factor in Security", Computers & Security, vol. 24, no. 6, pp. 425-426.

Siponen, MT 2000, "A Conceptual Foundation for Organisational Information Security Awareness" Information Management & Computer Security, vol. 8, no. 1, 2000.

Stanton, JM, Jolton, J, Mastrangelo, PR & Stam, KR 2004, "Behavioural Information Security: Two End User Survey Studies of Motivation and Security Practices" Proceedings of the Americas Conference on Information Systems (AMCIS), 5-8 August 2004, New York, USA.

Taylor, M & Murphy, A 2004, "SMEs and eBusiness", Journal of Small Business and Enterprise Development, vol. 11, no. 3, pp 280-289, 2004.

Van Niekerk, JC & Von Solms, R 2003, "Establishing an Information Security Culture in Organisations: an Outcomes-based Education Approach", Proceedings of ISSA 2003, 3rd Annual IS South Africa Conference, Johannesburg, South Africa, 2003.

Von Solms, B 2000, "Information Security - The Third Wave?" Computers and Security, vol. 19, no. 7, pp 615- 620.

Vroom, C & Von Solms, R 2004, "Towards Information Security Behavioural Compliance", Computers & Security, vol. 23, no. 3, pp. 191-198.

Warren, MJ 2003, "Australia's Agenda for E-Security Education and Research", Proceedings of the TC11 / WG11.8 3rd Annual World Conference on Information Security Education (WISE3), Naval Post Graduate School, Monterey, California, USA.

Zakaria, O & Gani, A 2003, "A Conceptual Checklist of Information Security Culture", Proceedings of 2nd European Conference on Information Warfare and Security, 30 June -1 July 2003, Reading, UK.

How Well Are Information Risks Being Communicated To Your Computer End-Users?

M. Pattinson[1] and G. Anderson[2]

[1] University of South Australia, Australia
[2] Anderson Analyses, Australia

Abstract

The authors of this paper adopt the premise that an individual's perception of the risks associated with information systems significantly influences the likelihood and extent to which she or he will engage in risk-taking behaviour when using a computer. Furthermore, they believe that the manner in which information system risks are communicated to the computer end-user can affect a change to his or her perception of the risks. Although there are numerous ways in which the communication of risk can be manipulated, this paper focuses on the use of graphics and symbols embedded within information security risk messages. Also outlined is some preliminary research conducted by the authors in an attempt to provide some much-needed evidence-based research relating to human aspects of information security and assurance.

Keywords

Information Security (InfoSec), Risk Perception, Risk Communication, Semantic Differential (SD).

1. Introduction

The "Conference Concept" for the inaugural international conference on Human Aspects of Information Security and Assurance, July 2007 states:

"It is commonly acknowledged that security requirements cannot be addressed by technical means alone, and that a significant aspect of protection comes down to the attitudes, awareness, behaviour and capabilities of the people involved.......Ensuring appropriate attention and support for the needs of users should therefore be seen as a vital element of a successful security strategy." (HAISA, 2007).

We seem to have reached a point in the information security (InfoSec) lifecycle where considerable literature exists that asserts that there is more to managing information security than simply focusing on hardware and software vulnerabilities.

Authors such as Schneier (2000 & 2004), Pincus (2005), Heiser (2005) and numerous others have been saying for a number of years that human factor aspects are equally important, if not more important, in terms of achieving an acceptable level of information security within an organisation.

To the present authors it appears that the above assertion is more often proclaimed a fact than is actually shown to be the case with the support of empirical evidence. For many researchers it is as though it were sufficient to nod in the general direction of human factors as a casual explanation, without necessarily delineating precisely what type of human factors under exactly what type of circumstances are likely to have a significant impact.

Some human factors that have the potential to impact upon the security of an organisation's information systems are:

- Organisational policy & risk culture
- Individual propensity to take risks
- The theory of risk homeostasis
- The bystander affect
- Familiarity with the communication
- Individual perception of the risks

- Age, gender, position in the organisation
- Cost of compliance
- Amount of education & training
- Individual cognitive style
- Experience
- How well the risks are communicated

Some of these factors relate to surroundings and conditions, some are considered sociological and others are related to the person's upbringing, culture or experience. This list is by no means exhaustive, and furthermore, this paper does not attempt to address all of these factors, but focuses on only two, namely, individual perception of the risks and how well these risks are communicated.

More specifically, the focus of this paper is more on the risk perceptions of computer end-users than it is on their risk-taking behaviour. The principle premise being that if computer end-user perceptions of the risks associated with information security threats are heightened, then it is likely they will exhibit more desirable behaviour.

Consequently, the aim of this paper is twofold. The first aim is to present the argument that the manipulation of risk communications by incorporating human factor variables can influence the information risk perceptions of computer end-users. In turn, this has the potential to improve end-user risk-taking behaviour. The second aim of this paper is to describe and discuss some pilot study research that attempts to ascertain whether the embedding of symbols or graphics within information security messages achieves a positive shift in the risk perceptions of computer end-users.

2. Risk Perception

The manner in which people see the risks associated with information security determines what decisions they will make regarding the actions they will take (or not take) in conjunction with whatever security measures their particular organisation has put in place. Unfortunately, to date, not much is known about the perceptions that computer end-users hold concerning information systems risk.

However, research into risk perception in general has identified some important factors. The influence these factors have on risk perception is considered to be a function of the extent to which the risk is viewed as (a) voluntary, (b) under control, (c) representing a threat or catastrophe, or (d) having potential for a reduction in gains, or an increase in losses (Heimer, 1988).

The literature on risk perception seems to be devoid of research into its prevalence in the information security domain. However, in terms of general risk perception research, there are a number of articles and studies that look at factors that influence risk perception. For example, Bener (2000) claims that there is a range of social, cultural and psychological factors that contribute to risk perception. Additionally, Otway (1980) lists other factors that shape risk perception such as the information people have been exposed to, the information they have chosen to believe and the social experiences they have had, to name but a few.

The media plays a significant role in influencing people's perception of information system risk. One only has to look at the impact of the terrorist attack on the world trade centre twin towers on September 11, 2001. Another example is the reporting of the phishing software that logs keystrokes and subsequently acquires IDs and passwords to enable access to banking information.

A good practical example of risk perception relates to the process of backing up our personal data. Assume that you are writing a large, but very important business report for your senior management and it is taking many days and much research effort. How often do you backup your work? What is your perception of the risk that you could lose all the good work you have done because of some computer problem or whatever? Some people have no appreciation of the intricacies of a computer and what can go wrong - these people are blithely unaware of the risks of losing everything. Yet it has probably happened to all of us at least once!

On the other hand, there are also informed people who are aware of the unpredictability of computers and that they sometimes crash for no apparent reason. Such people will back up regularly and to various mediums. In the end, we do personal backups to the extent that we are confident that we won't lose anything or any time. This is where we differ as individuals. Some people are risk-takers by nature and feel that they can rely on the automatic server backup that occurs every hour. On the other hand, some of us are more conservative and backup almost too often, just to be sure.

One of the factors that is purported to have an influence on risk perception is the way in which the risk message is communicated to computer end-users and IT management. Bener, (2000) claims the manner in which risk is communicated within an organisation substantially influences the risk perception of the different individuals within that organisation. Lippa (1994) put forward a similar view, claiming that an individual's perception of risks is shaped by the way in which risky situations are communicated to them within a particular organisational context.

3. End-user Risk-taking Behaviour

For the purposes of this paper, the term 'end-user risk-taking behaviour' refers to behaviour that ranges from the very risk averse (or very good) behaviour through to the very risk-inclined (or very bad) behaviour and can be either deliberate or accidental. A selection of such behaviours is shown below:

Risk-averse behaviour (deliberate)	Neutral behaviour (accidental)	Risk-inclined behaviour (deliberate)
• Always log-off when computer unattended	• Leaving a computer unattended	• Installing/using unauthorised software
• Disallow email attachments from unknown sources	• Opening unsolicited email attachments	• Create & send SPAM email
• Install more than one anti-virus software package & update regularly	• Not installing anti-virus software	• Writing & disseminating malicious code
• Change password regularly	• Sharing ID's & passwords	• Hacking into other people's accounts
• Vigilant in recognizing and approaching unauthorized personnel	• Not being vigilant re unauthorised personnel	• Giving unauthorized personnel access to authorized precincts
• Back up work regularly	• Not backing up work often enough	• Theft or destruction of hardware or software
• Always report security incidents	• Not reporting security incidents	• Conducting fraudulent activities
• Install firewall	• Accessing dubious web sites	• Executing games on company equipment

Recent research by Stanton, Stam, Mastrangelo & Jolton, (2005) analysed the various types of computer end-user behaviour and developed a taxonomy of six behaviour categories which can be aligned to the columns above as:

Aware Assurance Basic Hygiene	Dangerous Tinkering Naïve Mistakes	Intentional Destruction Detrimental Misuse

4. Risk Communication

As with other aspects of risk in general, risk communication has been variously defined by numerous authors. For example, (O'Neill, 2004) defines it as"…an interactive process of exchanging information and opinions between stakeholders regarding the nature and associated risks of a hazard on the individual or community and the appropriate responses to minimise the risks. The key behavioural change lies in risk communication designed to change people's perception of the risk and to increase their willingness to manage the risk." (p. 14).

Similarly, the USNRC, (1989) defines risk communication as "an interactive process of exchange of information and opinion among individuals, groups and institutions. It involves multiple messages about the nature of risk and other messages, not strictly about risk, that express concerns, opinions and reactions to risk messages or to legal and institutional arrangements for risk management" (p. 21) (as cited in Bener, 2000 & Backhouse et al, 2004).

For some time, the importance of communicating risk effectively has been of concern to those in the health industry, particularly in relation to risks in pharmacotherapy. Coleman (2005), in a paper on presenting information on risks associated with prescribing medicines and drugs, sees appropriate risk communication "as one of the most important approaches used today to minimise risk" (p. 513). He strongly advocates that the presentation of information on risks should be as simple and as user-friendly as possible. Although Coleman is referring to risk information relating to medication and drug therapy, the present authors believe that these principles are also applicable to risks relating to information security.

Potential threats and their subsequent risk to an organisation's information systems need to be communicated to all levels of computer end-users, from the order clerk to the application developer to the IT support person to senior management and the C-suite executives. Some common forms of risk communication include, for example:

Security awareness seminars	Web pages
Standard email memos	One-on one discussions
Notice board memos	Group meetings
Phone calls	Flyers

There is a constant problem for anyone designated with the task of organising such activities. Namely, what might have proven to be an appropriate technique in a one-on-one discussion may not necessarily prove to be as useful in an email message or a seminar presentation. In other words, different forms of risk communication require a considerable amount of thought by the sender in terms of how to achieve maximum effectiveness when he or she uses a particular communication medium.

Furthermore, it should be noted that the impact of a communication pertaining to a risk or a hazard is not always a direct result of the design of that communication. There are a number of additional factors that can render a message to be ineffectual. For example, familiarity with the message, that is, repeated exposure to the message, has been shown to create automatic behaviour and a total disregard for the message. This phenomenon is sometimes referred to as 'experience with the message' and gives the impression of apathy. Similarly, the issue known as 'cost of compliance' can also appear to be end-user apathy when in fact the person may have made a conscious decision not to take heed of the message regarding a risky situation (OSHA, 1997; Visual Expert, 2003). These two issues are appreciated by the authors but are beyond the scope of this paper, which is predominantly concerned with how we might communicate risk better.

5. Communicating Risk with Graphics & Symbols

The topic of 'effective presentation of information' has been extensively studied and researched for many years in many diverse environments. In particular, marketing professionals are well versed in the styles and methods that can be used to 'get the message across' to consumers, customers, boards of management, etc. Also, educationalists have conducted a plethora of research relating to the presentation of information in an attempt to improve learning outcomes. One of these techniques is to use appropriate symbols, pictures, graphics, colours etc embedded within advertisements, reports, memos, emails and presentation slides. The design of children's books is another example of how symbols and pictures can be used to maximise the understanding by the reader (Bang, 1991).

There is no apparent evidence of literature relating to the presentation of information concerned with the topic of information security risk. If risk communication is such an important tool in mitigating information risks, then it seems that there is a current hiatus in this research area. What is the most effective means of sending a broadcast email to all staff? How should it be worded?, how often should it be sent?, when should it be sent?, what colour should the font & background be? These questions and many more need answers based on sound theory supported by relevant empirical evidence in a typical evidence-based research approach that is most predominant in the field of health care.

The following sections detail some of the more recent field work the present authors have conducted, focusing almost entirely on the presentation of email messages that incorporate a graphic or symbol within the main body of the message. The impetus for this work was the observation that email communications being sent to computer end-users about information security issues and warnings tended to be almost exclusively concerned with achieving some type of behavioural outcome. Only in a relatively few cases did the originator of the message appear to be attempting to evoke in its recipients, any sense of fear, anxiety, dread or danger regarding the likely consequence of the security threat. In other words, while it was not a universal finding, many such messages were devoid of any evidence that the originator carefully selected his or her words for their appropriate connotations, or used symbols known to have an association with such commonly experienced human emotions.

6. Research

Two pilot studies were undertaken. The objective of each study was to establish whether the embedding of a relevant graphic relating to some known aspect of information security, when placed inside an information security message, would have any influence on the information security risk perceptions of any individual to whom the message was being communicated.

To this end, a one-page survey form, containing both a risk message and a semantic differential (SD) grid, was designed for each study. The SD grid was designed to be completed by the message recipient to provide an idea of his or her perception of some of the emotional aspects of the message. By way of explaining the SD grid procedure to the survey respondents in each study, they were provided with a sample grid using the concept/heading Global Warming Debate as the entity or thing to be considered, as shown below.

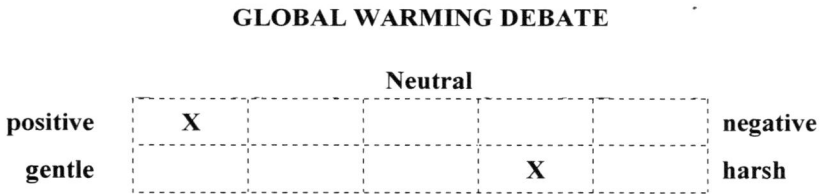

GLOBAL WARMING DEBATE

	Neutral				
positive	X				**negative**
gentle				X	**harsh**

Figure 1: Sample semantic differential grid used in each study

The survey form used to generate the results of our first study came in two versions. Version A had no graphic embedded and version B had the graphic embedded behind the complete message. The research subjects (i.e. survey participants) for this first study, were undergraduate students of the University of South Australia. There were two classes of students for this course, each at a different campus. The first class (of 35 students) was given version A of the form, that is, the one without any graphic and the second class (of 40 students) was given version B of the form.

The survey form used in our second study also consisted of two versions. In this instance however, each message contained a graphic. The difference concerned its placement. That is, Version A had a graphic embedded above the salutation of a supposed email message, while Version B had the same graphic embedded following the signature at end of the email message. In this instance, 36 Masters students from the University of South Australia participated.

The objective of the first study was to determine the extent of the emotional impact of an information security message relating to fake emails, i.e. the phishing threat and subsequent risks. The responses between the two groups of students, namely those who got the message without an embedded graphic and those who got the message with an embedded graphic, were compared.

The objective of the second study was to determine the extent of the emotional impact on a message recipient when a graphic associated with the detection of a computer virus was placed either at the beginning of an email message, or at the end of the message.

In both studies, the method of eliciting a response from each participant involved the use of a type of semantic differential (SD) grid. In many instances this procedure has been employed as a method for eliciting attitudinal responses to an issue, item or event. This SD grid consisted of 10 scale items, however, four of these acted as "filler items". Our main concern was in differences between the student responses to the six scale items meant to elicit reactions in respect to what are known as the Evaluation, Potency and Activity (EPA) dimensions. In general terms, the responses given would give indicate how the participants viewed the security message they were given in terms of its status, power and expressiveness. In more specific terms, the responses were an indication of the extent that each individual student saw the information security message as:

a) good or bad for them
b) strong or weak with respect to them, and
c) as an active or passive thing.

The following figure is a copy of the SD grid used in both studies. For the purposes of this paper, the E-P-A designation for the 3 pairs of relevant scales are is on the left-hand side.

		Extremely	Somewhat	Neutral	Somewhat	Extremely	
A	active						passive
	calm						excitable
P	strong						weak
	relevant						irrelevant
E	beautiful						ugly
A	fast						slow
E	valuable						worthless
	hard						soft
	clever						dull
P	heavy						light

Figure 2: Actual semantic differential grid used in each study

6.1 Research Results

On completing an analysis of the responses to the SD for the first study, no significant differences were detected between the groups with respect to any of the six scales. That is, the data obtained from the respondents who received the phishing message contained within an embedded graphic, in proportionate terms, did not differ significantly from the data obtained from the respondents who received the same message, but without the addition of an embedded graphic. Not surprisingly, when the same procedure was carried out after combining the responses to each of the two scales that made up the Evaluation, Potency and Activity dimensions respectively, again no significant proportionate differences between the two groups was found.

A number of explanations could be put forward to account for these findings. Perhaps the most plausible explanation is that the connotations inherent in the wording of the message were sufficient to get its negative import across - so much so that the graphic provided relatively little by way of additional emotion arousing effects.

As was the case with our first study, on completing an analysis of the responses to the SD for the second study, no statistically significant differences were detected between the groups with respect to any of the six relevant scales. That is, the data obtained from the respondents who received the message with the graphic placed at the beginning, did not differ significantly from the data obtained from the respondents who received the same message, but for whom the graphic appeared at the end. After combining the responses to each of the two scales that made up the

Evaluation, Potency and Activity dimensions respectively, again no significant proportionate differences between the two groups was found.

Although none of the results obtained met the criteria for statistical significance, which is not perhaps surprising given the relatively small sample size, nevertheless it seems that the differences were large enough for the present authors to be convinced that the SD measures used are indeed appropriate for larger and broader purposes.

7. Conclusion

The aim of this paper was, firstly, to discuss how the risk perceptions of computer end-users may be influenced by improving the process of risk communication by embedding symbols and graphics within information security messages. The second aim was to describe some pilot study research that the authors have conducted in an attempt to ascertain whether the embedding of symbols and graphics within information security messages achieves a shift in the risk perceptions of computer end-users.

The authors believe that if the effectiveness of the various forms of risk communication within an organisation can be increased, then the general perception of the risks to the information systems will be more realistic. This is in line with Heiser's (2005) claim that "After political issues, risk perception issues represent the biggest challenge for the security professional. Accurately understanding risk and effectively communicating that understanding to others is core to any risk management role".

There are many ways in which information risk communication could be made more effective. For example, in previous papers and field work the present authors have attempted to show how the concept of "message framing", in line with message recipient's cognitive style could be used. This paper, on the other hand, attempts to show how the use of graphics and symbols could be used to convey risk messages more effectively.

As a final point, it must be emphasized that this paper does not in any way attempt to provide any 'silver-bullet' solutions for management in terms of what they can do towards managing information risk - this was not the aim of this paper. However, it does outline research that is being undertaken by the authors at the time of writing, the ultimate objective of which is to subsequently advise management on how they can communicate information risk simply and more effectively to achieve the final outcome, being the mitigation of actual risks, as shown in Figure 3 below.

Figure 3: Logical hierarchy of risk outcomes

References

Backhouse, J., Bener, A., Chauvidul, N., Wamala, F. & Willison, R., 2004, "Risk Management in Cyberspace", Available at http://www.foresight.gov.uk/Previous_Projects/Cyber_Trust_and_Crime_Prevention/Reports_and_Publications/, viewed 27 April 2005.

Bang, M., 1991, *Picture This, How Pictures Work*, Bulfinch Press, Little, Brown and Company.

Bener, A. B., 2000, "Risk Perception, Trust and Credibility: A Case in Internet Banking", PhD thesis, London School of Economics and Political Sciences, Available at http://is.lse.ac.uk/research/theses/default.htm, viewed 27 April 2005.

Brown, S. L., 2005, "Relationships between risk-taking behaviour and subsequent risk perceptions", *British Journal of Psychology*, Vol. 96, pp. 155-164.

Coleman, J. J., 2005, "Presenting Information on Risks", *Journal of Clinical Pharmacy and Therapeutics*, Vol. 30, pp. 511-514.

HAISA, 2007, "Conference Concept", International Conference on Human Aspects of Information Security and Assurance, Plymouth, UK, July, 2007, Available at http://www.haisa.org/, viewed 12 January, 2007

Heimer, C. A., 1988, "Social Structure, Psychology, and the Estimation of Risk", *Annual Review of Sociology*, Vol. 14, pp. 491-519.

Heiser, J. G., 2005, "Read at your own Risk", *Information Security,* Sept 2005, Layer 8, Tech Target IT Media.

Lippa, R. A., 1994, *Introduction to Social Psychology, Second Edition*, Wadsworth (Belmont, CA).

O'Neill, P., 2004, "Developing a Risk Communication Model to Encourage Community Safety from Natural Hazards", paper presented at the Fourth NSW Safe Communities Symposium, Sydney, NSW.

OSHA, 1997, *Hazard Communication: A Review of the Science Underpinning the Art of Communication for Health and Safety*, US Department of Labor, Occupational Safety & Health Administration.

Otway, H. J., 1980, "Risk Perception: A Psychological Perspective", in M. Dierkes, S. Edwards & R. Coppock, (Eds.), *Technological Risk: Its Perspective and Handling in Europe*.

Pincus, J, D., 2005, "Computer Science is really a Social Science", Microsoft Research, Available at http://research.microsoft.com/users/jpincus/cs%20SocSci.html, viewed 14/01/2007.

Schneier, B., 2004, "The People Paradigm", Available at http://www.csoonline.com/read/110104/counsel.htm, viewed 20/01/2006.

Schneier, B., 2000, *Secrets & Lies: Digital security in a networked world*, John Wiley & Sons, NY, USA.

USNRC, 1989, *Improving Risk Communication*, National Research Council, Committee on Risk Perception and Communication, Washington, D.C., National Academy Press.

Visual Expert, 2003, "Are Warnings Effective?" Visual Expert Human Factors, Available at http://www.visualexpert.com/Resources/dowarningswork.html, viewed 06/04/2007.

Information Security Awareness: Towards a Generic Programme

H. Mauwa and R. Von Solms

Nelson Mandela Metropolitan University, Port Elizabeth, South Africa
Email: hope.mauwa@nmmu.ac.za; rossouw@nmmu.ac.za

Abstract

Basing information security awareness programmes on existing information security policies in organizations is a sound approach, since these policies are seen as the basis for effective information security. But this approach does not satisfy the needs of organizations that do not have such policies in place. Therefore, another approach, which does not entirely depend on existing policies, is needed so that organizations, even those without the policies, can implement such a programme.

Keywords

Information Security Awareness Programmes, ISO/IEC 17799, ISO/IEC 13335-3.

1. Introduction

In today's computing environment, awareness programmes now play a much more important role in organizations' information security programmes because the maintenance of effective security is more dependent than ever on the vigilance of users. Even though awareness programmes have become increasing important, the level of awareness in most organizations is still low. The current approach of developing these programmes recommends that they should stem directly from information security policies already existing in organizations (Du Plessis & Von Solms, 2002).

It is the objective of this paper to argue that the most effective type of information security awareness programme is a generic type, which is suitable for most organizations and does not depend entirely on existing policies in organizations.

In order to accomplish this, this paper will look at several issues, including the role that information security awareness programmes play, in order to gain an understanding of the impact they have on information security. The current approach to the development of these programmes will be discussed to highlight its limitations. Once this has been established, an alternative approach will be proposed by examining the topics discussed in information security awareness programmes.

Then, sources used to identify the contents for the proposed approach will be discussed. Finally, topics that can form part of the contents for the proposed approach will be identified based on the above studied sources.

2. Why Information Security Awareness?

Information security awareness efforts are designed to change behaviour or reinforce good security practices, and they provide a baseline of security knowledge for all users, regardless of job duties or positions (Du Plessis & Von Solms, 2002). Security awareness allows individuals to recognize information security concerns and respond accordingly. Courtney Gilbert (2003) described security awareness as a learning process, which changes individual and organizational attitudes and perceptions so that the importance of security and the adverse consequences of its failure are realized. Thomson and Von Solms (1998) motivate that information security awareness gives employees the necessary knowledge to maintain security by ensuring the confidentiality, integrity and availability of information.

Information security awareness focuses on developing an organizational culture that is both aware and capable of responding to security-related risks. It aims at changing the way employees behave towards an organization's vital information and cultivating an information security culture throughout an organization. The way in which people work with information assets in their daily job functions eventually becomes the way things are done in an organization, and this eventually becomes part of the culture of an organization (Du Plessis & Von Solms, 2002).

Achieving this level of understanding represents a major challenge because no amount of technology can reduce the overriding impact of human complexities, inconsistencies, and peculiarities (Ernst &Young, 2004). Ernst and Young (2004) claim that any strategy that overlooks this realization is inherently flawed. With proper awareness, employees become the most effective layer in an organization's security defence.

With the important role that these awareness programmes play in organizations' complete information security programmes, experts have developed guidelines to assist organizations in developing them.

3. The Current Approach to Security Awareness

The current approaches to the development of information security awareness programmes need to be examined. Studying these current approaches will assist in understanding the effect such programmes have on various organizations.

3.1 Guidelines and Standards

The current guidelines recommend that awareness programmes should be developed, based on the security policies and procedures currently in place in organizations.

This is advocated prominently in current information security guidelines and standards. Two such standards are ISO/IEC 17799:2005 and ISO/IEC 13335-3:2005. This is because management instructions, i.e., policies, are mainly seen as the basis for effective information security within an organization (ISO/IEC 13335-1, 2004).

It has to be said that every organization is unique, and as such, different organizations have different management instructions about how they should be run. Therefore, the awareness programmes that stem from these management instructions also differ from one organization to another. This could be called a company-specific approach to information security awareness, since it is based on elements that are very specific to a particular organization (Du Plessis & Von Solms, 2002).

Despite the illustrated importance of information security awareness and the widespread acceptance of this fact in current guidelines and standards, the level in most organizations is still low, according to some of the recently conducted surveys (Ernst & Young, 2004; Deloitte Touche Tohmatsu, 2005).

3.2 Limitations of Current Approaches

According to the *Global Information Security Survey* by Ernst & Young (2004), respondents named the *"lack of security awareness by users"* as the top obstacle to effective information security; however, only 28% listed *"raising employee information security training or awareness"* as being a top initiative in 2004. In the *Global Security Survey*, conducted by Deloitte Touche Tohmatsu – Australia (2005), respondents pointed to a host of continuing challenges to their businesses. One of the most prominent among them was the *"lack of employee awareness and training"* - (48%). According to the same survey, overall, security awareness and training implemented, or maintained, decreased from 77% in 2004 to 65% in 2005.

A possible reason for such a lack of awareness programmes in organizations could be the approach used to implement such programmes (Du Plessis & Von Solms, 2002). As pointed out in the last section, both ISO/IEC 17799:2005 and ISO/IEC 13335-3:2005 stress the need for implementing them, based on the information security policies and procedures already in place. But not all organizations have these policies in place. A recent survey conducted by PricewaterhouseCoopers LLP (2004), *Information Security Breaches Survey 2004*, reveals that a third of all companies and two-thirds of large businesses in the United Kingdom now have information security policies. This means that only those organizations would have a basis on which to formulate their information security awareness programmes.

The current lack of awareness programmes in most organizations suggests that a problem exists with the traditional method of basing awareness programmes on the policies and procedures already in places   (Du Plessis & Von Solms, 2002). Therefore, an *alternative* approach to the development of information security awareness programmes has to be developed that will not depend entirely on existing policies.

4. A Generic Information Security Awareness Programme

An examination into the different areas of security knowledge covered in awareness programmes reveals that some aspects are company-specific while others are generic components that are non-company-specific.

Company-specific information includes an organization's information security policy's contents and specific procedures. Policy documents are different for different organizations, since the goals and directions are also different. As such, employees of different organizations are, therefore, educated by different awareness material concerning their organization's policies. Procedures are based on the broad guidance provided by policies, and as such, they are much more specific to every organization. It is through policies and these procedures that employees within a specific organization are guided in their role of securing the organization's information technology environment (Du Plessis & Von Solms, 2002).

Du Plessis and Von Solms (2002) argue that the focus is not only on educating employees on the policies of their organization, but also on changing their behaviour and cultivating an information security culture throughout the organization. To achieve this, an information security programme would include aspects other than only the organization's policies. Such aspects include general procedures, basic information technology concepts, threats to and vulnerabilities of computer systems and the importance of protecting information in today's business environment, which tend to be the general and common aspects that affect most organizations. Generally, these aspects are part of a company-specific content but could be catered for in a non-company-specific way. Such an approach to implementing an awareness programme can be called a generic approach to information security awareness (Du Plessis & Von Solms, 2002).

In most organizations an information worker needs to be aware of the general information threats and vulnerabilities that exist today, specifically when using electronic means to transact business processes, and it is these aspects that should form part of a generic information security awareness programme.

Having examined what would constitute a generic programme, several sources were studied in order to formulate its actual contents.

5. Towards a Generic Information Security Awareness Programme

Several internationally recognised sources, information security awareness programmes located on the Internet and a survey conducted by the authors were used to identify the contents of a generic information security awareness programme and to ensure that the foundation on which it is based is as broad as possible.

5.1 The Standards

The ISO/IEC 17799:2005 and the ISO/IEC 13335-3:2005 were used because they comprehensively cover awareness programmes. Both standards recommend that these programmes should reflect on the contents of a corporate information security policy, and should cover all objectives of an information security plan. The ISO/IEC 13335-3 goes on to say that the programme should ensure that the IT staff and the end-users have enough knowledge of the hardware and software systems to understand why safeguards are necessary, and to know how to use them correctly.

5.2 The Internet

Some awareness programmes offered on the Internet were studied thoroughly to gain more insight into the topics covered in them. A well-known one is the SANS Security Awareness Programme.

This covers general security areas affecting most organizations, such as passwords, computer viruses, malicious codes, personal use and gain, data backup and storage, incident response, environmental security, inventory control, physical security and social engineering. It also reports on true-life stories that have happened to people and organizations to demonstrate and reinforce the importance of the concepts covered. Each example demonstrates the consequences of simple mistakes or lapses in information and computer security.

5.3 The Authors' Survey

Having studied what is covered in the international information security standards and the Internet, a questionnaire was drafted and sent out to some well-known South African organizations known to follow sound information security principles. The main aim of the survey was to solicit ideas on what their managements recommend for inclusion in a generic programme.

It is important to point out that the organizations that were selected and participated in the survey operate in diverse industrial sectors: mining, manufacturing, food and beverages, education, communications and IT. This was done in order make sure that the identified content is suitable for interdisciplinary organizations.

The guidance and recommendations provided by the above sources and the survey are sufficiently broad to identify and base the contents of a generic programme on them.

6. Generic Contents of an Information Security Awareness Programme

It is important to bear in mind that general and common aspects affecting most organizations' employees would need to be included when identifying the topics for a generic programme. Any company-specific information, such as information security policies, guidelines and procedures, would only be introduced to the employees to make them aware of their existence and encourage them to find out more from their respective organizations. Based on the guidance and recommendations from the sources studied and the survey, the following broad topics were identified as part of the contents of a generic information security awareness programme:

- Data backup and storage
- Social engineering
- Remote/mobile worker security
- Malicious code security
- Password security
- E-mail security
- Physical and environmental security
- Computer ethics
- Privacy and confidentiality
- Paper-copy document security
- Accountability and responsibility
- Anti-virus software and firewalls
- Information security policies, standards and procedures.
- Information risk management
- Contingency planning
- Incident management
- IT laws, regulations and standards
- Computer auditing
- Change management.

It is important to point out that a generic awareness programme has to compromise the scope of the material that it presents in order to satisfy the primary goals of keeping the programme generic. All that the generic approach tries to achieve is to provide a baseline of awareness by educating the employees on the essentials of information security. Having such a baseline in place can provide organizations with the assurance that some basic level of awareness exists among employees.

7. Conclusion

It has been established that the general approach of basing awareness programmes on security policies and procedures already in place in organizations is a limiting factor: if organizations do not have them, they do not have a basis on which to support awareness programmes. This has contributed to the current low level of information security awareness in most organizations.

The contents of awareness programmes identified on the Internet were examined, and it was realized that these programmes contain a generic component that is company-independent. Therefore, a generic approach, which does not depend entirely on existing company policies and procedures and caters only for this non-company-specific component, was further investigated and proposed. The actual contents of the generic programme were also formulated using guidance from the ISO/IEC 17799:2005 and ISO/IEC 13335-3:2005, the Internet and the survey that was conducted with some South African organizations. These sources were used to make sure that the foundation on which the contents of the generic programme are based is as broad as possible.

The generic approach allows for the creation of an awareness programme that would be suitable for most organizations, even those without security policies and procedures. As such, it is expected to improve the level of awareness programmes in organizations. It must be noted though, that such a generic information security awareness programme, as suggested in this paper, should be augmented eventually by some contents to cater for the company-specific information that cannot be included in such a programme.

References

Deloitte Touche Tohmatsu - Australia. (2005). *2005 Global Security Survey.* Retrieved August 21, 2005, from http://www.deloitte.com/.

Du Plessis, L. & Von Solms, R. (2002). *Information Security Awareness: Baseline Education and Certification.* Baccalaureus Technologiae. Port Elizabeth: Information Technology Department, Nelson Mandela Metropolitan University.

Ernst & Young. (2004). *Global Information Security Survey 2004.* Retrieved August 21, 2005, from http://www.ey.com/global/.

Gilbert, C. (June 2003). *Developing an Integrated Security Training, Awareness, and Education Program.* GSEC Practical Assignment version 1.4b Retrieved August 8, 2005, from http://sans.org/rr/whitepapers/awareness/.

ISO/IEC 13335-1 (2004). *Information Technology - Security Techniques - Management of Information and Communications Technology Security.*

PricewaterhouseCoopers. (2004). *Information Security Breaches Survey 2004.* Retrieved August 21, 2005, from http://www.infosec.co.uk/.

Thomson, M. & Von Solms, R. (1998). *The Development of an Effective Information Security Awareness Programme for Use in an Organization.* Magister Technologiae. Port Elizabeth: Information Technology Department, Nelson Mandela Metropolitan University.

Von Solms, B. (2000). Information Security - The Third Wave? *Computers and Security* 19(7): pp.615-620.

User-Centered Security Applied to the Development of a Management Information System

M. Nohlberg[1] and J. Bäckström[2]

[1] School of Humanities and Informatics, University of Skövde, Skövde, Sweden
[2] Department of Computer and Information Science, University of Linköping,
Linköping, Sweden
e-mail: marcus@nohlberg.com

Abstract

The purpose of this study has been to do a user-centered security development of a prototype graphical interface for a management information system dealing with information security. The interface was perceived as successful by the test subjects and the sponsoring organization, Siguru. The major conclusion of the study is that managers use knowledge of information security mainly for financial and strategic matters which focus more on risk issues then security issues. To facilitate the need of management the study presents three heuristics for the design of management information security system interfaces:

1. Provide overview information very early in the program.
2. Do not overwhelm the user. Managers are not interested in the details of information security, but if they need details, they should be provided in a logical place.
3. Provide information in a way that is familiar to the manager. Provide contextual help for expressions that must be presented in a technical way.

Keywords

User-Centered Security, Management Information System, Usability.

1. Introduction

While security has been a concern almost since the beginning of the history of computers, it is during the last couple of years that the problem has been communicated to a broader audience than merely systems administrators and technicians. Security has been a major operational issue for a long time, and the costs have continued to rise, as have the number of incidents. In 1998, 32% of British companies suffered some kind of information security incident, and in 2004 that number had risen to 74 % of all companies and 94 % of the major companies (Department of Trade and Industry, 2004).

New laws and regulations such as Sarbanes-Oxley make managers more responsible for security. The widespread media coverage of viruses, DOS-attacks, computer crime etc. also adds to the attention paid to security. Business partners and stakeholders demand good information security if they are going to conduct business with a company (Rasmussen, 2002). This all makes security a business problem.

Many managers are neither technicians nor particularly knowledgeable in information security. Most of their knowledge comes distilled from a specialist who informs them about the current situation, as discussed by the authors in a previous paper (Nohlberg & Bäckström, 2007). Managers only receive second-hand information since they themselves are unable to get any kind of impartial data from the organization using the systems they have today. From the point of view of managers this makes security vastly different from, for instance, economical data that can be found from several sources in a company. The few security solutions that gives some general security information aimed towards users rather than specialists are often regarded as too complicated or too difficult to use, as is understood from the authors' professional experience and as discussed more in general by Furnell et al (2006). Hence, there is a need for an application that provides managers with an overview and understanding of information security that is aimed towards their specific needs and interests. This approach also fits well with the strive to avoid "The 10 deadly sins of information security", as argued by von Solms & von Solms (2004), where security is argued to be a corporate governance responsibility, as well as a business issue.

The purpose of this study was to construct a usable interface for information security-monitoring software with upper-level managers as target users. In order to construct a usable interface, it was important to get to know the users, their situation, their view on information security, and what kind of information they need.

This study was supported by the company Siguru, a small start-up company developing information security software, and is a part of the development process for the forthcoming product.

2. User-Centered Security

Almost as long as we have had computers and computer networks, there has been an ongoing work with development of programs to make them more secure. The focus of this work has been to generate powerful tools to protect our systems. The same attention has not paid to making the users understand the programs and making the same people understand the importance of a secure behavior when using computers and computer networks (Whitten & Tygar, 1998; Flechais & Sasse in Cranor & Garfinkel 2005; Dourish & Redmiles, 2002).

Since the mid-nineties there has been a growing interest among researchers in the information security-area who has called for a more user-centered approach to information security. There is a growing amount of articles on the subject (E.g. Simon & Zurko (1996); Holmström (1999); DePaula et al. (2005)).

The term "user-centered security" was coined by Simons & Zurko (1996) at the proceedings of the ACM-conference in 1996, and it can be seen as a key component of the movement for user centered development of information security applications. The term refers to "Security models, mechanisms, systems and software that have usability as a primary motivation or goal" (Simon & Zurko, 1996, page 27).

3. Design Principles for Development of Information Security Applications

The same basic principles of usability that apply to other applications apply to information security applications. A great foundation for all usability design is the design principles developed by Donald Norman (Norman, 2002). They describe a number of heuristics that is likely to enhance the usability of a product, i.e.:

- Feedback, giving the user some sort of information of what his or her action has lead to will make the user more aware of the status of the system.
- Visibility, it is easier to label a control that only has one function. The label of a control can be used by the user to remember the controls' function. If a control has many functions there is an immediate risk that the labeling will be ambiguous.
- Constraints, if the designer is able to constrain the number of actions that a user can carry out at a specific moment, the designer is also able to minimize the number of errors that the user can carry out at the same moment.

Other principles specifically considered in this project are described below.

According to Berson (in Carnor & Garfinkel, 2005), as little text as possible should be used to explain facts to the user. At the same time, it is important for the user to understand what is being communicated by the design, though the amount of text should be kept at a minimum. Every word, button and pixel should have a pedagogic ulterior motive (Berson in Carnor & Garfinkel, 2005).

The complexity of the interface should be kept as low as possible. It is also important *not* to design an application for all potential tasks that a user might be willing to undertake. The design should rather focus on the tasks that the user is most likely to undertake (Berson, 2005).

An interface which gives the users too much information, information at the wrong time or in an unsuitable way, will be perceived as confusing by the user. If the amount of information is too small, there is a risk that the user will not discover potential security threats (Long & Moskowitz, 2005; Berson, 2005).

Teach the user simple tricks. For instance, in the web browser Firefox, the address bar turns yellow when the user enters a site that uses SSL (a protocol for transmitting data safely over the Internet). The user knows that the current page is a secure site when he/she sees this, without having to interact with numerous dialogue boxes (Berson, 2005). Using simple tricks like this is mainly positive, though the designer has to continuously consider whether the user really needs this information about the program. A clue about when to use these tricks is when there is some change in the state of the program that the user needs to know about (Berson, in Cranor & Garfinkel, 2005).

4. Method

The first task was to learn what the potential users of the product would actually want to know about security. This was learned through a number of interviews and by scenario testing, described in more details in a previous paper (Nohlberg & Bäckström, 2007). The results showed in general a specific interest in knowing about security from a financial and strategic perspective, grouped in sections of security information, rather than an interest in detailed data. In fact, security was perceived by the managers mostly as financial risks.

An interview was made with representatives from the sponsoring company, Siguru, in order to get a broader understanding of the product the interface was supposed to be used with, its limits and possibilities. This formed the first guidelines on how the interface was supposed to be designed.

When the information from the interviews was collected, a "lo-fi" prototype was constructed on paper. The design of the prototype was created on the basis of the information from the interviews and information regarding the design of interfaces that was found in the literature survey. The "lo-fi" prototype was made by hand drawings on paper, in order to quickly generate a sketch of the interface while at the same time communicating to the subjects that this was an early prototype in hopes of making them more willing to give improvement suggestions.

User tests on the lo-fi prototype were made on potential target users. The first subject was in charge of the information security in a major governmental organization in Sweden. The second subject is the chairman of an information security company. The two subjects did not take part in the interviews. The user tests were recorded with a video camera. The tests consisted of six tasks and ten questions. The tasks were conducted first (except for the first question "What are your impressions of the first page") and were then followed up by questions.

The user tests were analyzed through a task log. The purpose of the task log was to find out where the test persons experienced difficulties with the prototype, why they experienced these difficulties, and what could bee done to eliminate these difficulties (Hackos & Redish, 1998). Through this procedure, it was possible to find concrete improvements of the interface as well as investigate the test person's mental model of how the system should work.

The "lo-fi" prototype was updated to a "hi-fi" prototype with the feedback from the interviews, the results, and the inferences from the "lo-fi" tests taken into consideration. The "hi-fi" prototype was interactive and built using Macromedia Flash. The prototype thus emulated a working interface and the tests were done on a computer, in contrast to the tests done on paper with the "lo-fi" prototype.

The "hi-fi" tests were carried out on three potential end product users. The users all had management positions within their company. The first two test persons are managers of a science park, while the third person is the MD of a mobile application company. The persons in the user tests for the "hi-fi" prototype had not taken part in the interviews nor the user tests on the "lo-fi" prototype. The user tests were recorded with a video camera.

The user tests consisted of five tasks and thirteen structured questions connected to the tasks that had been performed. The questions were then complemented with follow up questions depending on the answers of the interview subjects. The user tests were analyzed through a task.

The "hi-fi" prototype tests resulted in an updated design of the interface and a number of requirements for how the program should behave and how it should be implemented in the organization, as well as a set of design heuristics.

5. Results

In this section the three stages of development are presented, represented also by figures. These figures show only a small part of all the screens in the product, and are of course in higher resolution and color in the actual software. The data displayed in the figures are to visualize the software UI, and does not represent any actual organization. The features and functions behind the data are proprietary to Siguru, and thus not discussed further here. Where the decisions have been made with a basis in CHI literature, it is referenced, in other cases it is decisions made during the study with conclusions from the prototypes as a background.

The "lo-fi" prototype, as seen in figure 1, was constructed with support from theory and information gained through interviews. The major design decisions that were supported by theory and the interviews were:
Every piece of information is (in most cases) just one or two clicks away. This is made possible through the flap system and supports "recognition rather than recall" (Nielsen, 1994).

Three flaps were added, policy, education and inventory, in order to match the typical managers mental model of information security, which was found during the interviews and the scenario attached to the interviews (Nohlberg & Bäckström, 2007).

Information that was not regarded to be highly important for the novice users was hidden under the triangles to support Nielsen's principle of minimalist design (Nielsen, 1994). This was also done to minimize the amount of text and pictures, which would lead to reduced complexity and reduced clutter. Through this, the user primarily gets an overview of the current situation rather than details, which was one thing the interviewees said they wanted.

The language was adjusted to suit managers rather than technicians.

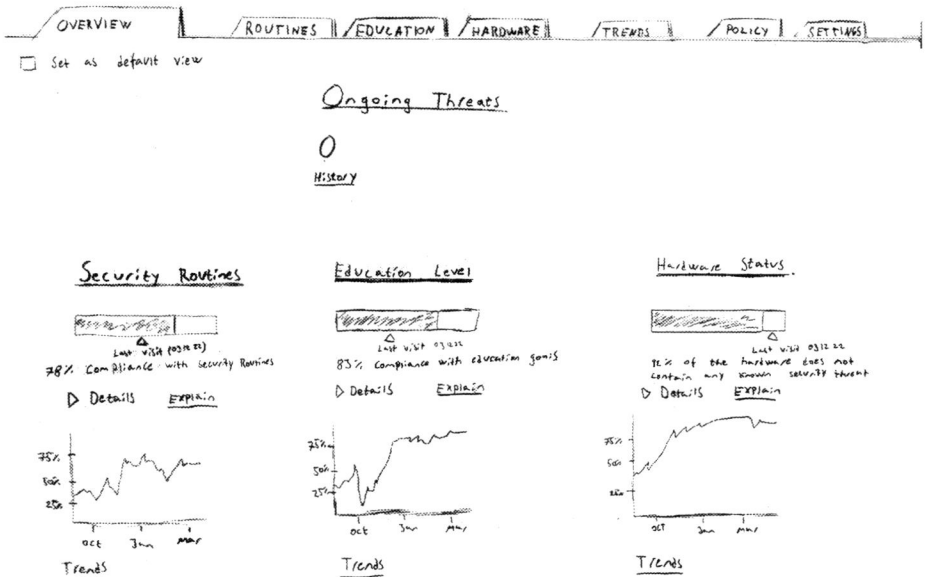

Figure 1: The "lo-fi" version of the overview page

The "lo-fi" prototype, as seen in figure 1, was developed on paper and tested. The major points of the feedback from the subjects where:

- The subjects preferred to have as little information as possible at the beginning, but also stressed that it was important to be able to access additional information in an easy way.
- The subjects want to be able to review why an incident happened and what can be learnt/improved from that. Because of that the history should include when and why the incident did happen, how much harm was done, what it cost, and other specific conditions at the time the incident happened.
- The subjects want to be able to see different threats that occurred at a certain time/period so that they can make strategic decisions based on this information. Therefore the history page should include an option that lets the user compare the threats during specific periods.

- It is important for managers to see the consequences of their investments in information security. Therefore a flap for money and resources was added to the "hi-fi" prototype.
- The subjects want to be able to see how severe a single threat/attack has been to the organization to make new decisions based on this information. Therefore the threats part of the inventory should include "consequences" of threats.

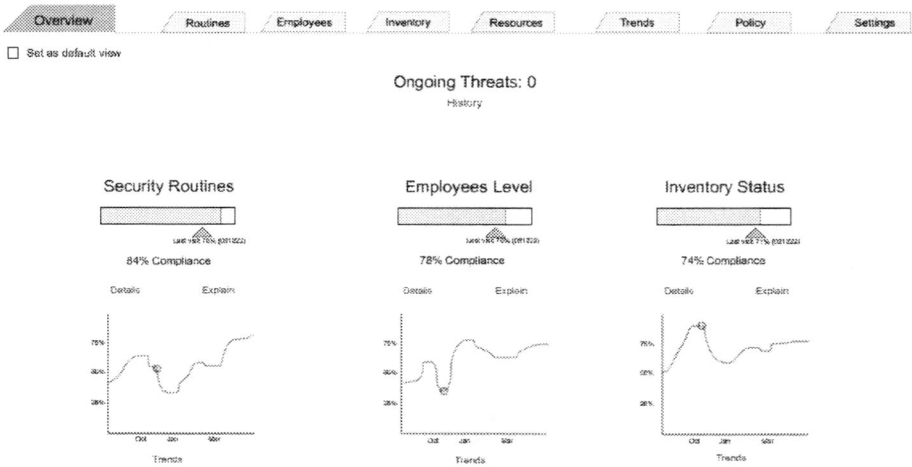

Figure 2: The "hi-fi" version of the overview page

The "hi-fi" prototype was developed further based on the results of the "lo-fi" tests and the interviews mentioned above; a screenshot can be seen in figure 2. The major points of feedback gained from the subjects were:

- A contextual help for each function that the users can access at any time will enhance the interaction with the system and provide guidance to the users when they need it.
- If the colors of the bars change depending on the status of the bar (e.g., if the value of a bar is critical, it should be red), then the users will easier interpret the value of the bar. Therefore if a value of a bar is acceptable, it should be in one color, if it is not acceptable it should be in another, and if it is close to not being acceptable it should be in a third color.
- When a user expands information that concerns a single subject, it should be made clear whether the information that he is expanding is connected to the information above or if it is new information. Therefore information that gives an overview of something should be made clearer and separate from information regarding one individual person

- According to the subjects it is important to be able to use the software to follow up the goals of the company, expenses etc. and thereby facilitate their ability to make strategic decisions. Therefore the trends graph should have an indication of how the different values relate to the reference values of the company. All the subjects stressed that it was very important that the program should support strategic and financial decisions, since that is a very important aspect of managers' responsibility.
- All subjects were satisfied with the amount of information that the interface presented.
- All subjects stressed that it was important to involve their subordinates in the system. By doing this they were likely to be more motivated to act in a secure way and at the same time they won't feel as monitored as they would feel if they were not involved.

All the subjects stressed that the information that was important to managers was information that gives an overview of the current situation rather than information that gives details about information security, and that the information should be presented using a vocabulary that managers can understand.

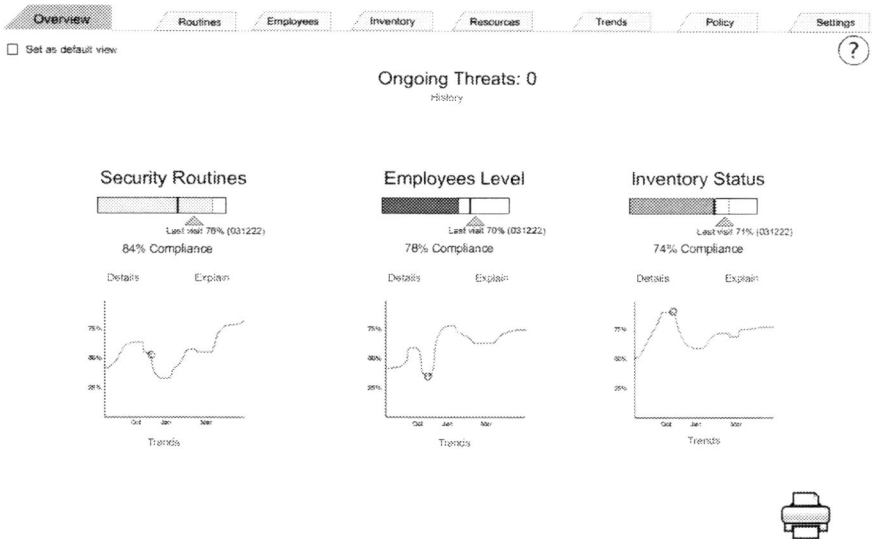

Figure 3: The final version of the overview page

This input was used when developing a final version of the interface; a screenshot of the final version can be seen in figure 3 above.

6. Conclusions and Discussion

Managers are interested in security, but often find it hard to grasp the knowledge needed to fully understand and to make decisions about security. Therefore the information given to managers about security should be adapted to the specific needs of the target audience, rather than the technical possibilities or the requirements of technical personnel. This project has found several key characteristics of what managers' wants to know about security:

1. Managers are more interested in the overall status of the information security of the company than the details. This does not make managers uninterested in details, but they only want them when they need them, and they tend to group together areas of information security.
2. Managers consider information security on a more strategic and financial level than security specialists tend to do, focusing more on risks.
3. Managers do not only see security from the perspective of security, but also considers the possibility of making other gains, such as increased efficiency, minimized downtime etc.

In order to cater to the specific needs of managers, three design heuristics for user centered security design aimed at managers were developed during development of the interface. They were based on the works of Norman (2002) and further developed in this context:

1. Provide overview information very early in the program. The typical manager does not have the time or the knowledge to make this overview by himself/herself.
2. Do not overwhelm the user. Normally a manager is not interested in the details of the information security and/or does not have time to read this sort of information. If the manager wants the information, the manager is likely to find it.
3. Provide information in a way that is familiar to the manager. Use wordings that the user understands. Provide contextual help for expressions that must be presented in a technical way.

This project aimed towards developing an interface to display security related information to managers. The user centered process for creating the interface has been successful. The concept and the interface have been appreciated by both the subjects and the company, and are now going to be used as the basis for developing the actual "Siguru"-product.

From a managerial perspective, it is important to know where the educational and economic resources should be spent to secure proper information security in the entire organization. This kind of information security information systems might be able to prevent people from acting in an insecure way, since it will help managers to make the right investments, be they in technology, resources, or education.

In the future, the Siguru-software will also consist of an education module, to be used by each and every employee. This is believed to help the employees to educate themselves in security, as well as improve general awareness of security. With a management information system like the one proposed in this study as a foundation, security education can be transformed from a mere sidetrack to a critical process, the same way that information security might be transformed; by helping the decision makers understand, and be active in the process. Information security might finally be integrated in the normal decision processes of managers. That is the first step to get a really secure organization – when those making the decisions both care about security and understand it, and a good way to stop committing the 10 deadly sins of information security management (von Solms & von Solms, 2004).

7. Acknowledgment

The authors would like to thank the subjects for giving freely and willingly of their time. The authors would also like to thank colleagues and friends for support during the process, in particular Benkt Wangler, Stewart Kowalski, Thomas Ekström from The Logic Planet AB and Alexander Backlund.

References

Berson, J. (2005), *Zone Alarm: Creating Usable Security Products for Consumers*, in Lorrie, F.C. and Simson G., *Security and Usability*, O' Reilly Media, Sebastopol, CA.

Department of Trade and Industry (2004) "United Kingdom's Department of Trade and Industry's Information Security Breaches Survey 2004", www.pwc.com/uk/eng/ins-sol/publ/pwc_DTI-InfoSecutiry-Survey2004-Exec.pdf, (Accessed 10 May 2006)

DePaula, R., Ding, X., Dourish, P., Nies, K., Pillet, B., Redmiles, D., Ren, J., Rode, J. & Silva, F.R. (2005), "Two Experiences Designing for Effective Security", cups.cs.cmu.edu/soups/2005/2005proceedings/p25-depaula.pdf, (Accessed 15 November 2006)

Dourish, P. and Redmiles, D. (2002), *An approach to Usable Security Based on Event Monitoring and Visualization*, New Security Paradigms Workshop 02.

Furnell, S.M., Jusoh, A., Katsabas, D. and Dowland, P. (2006), *Considering the Usability of End-User Security Software*, Proceedings of 21st IFIP International Information Security Conference (IFIP SEC 2006), Karlstad, Sweden, 22–24 May 2006, pp. 307–316.

Flechais, I. and Sasse, A.M. (2005), *Usable Security*, in Lorrie, F.C. and Simson, G., *Security and Usability*, O' Reilly Media, Sebastopol, CA.

Hackos, J.T. and Redish, J.C. (1998), *User and Task Analysis for Interface Design*, John Wiley & Sons, Inc., New York, NY.

Holmström, U. (1999), "User-centered design of security software", www.hft.org/HFT99/paper99/Design/5_99.pdf, (Accessed 10 October 2006)

Long, C.A. and Moskowitz, C. (2005), *Simple Desktop Security with Chameleon*, in Lorrie, F.C. and Simson, G., *Security and Usability*, O' Reilly Media, Sebastopol, CA.

Nielsen, J. (1994), *Heuristic evaluation,* in Nielsen, J., and Mack, R.L., *Usability Inspection Methods,* John Wiley & Sons, New York, NY.

Nohlberg, M., Bäckström, J. (2007), *Talking Security to Management: How to Do it.* Unpublished paper submitted for review.

Norman, D. (2002), *The Design of Everyday Things,* Basic Books, New York, NY.

Rasmussen M. (2002), "IT-Trends 2003: Information Security Standards, Regulations and Legislation", images.telos.com/files/external/Giga_IT_Trends_2003.pdf, (Accessed 5 August 2006)

Simon, R.T and Zurko, M.E. (1996), *User-centered security,* Proceedings of the UCLA conference on New security paradigms workshops September 17 – 20, portal.acm.org/citation.cfm?id=304859, (Accessed 5 August 2006)

Von Solms, B., Von Solms, R. (2004), The 10 deadly sins of information security management, *Computers & Security* 23 (5), pp. 371 – 376.

Tygar, J.D & Whitten, A. (1998), "Usability of Security: A Case Study", reports-archive.adm.cs.cmu.edu/anon/1998/abstracts/98-155.html, (Accessed 2 August 2006)

Vulnerable Groups and the Impact of Technology upon Personal Privacy

S.Atkinson[1], C.Johnson[2], and A.Phippen[1]

[1] Network Research Group, University of Plymouth, Plymouth, United Kingdom
[2] University of Plymouth, Plymouth, United Kingdom
email: shirley.atkinson@plymouth.ac.uk

Abstract

Privacy for the individual has become more of a concern as use of the Internet increases. Social websites that facilitate sharing of photographs and personal information potentially increase the risk of harm through harassment and bullying thus leading to serious physical or mental harm. Vulnerability is perceived in new technological development and privacy enhancing technologies (PETs) do not fully address the vulnerability issue. This research presents a view of privacy issues for two vulnerable groups, teenagers and domestic abuse survivors and concludes with how technology might address some of the vulnerability issues.

Keywords

Privacy, Vulnerability, Domestic Abuse, Teenagers, Technology.

1. Introduction

The intersection between personal data with Internet connectivity and the resultant potential for harm is an area of increasing concern. The media make much of the potential threats to privacy (BBC News, 2006, Ward, 2006a, Ward, 2006b) highlighting the latest technology and the potential for harm. Privacy activists utilise the Internet to promote their campaigns for confidentiality and protection of personal data (Caspian 2004, The Big Opt Out 2006, No2ID 2007, Spychips 2007). Furnell (2005) highlights the issues faced by Internet users, suggesting that the primary threat motivations are usually "mischief or money".

However a more serious potential for harm is seen with harassment and bullying coexisting with identity theft. These examples of criminal behaviours are exacerbated by the ready availability of personal information. Social networking websites have been linked to murder (Wired News, 2006); Bocij (2004) identifies the Internet as a tool for stalking behaviour; Southworth et al (2005) illustrate how domestic abuse is made easier with modern technology; and Mitchell et al (2005) and Hughes (2003) observe how the Internet has facilitated sexual exploitation of women and children.

The combination of this serious potential for harm with the evolution of the Internet into a more social space and the convergence of mobile phones with the Internet, leads to some disturbing issues. Websites share photographs, information, arrangements to meet friends and online diaries or 'blogs'. Both the European Commission (EU) and the UK Home Office have taken action to address the issues for harm: the EU Safer Internet Programme (2006) unites European countries aiming to provide a safer online environment for children; the Home Office initiated the Child Exploitation and Online Protection Centre (2006). Government education campaigns (Fiveash, 2006), and researchers (Bocij, 2006; CRU, 2006) give advice that centres around keeping personal information private. However, here lies the dichotomy, young people should keep their information safe, but they want to share it with their friends using the technology that is part of their social world.

This paper presents an outline of technological approaches to privacy and their limitations before presenting the study into the issues faced by inviduals for whom privacy is of serious concern. The findings from the study are presented followed by a discussion on how technology might be utilised to address some vulnerability issues.

2. Technological Solutions

Privacy enhancing technologies (PETs) and privacy aware technologies (PATs) attempt to address some of the concerns surrounding the control of personal information: PETs minimise or eliminate the collection of identifiable data (HISPEC, 2002); PATs are designed, developed and deployed with privacy in mind (Cannon, 2004). Limiting factors are seen in the deployment and usage of PETs: weak tools within distributed systems (Goldberg, 2003); explicit choice between anonymity and identity (Burkett, 1997); and lack of awareness of threats by the individual (Furnell, 2005). Those in favour of PATs suggest better protection is afforded when privacy measures are incorporated into design (Givens, 2000), or when technological and social approaches are combined to provide the best privacy toolkits (Goldberg 2003, Raab 2004).

Garfinkel (2000) suggests that developers create naturally privacy invasive solutions by ignoring the need to protect personal information, leading to lack of control for the individual. Solove (2004) also describes technology as creating an "architecture of vulnerability" where individuals are placed at risk, yet powerless to take any action, giving identity theft as an example of this. The Fraud Advisory Panel (2005) identify technology as providing new approaches for fraudulent behaviour, changing the boundaries of how criminal behaviour takes place. Disclosure (Dinev and Hart, 2004) and lack of control of personal information (Margulis, 1977) has been directly linked to issues of vulnerability.

One issue to emerge from criticisms of the technological approach is how best to inform design. To this end, Raab and Bennett (1998) propose that studying privacy issues for vulnerable groups would enhance the technological design for personal privacy protection.

3. Study of Potential for Harm

Two groups of individuals were chosen as those who most exhibit issues of vulnerability: Domestic abuse survivors (hereafter referred to as Survivors) and Teenagers. For these groups the lack of control of personal information has some serious consequences: Survivors are at most risk when they decide the leave an abusive relationship (Women's Aid, 2002); Teenagers make full use of the Internet as a social networking tool and are considered most at risk from predatory behaviour (Magid, 2004).

3.1 Methodology

Qualitative approaches to collecting information were adopted as the most appropriate way to study the social context (Dahlbert, 2004) and to gain an understanding of how the different complexities involved were experienced (Feenberg, 1999). Semi-structured interviews were held with: refuge managers; providers of Survivor's outreach services; and probation and police officers. Front line staff were selected as those best able to give an overview of the situation without being under emotional duress. Focus groups were held involving 105 teenagers from the South West of England, with an average age of 14.7 years and a fairly even gender balance. An online questionnaire distributed through snowball sampling collected opinion about different privacy scenarios concerning the Internet.

4. Findings

Whilst the issues for Survivors and Teenagers fell into different categories, there were some similarities. Tracking of Survivors was felt to be the primary concern, whether technologically assisted or through methods best described as "social engineering" (Mitnick and Simon, 2003). Teenagers did not see any problems with sharing their personal information on specific websites, but they did view with suspicion websites that wanted to gather personal information for which there was no obvious reason. Some described unwanted contact and how they had dealt the situation.

4.1 Survivors

As Abrahams (2007) highlights the safety of Survivors relies heavily upon protecting the security of the refuge, ensuring that even inadvertent actions do not compromise safety. Of primary concern therefore, was how technology provided abusers with the tools and information necessary to carry out abusive or controlling behaviour. Tracking of safe houses or refuges through divulging of address information;

continuation of harassment and controlling behaviour through the use of mobile phones; residents use of the Internet in refuges; and data protection controls of third parties were all expressed as concerns.

4.1.1 Tracking

Examples of tracking were given where location information had been gleaned through Internet resources or mobile phones. One woman had been traced through her Internet banking, it was not beyond the realms of possibility that pin numbers and personal questions were known or easily calculated by an intimate partner. In another situation, a perpetrator had access to data held in the Drivers Vehicle Licence Authority (DVLA) database which was provided to his place of work through an Internet connection. The registration number of the support workers car was traced which in turn provided the address. The perpetrator was therefore able to discover which refuge the Survivor had fled to.

One respondent described the elaborate security details that the support services had created, only to be overturned by a member of staff at a utility company divulging the address.

> "She'd had high level security around moving in ....He'd got the address from the gas board because he rang and said that he was aware that they'd turned it off but unfortunately he couldn't remember the house number and they actually gave the full postal address. The lengths that that woman had gone to, ...even the removal men didn't know the address they were taking her to until the van was laden. ....That is awful when somebody has gone to that length to be safe and it's been taken away. For three days they'd had the only peace of mind that they'd ever known, and even then, they were anxious about going out to the shops or anything. Then there he was on the door. He actually said that was how he tracked her down."

Mapping websites such as Google Earth, multimap aerial photographs, upmystreet.com and 192.com caused concern for refuges because of the way that the Royal Mail allocate post box numbers. P O Box postcodes are allocated according to the address of the property, not the nearest post office. The mapping websites show exactly where in the country the postcodes are located and provide aerial images in some cases. One manager of a refuge spoke of her despair at trying to remove their postcode from a mapping website.

> "it just makes a mockery of everything that we try and achieve in terms of confidentiality and secrecy and just to think anybody could log on to that website and have a pretty good idea of where we are, and the fact that we can't get it removed either."

4.1.2 Mobile Phones

Mobile phones were considered problematic in providing constant communication between the Survivor and the perpetrator as well as issues surrounding location tracking. One refuge manager described how mobile phones almost negated the work that the refuge was trying to carry out.

> "In terms of the old days, if women fled they could get away from their partners without their partner knowing where they were .... Often the fact that women come with mobile phones and partners have access those numbers, means that there's all sort of different issues ....you do occasionally have situations........where a woman is in the refuge and they talk to their partners........which just seems a bit of an irony,.......in that they are in a refuge to get away from them in the first place, ...where he has attacked them and the police have come to get them, and they are actually talking to them."

Women in the refuges were encouraged to change their phone numbers and in most cases were provided with new Sim cards for their mobile phones. Despite this, two respondents described incidents where new mobile numbers had been discovered by the perpetrators. Mobile phones were also common presents to children of the relationship and therefore caused concern over location tracking services being used. One outreach support worker described how survivor's mobile phones would often be checked by perpetrators.

> "Most women who have mobile phones will say that they're partners check their phones, they check them for numbers, they randomly ring the number, they'll answer them"

In addition to these actions, the support worker was certain that a client of hers had been traced using her mobile phone.

> "We've had problems in the past where, and I don't understand the technicality of it, but whereby partners of women who've got mobile phones have been able to actually track where they are from the phone."

4.1.3 Data Control

For those remaining within the home environment, emails and Internet history being monitored were a well known issue. Survivors were described as being more likely to be fooled by spam and phishing emails.

> "When you see things like that it is, especially if you are vulnerable, you can sometimes be easily swayed."

Other forms of harassment were described where personal details had been posted by perpetrators to advertise sexual services.

Within refuges computing facilities were provided to Survivors primarily for two reasons: housing authorities were now using online bidding for housing; and resident's children needed access to assist with their education. However, two new problems were identified:

- personal information was freely divulged by the residents about themselves and about other residents.
- Gambling, pornography, online dating websites accessed.

The effectiveness of privacy controls utilised by third parties storing personal data about service users was raised as a concern. The effect of the Freedom of Information Act had been felt when one perpetrator had used the right of access to information to discover the safe-house location of the family. In another situation the support worker had to take great care over how rehousing information was to be held:

> "a woman working for the local authority who wanted to access our service who's partner worked for the city council too, and was very anxious about what we held on computer and what information we sent in. Because we were assisting with rehousing and they were actually anxious about who had access to that information within the city council, whether it was held and maintained in that individual section, or whether it would be accessible because her partner was in a position where she thought he may be able to find out that information. So there has been a number of cases like that I think where people have been anxious."

4.2 Teenagers

The findings from the focus groups were very much in keeping with what was expected: 83% of young people interacted online; 62% gave out personal information as part of a registration process. What was noteworthy was that 27% expressed concern about having given out information. Figure 1 illustrates a fairly even gender split of those who signed up and those who were concerned.

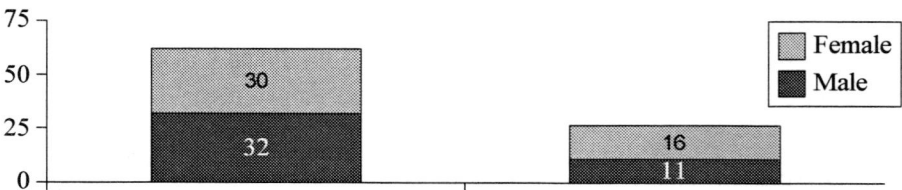

Figure 1: Gender split on divulging Personal Information

4.2.1 Internet Usage

The majority of young people said they made use of the Internet for: homework; revision; referencing Wikipedia; searching for information for work; school work; and coursework. Social uses were described which included interaction with friends; playing games; and downloading music or videos. Connecting with friends from school was a major activity with only one person admitting to using the Internet to meet new people. Control measures were utilised on occasion where the ability of messaging software to block people was utilised.

52 different websites were listed as having collected personal information from the respondents, with the top three being social networking sites. The most common sites were MSN Space, Bebo, and My Space which have differing privacy approaches. My Space made it easy to find people by school and allowed a search for young people between the ages of 16 and 18, however with Bebo a search could not be made of a young people at a specific school unless invited by somebody who was already a member. At the time of researching the websites, MSN Spaces was upgraded to Windows Live Spaces which appeared to have stronger privacy controls allowing different public and private profiles to be created.

Most young people knew that large amounts of information should not be given out, one respondent passed comment on the apparent naivety of individuals who posted large amounts of personal information on the web, suggesting that these must be younger people who did not have an idea of the potential dangers. This protection of information also related to websites that collected quantities of personal information during the registration process. Many young people evaluated the websites to determine which requests for information were really necessary.

> "…... Or rather, it concerns me how much some websites ask for when I can't see why they would need the information or if a website asks for an email address for what would appear to be to gain nothing particularly. I don't give my information to them. I use my hotmail"

Mandatory fields collecting personal information that were considered to be in excess of what was necessary, were circumvented with false information or aliases frequently used. One respondent described making up a false address in order to circumvent the need for American zip codes. Multiple email addresses were used in some cases, one for signing up to websites, and another for personal use.

4.2.2 Bad Experiences

Most teenagers answered "No" when asked if they had any bad experiences using the Internet with two notable exceptions. One described looking for information about a basketball team, and on clicking the hyperlink being confronted with pornography; another described pornographic material sent to his hotmail account which had to be shut down.

Being contacted by strangers through MSN Instant Messenger was mentioned in five different groups, but was not explicitly considered to be a bad experience. One group of girls described men discovering their email addresses on the Internet, making contact and suggestive remarks; one student could trace the increase in spam emails to when his friend had published his email address on the Internet; another described an interaction through MSN with somebody who at first appeared to be a friend of theirs, but later transpired not to be; another girl described how her suspicions were aroused when conversing with somebody claiming to be 13 years old saying:

> "This guy, like * he added me and I just accepted him thinking oh, I don't know who it is. He said he lived far away. He said where do you live, and I goes **, and he said where's that? and he didn't know. So I thought, everyone knows where ** is and he said I don't . Then I said how old are you and he said he was 13. Then he like showed a picture and he looked loads older, and then started saying like loads of weird things to me, so I thought, then I showed my mum and she said there's no way he's like 13 and stuff like this."

Being contacted by strangers was not the only thing to make some young people feel vulnerable. Another person described taking part in an online game which included a large number of players speaking French. As he did not speak French he could not understand what they were saying, but noticed his name being mentioned many times, which in turn led to his feeling very insecure.

Three people described financial losses: one had an e-bay purchase that went wrong; another had a credit card fraudulently used through e-bay; and the final one was from a prize draw scam.

> "It said we'd won something, then we clicked on it and then it says you ring up. So we rang up and then it said, give the bank details. We'd done it before and it's just then she got scammed over thousand pounds and lost pounds from her bank account. But then the bank could do nothing about it."

5. Discussion

The findings illustrate the effects on individuals when personal information is released, whether they have explicilty released the information themselves or another party has done so. Previous work by Margulis (1977) and Dinev and Hart (2004) correlated the release of personal information to vulnerability, the more personal information released, the more vulnerable an individual becomes. Considering that measure in terms of risk measurement, each instance of personal information released by the individual or by a third party, can therefore be seen in terms of increasing the risk. Risk measurement, risk assessment and risk management techniques can therefore be applied to control the amount of personal information and thus reduce the risk.

Reducing the risk links well with the approach advocated by Clarke (1995) in Situational Crime Prevention (SCP). SCP is where the opportunity for specific categories of crime are reduced. This looks primarily at offender reactions in different situations where the risk of being caught or convicted is high, then the benefits of committing the crime have to be high for them to offend. The Internet combined with the anonymity provided by some PETs has enabled the abuse of information to happen with reduced risk detection.

Current PETs do fit into this situations of risk assessment, or management. Young people wish to share their information with others for social networking purposes and will circumvent various filtering controls and constraints; personal information has to be divulged during certain transactions; government public records are published; many situations have an unequal power balance against the individual, there are no other real alternatives but to give out the information. Therefore PETs that rely on making individuals choose between anonymity or identity are not suitable, they do not fit this context.

If the approach is taken whereby technology enables and empowers the individual to take more responsibility for their actions, a reduction in risk should follow. This approach is seen with the current health and safety approach in this country. The UK Government has enacted legislation to enforce safe practice within the workplace, The Health and Safety at Work Act, 1974; business and employers have a duty of care to their workforce and to their customers; and individuals have a duty to act in ways that continue that duty of care to both themselves and to others.

PETs could be created to combine the monitoring of the release of personal information in such a way that individuals had control over it, they could return to where they gave out the information and perhaps be able to take steps to remove it should they wish. Personal information held by other parties could also be monitored. This approach needs to be embedded into everyday tools which are intuitive and easy to use, that do not require very much in the way of mental overhead for the individual.

To achieve this approach, the next phase in this research is to create a prototype browser plug in that allows individuals to keep track of where they have given out their personal information, where information is stored about themselves and links to current advisory sites to help them make decisions.

6. Conclusion

The findings from the two groups has illustrated the different risks that occur from the release of personal information. Readily available tracking technologies; release of personal details; divulgence of information by third parties all combined causing different threats. In the case of Survivors, often the impacts were felt even though they did not themselves engage with the technologies.

Teenagers made good use of the web in a predominantly social manner. The use of messenger and social networking websites illustrated a significant amount of personal information being divulged. Teenagers demonstrated their proficiency at making use of the software controls provided or by providing false information to circumvent excessive collection of personal data.

To address the current criticisms of PETs technological solutions need to allow individuals the ability to minimise their risks, that are inutuitive and relevant to the situation in which the individual finds themself. In this regard, PETs could then be seen to fulfil a role in controlling the risks for the potential for harm.

The purpose of this research has been to explore the privacy issues faced by the more vulnerable members of society. The issues highlighted in the study where individual's have been exposed to a risk of harm, or where privacy has been eroded through an individual's own use, or another's use of technology, form important elements for consideration when considering the impact of technology upon privacy. These useful pointers can be used by designers of technology and software; for policymakers and for those who have a moral responsibility for individuals.

Future work will involve a study of how technology may combine with other social and human factors to bring about a reduction in the elements of risk faced by the two vulnerable groups used in this study.

References

Abrahams, H, (2007), *Supporting Women after Domestic Violence*, Jessica Kingsley, London.

BBC News, (2006), *"Privacy fears hit google search"*, 10th February 2006,
http://news.bbc.co.uk/1/hi/technology/4700002.stm (accessed 30 November 2006)

Bocij, P, (2004), *Cyberstalking*, Praeger, Conneticut

Burkett, H, (1997), "Privacy-Enhancing Technologies: Typology, Critique, Vision", In Agre, P.E., and Rotenberg, M (Eds), *Technology and Privacy: The New Landscape*, MIT Press, London

Cannon, J.C., (2004), *Privacy What Developers and IT Professionals Should Know*, Addison Wesley Professional, Harlow

Caspian (2004), "Consumers against supermarket privacy invasion and numbers", www.nocards.org, (accessed 31 March 2007)

Clarke, R.V., (1995), "Situational Crime Prevention, Building a Safer Society: Strategic Approaches to Crime Prevention", *Crime and Justice*, Vol. 19, pp. 91-150

CRU, (2006), *Internet Safety Zone*, Cyberspace Research Unit, University of Lancaster
http://www.internetsafetyzone.co.uk/root/default.htm (accessed 30 November 2006)

Dahlberg, L., (2004), "Internet Research Tracings: Towards Non-Reductionist Methodology",
JCMC, 9 (3) April 2004, http://jcmc.indiana.edu/vol9/issue3/dahlberg.html (accessed 30
November 2006)

Dinev, T. and Hart, P, (2004), "Internet Privacy Concerns and their Antecedents -
Measurement Validity and a Regression Model", *Behaviour and Information Technology*,
Volume 23, Issue 6, November 2004 pages 413-422

European Commission, (2006), *Safer Internet Programme*, Europe's Information Society,
http://europa.eu.int/information_society/activities/sip/index_en.htm (accessed 30 November
2006)

Feenberg, A, (1999), *Questioning Technology*, Routledge, London

Fiveash, K, (2006), "Internet safety talks for UK kids", *The Register*,
http://www.theregister.co.uk/2006/09/20/internet_children_safety/ (accessed 30 November
2006)

Furnell, S, (2005), "Internet threats to end-users: Hunting easy prey", *Network Security*, July,
pp5-9

Fraud Advisory Panel (The), (2005), *The Human Cost of Fraud: Seventh Annual Review*,
Fraud Advisory Panel,
http://www.fraudadvisorypanel.org/newsite/Publications/Publications_annualreports.htm
(accessed 30 November 2006)

Garfinkel, S, (2000), *Database Nation*, O'Reilly Associates, Sebastopol, CA

Givens, B, (2000), "Eight Reasons to be Skeptical of a "Technology Fix" for protecting
privacy", In *Proceedings of Computer Professionals for Social Responsibility*, University of
Pennsylvania, Philadelphia, http://www.privacyrights.org/ar/8skeptical.htm (accessed 30
November 2006)

Goldberg, I, (2003), "Privacy-Enhancing Technologies for the Internet, II: Five Years Later",
In *Privacy Enhancing Technologies*, LNCS Volume 2482/2003, Springer Berlin / Heidelberg

HiSPEC, (2002), "Privacy Enhancing Technologies State of the Art Review",
www.hispec.org.uk, http://www.hispec.org.uk/public_documents/7_1PETreview3.pdf
(accessed 30 November 2006)

Home Office, (2006), "Child Exploitation and Online Protection Centre",
http://www.ceop.gov.uk/ (accessed 30 November 2006)

Hughes, D.M., (2003), "Prostitution online", *Journal of Trauma Practice*, Vol 2. No 3/4,
2003, pp115-132 http://www.uri.edu/artsci/wms/hughes/internet.pdf (accessed 30 November
2006)

Magid, L, (2004), "Teen Safety on the Information Highway", *National Center for Missing and Exploited Children*, http://www.safeteens.com/safeteens.htm#Guidelines_for_Parents_0 (accessed 30 November 2006)

Margulis, S.T, (1977), "Conceptions of Privacy: Current Status and Next Steps", In *Journal of Social Issues*, 33. 5-10

Mitchell KJ, Finkelhor D, Wolak J, (2005), "The Internet and family and acquaintance sexual abuse", Child Maltreatment, 10 (1): 49-60 FEB 2005

Mitnick, K. D.,Simon, W. L., (2003), *The Art of Deception: Controlling the Human Element of Security*, Wiley

No2ID (2007), "The NO2ID Campaign", www.no2id.net, (accessed 31 March 07)

Raab, C.D and Bennett, C.J, (1998), "Distribution of Privacy Risks: Who Needs Protection", *Information Society*, Vol 14, Issue 4, p 263-274

Raab, C.D., (2004), "The Future of Privacy Protection", *Cyber Trust and Crime Prevention Project*, http://www.foresight.gov.uk/Previous_Projects/Cyber_Trust_and_Crime_Prevention/Reports_ and_Publications/The_Future_of_Privacy_Protection/The_Future_of_Privacy_Protection.html (accessed 31 March 2007)

Solove, D.J, (2004), *The Digital Person*, New York University Press, New York

Southworth, C., Dawson, S., Fraser, C., Tucker, S., (2005), "A High Tech Twist on Abuse: Technology, Intimate Partner Stalking and Advocacy", *Violence Against Women Online Resources*, Minesota
http://www.mincava.umn.edu/documents/commissioned/stalkingandtech/stalkingandtech.html (accessed 30 November 2006)

Spychips (2007), "RFID 1984", www.spychips.com, (accessed 31 March 2007)

The Big Opt Out (2006), "NHS Confidentiality Campaign", www.nhsconfidentiality.org, (accessed 31 March 2007)

Ward, M, (2006a), *Radio Tag Study revealed at Cebit*, BBC, 10th March 2006, http://news.bbc.co.uk/1/hi/technology/4792554.stm (accessed 30 November 2006)

Ward, M, (2006b), *Wi-fi set to re-wire social rules*, BBC, 8th March 2006, http://news.bbc.co.uk/1/hi/technology/4770188.stm (accessed 30 November 2006)

Wired News, (2006), *Teens Reveal Too Much Online*, Associated Press, 5th February, 2006 http://www.wired.com/news/wireservice/1,70163-0.html (accessed 30 November 2006)

Womens Aid Federation of England, (2002), *Domestic Violence Statistical Factsheet 2002*, , http://www.womensaid.org.uk/dv/dvfactsh2002.htm

A Systemic Approach to Analysing the Implications of the Introduction of Biometric Passports

C. Hennell and V. Katos

School of Computing, University of Portsmouth, UK
email: {cheryl.hennell, vasilios.katos}@port.ac.uk

Abstract

This paper adopts a systemic approach to developing a holistic view in order to facilitate an understanding of the security and usability issues relating to the implementation and adoption of biometric passports. The main focus is to establish whether the proposed use of the biometric technologies should be used both for identification and authentication of the holder. Using the UK's National Identity Scheme (NIS) and National Identity Register (NIR) initiatives as a case study, we explore their proposals in the international context.

Keywords

Biometrics, Security, Usability, Rich Picture.

1. Introduction

It is a paradox that on a macro-scale we demand a freedom to live our lives and security from the governments that have the power to provide that security whilst on a micro-scale demanding that our personal civil liberties and privacy are sustained. Before 9/11 and enhanced since, the focus on terrorism and a need to protect national boundaries has gained momentum. Governments across the globe are passing laws that will support the introduction of identity cards (UK 2006) and the expedition of biometric passports (27 countries) in the name of protecting indigenous populations. The political and technical agenda sit outside the scope of this paper, however there are, as this paper will show, elements that are noteworthy of mention as they impact the human concerns over the use of biometric passport systems.

This paper addresses the question of whether biometric passports should be used as identification or authentication of the owner, and how this can be securely achieved. The paper is structured as follows: First we provide an overview of biometrics and the relationship with secure identification and authentication by mainly drawing on the work of UK Government bodies. We continue to discuss the relationship between security and usability of biometrics and the role of the user. Section 3 considers the UK Government proposals for implementing the information system to capture, store and process the biometric data. In Section 4, we discuss a selection of external factors that might impact the success of the biometric passport system. Section 5 presents a systemic view of the discussions in the previous sections to provide a holistic image of the conflicts, concerns and issues related to the introduction of biometric passports. Based on the systemic representation, we conclude with a justification for our proposal to improve usability and security of biometric passports for identification and authentication, in the UK.

2. Biometrics and the Government

Biometrics can be defined as the use of anatomical, physiological or behaviour characteristics to recognise or verify the claimed identity of a person. It requires the collection, processing and storage of a person's physical characteristics (Coventry et al, 2003). Biometrics have a long history and are inextricably linked with forensic sciences: many of the emerging biometric areas are based on mature forensic disciplines.

The use of biometrics as identification and/or authentication is not however a new concept. There are some indications that biometrics were used by the ancient Egyptians to routinely record distinguishing marks. Pharaohs certified decrees with thumbprints and workers on pyramids were identified by biographical data and biometric data such as distinguishing features. In 14th century China, children's palm and footprints were recorded for identification purposes (Roberts, 2005)]. It is the IT security use of biometrics for identification and authentication in that is the emerging technology.

Traditional passports contain limited biographical data on the holder stored in two machine readable lines of OCR-B typeface. The standard format, data elements, field length and check digits comprise the first security measure that International Civil Aviation Organization (ICAO) invented for a passport. The photograph is used to confirm identity of the holder (McMunn, 2005). The traditional passports are not tamper proof and subject to forgery. In 1997, at the request of the ICAO, the New Technologies Working Group began a systematic study of biometrics and their potential to enhance identity confirmation. Adopting a scientific, quantitative scoring approach, the study chose to evaluate different biometrics against the unique requirements of travel document issuance and inspection processes. In their review of biometric technologies, the ICAO assessed their compatibility according to seven criteria, including:

- compatibility with enrolment requirements
- compatibility with MRTD renewal requirements
- compatibility with MRTD machine-assisted identity verification requirements
- redundancy
- global public perception
- storage requirements
- performance

- The results of the study (McMunn, 2005), based on their overall ability to meet the comprehensive set of requirements, were categorized into three groups:
- Group 1: Face achieves the highest compatibility rating (greater than 85%);
- Group 2: Finger(s) and eye(s) emerge with a second-level compatibility rating (near 65%); and
- Group 3: Signature, hand and voice emerge with a third-level compatibility rating (less than 50%).

These outcomes provide the basis for the development of the biometric passports currently being introduced by different governments as a mechanism to improve security at national borders. The validity of this adopted practice depends on the usability of the biometric passport and the human acceptance.

3. Security and Usability

The passport is conceptually a security token, something the holder *has*. As discussed, the *token* stores data on the holder and the holder does not need to *know* what the data are to be able to use the token to cross borders. This token is not secure. It is not tamper proof and it may be lost. However, for the holder, it is easy to use. The introduction of biometric passports should maintain the ease of use whilst increasing the security for the individual and the nation. There is a direct, if inverse, relationship between security and usability. In general the more stringent the security, the more it interferes with the user's experience causing a decrease in the usability of the system (Garzonis et al, 2004). There has been recognition that user behaviour plays a part in many security failures: it has become common to refer to users as 'the weakest link' (Sasse et al, 2001). User acceptance and behaviour have a direct impact on the successful adoption and implementation of biometric systems. Traditional passports are tokens that may be universally owned. Biometric passports require a different set of properties.

Biometric modalities can be classified by five desirable properties:

- Universal (available on all people)
- Invariant (features extracted are non-changing)
- High intra-class variability (features extracted are different from each user)
- Acceptable (characteristic is suitable for use by everyone)
- Extractable (a sensor can extract the features presented in a repeatable fashion) (Clarke, 1994; Wayman, 2000; Coventry et al, 2003; Kukula and Elliott, 2006).

To acquire a traditional passport requires the completion of documents and the presentation of a photograph authenticated by a *trusted* person. In the case of biometric passports, holders are required to enrol onto the system and for their biometric data to be captured and stored. In different business applications, a different biometric might be more appropriate than others. The iris being used quite successfully where there is a high volume of people passing through a system, such as the expedited gate clearing at the airports (Courtney, 2005).

The introduction of biometric passports is being considered by governments across the world. The consensus of minimum data appears to be biographical in nature. Those biometric passports that have been considered appear to adopt the basic requirements of the ICAO, however, their implementation appears to be different. For example, Australia includes a PKI approach, whereas the Swedish passports use two chips (one for border control and one for accessing electronic services), unlike Singapore and Russia who use one chip.

However, some governments have decided to extend the scope in order to utilise the stored data for purposes other than purely border control. A particular case of interest is that of the UK government who appear to be using the introduction of the biometric passport to simultaneously develop the introduction of personal identity card.

3.1. The UK Government proposals

To further this discussion, we need to understand the UK Government proposals and intentions for the new biometric passport system. The UK Government has established a set of processes and procedures to set up a system to manage the biometric passports and identity card enrolments, data storage and data processing. This is known as the National Identity Scheme (NIS) (Home Office, 2006). In the plan they propose to deliver benefits in a number of key areas. These include securing national borders and tackling illegal immigration through effective identity management; reducing identity theft and identity fraud to fight crime and terrorism, and using the national identity scheme to protect vulnerable members of society, and to provide a shared data resource between government departments.

The Identity Cards Act 2006 outlines the main aims of the scheme as maintaining a secure and reliable record of facts about individuals in order to:

- prevent or detect crime;
- ensure national security;
- enforce immigration controls;
- secure the efficient and effective provision of public services; and
- enforce prohibitions on unauthorised working or employment (Garzonis et al, 2004).

The National Identity Scheme will be delivered by the Identity and Passport Service; the first Identity Cards are scheduled to be issued by 2009. The linking between the Identity Card and the issuing body provides an insight to the rationale for the collection and storage of both biographical data and biometric data for the biometric passports.

Biometric passports, including chips with the holder's facial biometric, were introduced in March 2006. These passports are in line with the standards set by the International Civil Aviation Organisation (ICAO) in May 2003, which nominated facial recognition as the primary biometric with iris and fingerprint as backup.

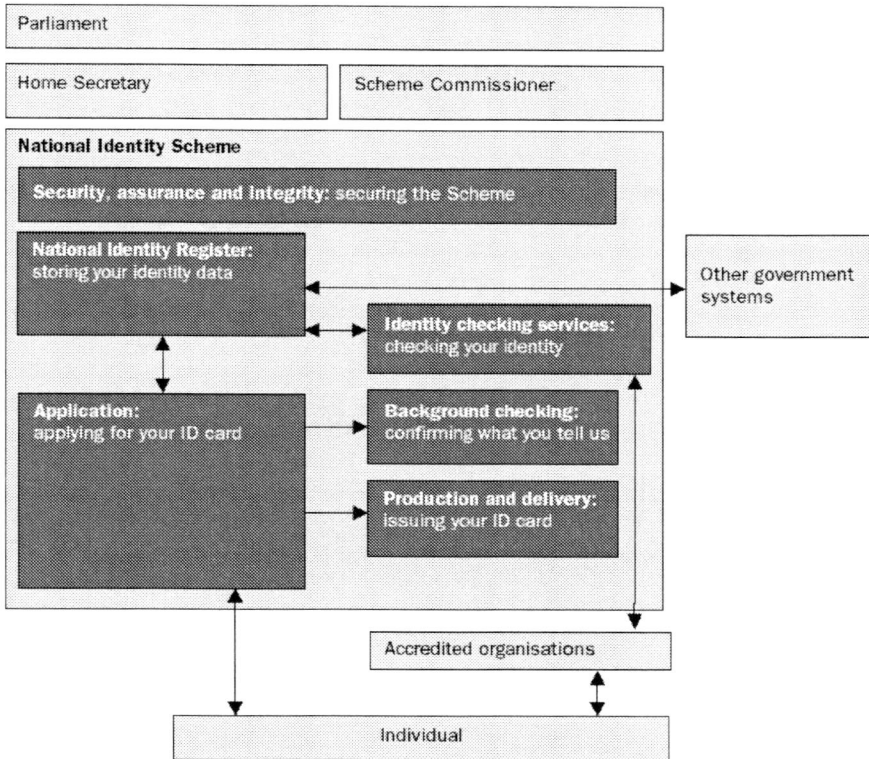

Figure 1: The National Identity Scheme model (source: Home Office, 2006)

The model clearly identifies the government's intentions to store biometric data alongside other personal and biographical data elements such as name, address and date of birth. The model also highlights the intention for the National Identity System to share this stored data with other government agencies. The government propose to store the data in a single logical database and on smart cards. Customised-of-the-shelf software modules will be used to process the data. The rationale for this approach is to simplify maintenance, to reduce risk and to highlight security violations as the data flows between the systems.

3.2. Issues

A number of studies have explored the technical perspectives relating to the various biometric devices, examining response times, Type I and Type II error sensitivity, data storage and retrieval times, and the cryptographic systems proposed to protect the data. Other studies have been conducted eliciting views from the general public through surveys to determine the acceptance levels by the British public of biometric passports. In the UK, the discussions relating to the biometric passport appear to be integrated with those of the introduction of the identity card. The latter has received a tide of negativity and overshadowed the introduction of the biometric passport. Whilst endorsing and supporting the need for an ID Card system, expert panel sessions and the LSE report have voiced concerns about the proposed system, and its ability to achieve its stated objectives within the current legislative and technology framework (Stevens, 2005). We need then to establish a secure system to identify and authenticate the holder of the passport to establish legal right of entry to the country. However, the authentication process is one of ensuring integrity, that the holder of the passport is who they claim to be.

Counterpoint to the usability claim of the biometric passport system as an effective and efficient security mechanism is the authentication of the holder. Herein lies the weak link to the perceived secure use of biometric passports. In order to gain a UK passport, the applicant needs to provide personal documents and data. This includes a birth certificate. Acquiring a birth certificate in not a difficult process and can now be undertaken on-line. Armed with a birth certificate and an application form, the applicant can assume the identity of any person. The biometric data will be captured, processed and stored on the biometric passport. As far as the system is concerned, the applicant's new identity is endorsed, with the biometric evidence as proof.

In the next section we consider a number of threat vectors related to the introduction of biometric passports.

3.3. Threat vectors

What does the biometric passport offer that conventional passports cannot? The passport demonstrates the owners' nationality and right to enter his/her own national boundaries. Whilst the traditional style passports have in the past been forgeable, it is intended that the introduction of biometrics should reduce this, strengthening the national border security.

It was mentioned earlier that in order for systems to succeed, the implementation must reduce 'the weakest link' – that of the human user. In this section we consider a number of external factors that initially appear to be unconnected. Collectively we perceive that these external factors create potential vulnerabilities which may be exposed to threat agents.

3.3.1 Identity Theft

The growing rate of identity theft, or at least the growth in the broadcasting of identity theft incidents have lead to public fear, uncertainty and mistrust. Many people have personally experienced financial loss and credit difficulties as a consequence of their identities being stolen. The public on the one hand are encouraged to protect their data both physical and soft, ensuring the use of strong passwords, firewalls and security software, and the secure destruction of identifying documentation such as household bills and credit card receipts. Ironically, on the other hand there is a perception that they are required to store all of their personal data and biometric data, the most sensitive personal data of all, on a digital chip in a single location, and of a questionable physical security. The difficulties faced in restoring one's financial status and credit rating, are challenging enough to provide sufficient convincing evidence of innocence. The challenges faced if ones complete biometric profile is stolen could be insurmountable.

3.3.2. Privacy and Human Rights

The UK Government's proposals to store unprotected biographical and biometric data on the passport chip may have serious personal consequences. Privacy International (2004) have stated that "The ICAO is aware, however, that there are contentious legal issues involved with the infrastructure for these passports, including the collisions between the goals of centralizing citizens' biometrics and protecting privacy laws, and with 'cultural practices'. Not only does this involve a central data store of fingerprints and photos (and face scans) that can be scanned against other databases for other purposes, but this sensitive information may be transferred to other countries when verification is required at border controls. The ICAO foresees that this information may be retained by these other countries. In essence, this may turn into a global distributed database of personal information.

3.3.3. Departures and Arrivals Airport Security

Since the events of 9/11, there has been a noticeable increase, decline and then increase (following 7/7 terrorist attacks in London) of security measures at UK airports. Baggage security, personal security checks and searches heightened slowing down the movement of passengers. However, automated biometric passport controls have been implemented which enable passengers to conduct their own passage through border controls. The microchip embedded in the passport can be read by a special chip reader, while digital signatures verify the data's authenticity, or reveal if the data has been tampered with (O'Brien, 2006).

In Singapore, the Automatic Border Control (ABC) System replaces the manual immigration clearance process with a more efficient and secure system, thereby eliminating human error while heightening security significantly. The automated operation uses a hybrid biometric authentication – NEC Facial Recognition and NEC Finger Identification - to reduce a previously 15-minute process of immigration clearance to mere seconds with the highest accuracy achievable today. The ABC

System also offers immigration authorities the added advantage of re-deploying limited resources to other important functions (NEC, 2005)]

For those airports without automated passport controls, the performance of the technical platforms will control the footfall through the arrivals and departures gates. In addition to the fully automated ticketing processes now offered by some airlines, the role of the human at the border controls appears fragile and diminishing. The reliance on technology for human identification and authentication is extending its reach.

3.3.4 Lost passports

As Reid states "With the old passport, we knew where we stood. If you lost it you knew you had lost it, but with the new, machine readable passports the story is very different. When you take a digital photo the image is, in effect, a code, which means that however many prints you make they are all exactly the same" (Reid, 2006). The loss becomes virtual and often undetected by the holder.

3.3.5 False Accept and False Reject

The choice of technology and the performance levels pre-determined will impact the usability and user satisfaction of the system. The level of sensitivity, the crossover error rate of such systems will govern the number of illegal entrants accepted and the number of legal entrants rejected. Either situation would be unacceptable to the individual concerned or to the wider public in the event of an illegal being granted entry contradicting all government promises.

4. Analysis of the problem – A Systemic Perspective

As for any proposed system, adopting a reductionist view analysing the elements in isolation creates a potential conflict in operations and diminishes potential system success. The systemic approach adopted here provides a holistic view of the issues previously discussed, collected and collated in a rich picture. Rich pictures offer a benefit over process models, capturing human thoughts, views, feelings, and drawing out the support and conflict relationships between the various elements within the system. The rich picture in Figure 2 was developed using data drawn from a wide range of documents including news reports, journal articles, white papers, discussion boards, security briefing documents and academic papers. These rich sources provide multiple perspectives from diverse backgrounds.

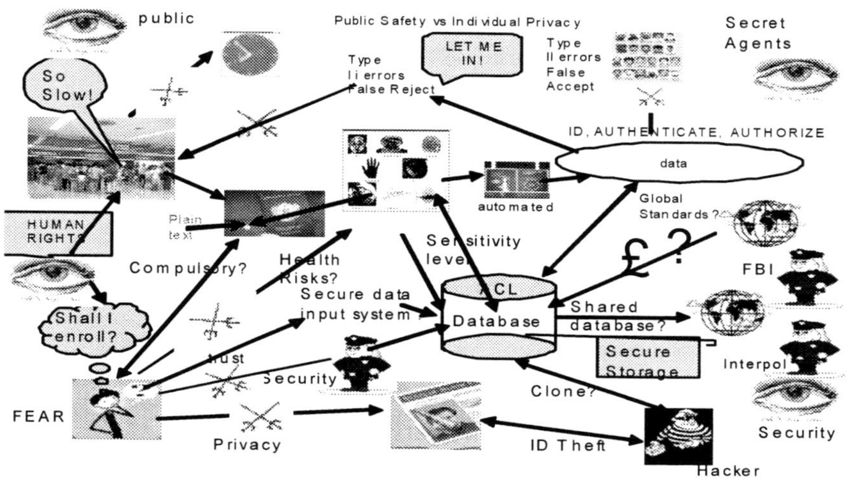

Figure 2: The rich picture

A number of issues become apparent when adopting a holistic view of the problem, as captured in the rich picture in Figure 3. As mentioned earlier in this paper, the main focus is to investigate whether biometric passports could be used for both identification and authentication purposes.

An obvious flaw in the whole approach is the assumption of the consideration of Type I and Type II errors in the security process. The calculation of the false rejection and false acceptance rate assumes that the biometric storage facility has not been tampered with. Consequently, the assumption of the adversary is limited to a person who is attempting or hoping to gain access as part of the false acceptance state of the system. Although the granularity of the analysis of the feasibility of a biometric system is increased with the introduction of additional metrics - such as the false match and non-match rates and the failure to acquire rate - a malicious adversary introducing protocol failures (say through spoofing) is not extensively studied in a biometric passport control system. In other words, the false acceptance and false rejection rates would have no significant meaning (other than user acceptance metrics) in the case of a biometric passport border access control system. This is because calculation of these rates needs to be performed in a "sterile" environment, where there is *a priori* knowledge on the validity and integrity of the authenticated subjects and the data they are holding. A malicious adversary by tampering successfully the biometric data storage would in effect invalidate the false acceptance rate, as it will not be possible to objectively calculate this metric. In addition, the false rejection rate could still be valid, but any failure to successfully authenticate would be treated as the system sensitivity rather than a security breach issue. Consequently, in order to overcome the spoliation of the false accept rate, authentication would need to be performed by other means, whereas the biometric data would be limited to supporting only identification.

The assumption of the malicious adversary was addressed at the Black hat Conference in Las Vegas, 2006. More specifically, Grunwald (2006) demonstrated that it is trivial to copy the biometric certificate from an open e-passport into a standard ISO 14443 smartcard using a standard contact-less card interface and a simple file transfer tool. In particular, Grunewald did not change the data held on the copied chip, which binds biometric data (e.g., photo) to identity data (e.g., name and date of birth), without invalidating its cryptographic signature, which means at present the use of this technique does not allow reprogramming of fake biometric data to match a different user. Grunwald also did *not* clone the Active Authentication functionality, an optional feature of the ICAO e-passport standard that some countries implement such that the embedded microprocessor is not only a floppy-disk-like data carrier for a biometric certificate, but also a tamper-resistant authentication token that can participate in a public-key-cryptography based challenge-response protocol. Nevertheless, Grunewald created international media headlines with his claim that such copying of the biometric certificate constitutes the creation of a "false passport" using equipment costing around USD$200.

Furthermore, a group of German privacy hackers have come up with a portable device that can wipe a passive RFID-Tag permanently. In this case the adversary would target the availability of the data, mounting a large scale denial of service attack, and this would have an impact to false non-match rate (Farrell, 2006).

The concerns regarding the implementation of biometric passports transcend national boundaries. "Nearly every country issuing this passport has a few security experts who are yelling at the top of their lungs and trying to shout out: 'This is not secure. .... There are lots of technical flaws in it and there are things that have just been forgotten, so it is basically not doing what it is supposed to do. It is supposed to get a higher security level. It is not." (Reid, 2006).

Whilst endorsing the need for biometric systems, the evaluation panels and the LSE report have voiced concerns about the proposed system, and its ability to achieve its stated objectives within the current legislative and technology framework (Stevens, 2005).

5. Conclusions

The implementation of biometric passports is unstoppable. Introduced in the wake of terrorist activity by governments on a global basis, individuals must accept them. The current approach to biometric passports is to strengthen its tamper resistance, increasing the effort and resources required in order to forge them. As discussed, this is not the case, since methods to crack the electronic data have been published. Thus it would appear that biometric passports cannot be used to authenticate the holder. As a direct consequence, the expectation that biometric passports would help in automating the border controls processes cannot be met, as identification and authentication would still require human intervention.

The usability of a biometric passport system requires the acceptance of all users that the system will protect their persona and provide an acceptable level of usability. To quell the anguish of future passport holders, the government need to instil confidence and the system must be fit for purpose. Instilling confidence in passport holders may be achieved through an appropriate education and communication mechanism. However, without the evidence of trust, the holders will adopt the biometric passport system reluctantly, not necessarily by choice but by force. It will take another nine years before the biometric passport system can be fully implemented.

From our analysis of the discussion, we conclude that biometric passports should contain sufficient data to enforce national border controls to establish the identity of the holder. To automate this activity and provide authentication, more secure approaches are needed. We propose a further study into the adoption of a number of potential cryptographic techniques such as one way hashes, one-way keyed hashes, Manipulation Detection Codes, to provide a secure, tamper proof environment to store the data.

References

Clarke, R. (1994). Human identification in information systems: Management challenges and public policy issues. Information Technology & People, 7(4), 6-37.

Courtney, K. (2005), Select Committee on Science and Technology, sixth Report, www.publications.parliament.uk/pa/cm200506/cmselect/cmsctech/1032/103205.htm

Coventry, L., De Angeli, A., and Johnson, G. (2003). "Usability and biometric verification at the ATM interface," Conference on Human Factors in Computing Systems Ft. Lauderdale, Florida

Farrell, N. (2006), German privacy hackers develop RFID zapper: Destroys passive RFID tags at a glance, The Enquirer, http://www.theinquirer.net/default.aspx?article=28737

Garzonis, S., O'Neill, E., Kostakos, V., Kaenampornpan, M. and Warr, A. (2004), A Novel Approach for Identification and Authentication of Users in a Pervasive Environment, proceedings of the 2nd UK-UbiNet Workshop, HCI Group, University of Bath

Grunwald, L. (2006), New Attack to RFID systems and their Middleware and Backends, Black Hat conference, Las Vegas, August

Home Office (2006) Strategic Action Plan for the National Identity Scheme: Safeguarding your identity
http://www.publications.parliament.uk/pa/cm200506/cmselect/cmsctech/1032/103205.htm#a4

Kukula, E. and Elliott, S. (2006) Implementing Ergonomic Principles in a Biometric System: A Look at the Human Biometric Sensor Interaction, www.biotown.purdue.edu/research/ergonomics.asp

McMunn, M. (2005) Machine Readable Travel Documents with Biometric Enhancement: the ICAO Standard, Optimizing Security and Efficiency Through Enhanced ID Technology ICAO MRTD Report, Inaugural Issue, Volume 1, No 1
http://mrtd.icao.int//downloads/publications/MRTD_Report/MRTD_Rpt_V1N1_2006.pdf

NEC (2005) NEC unveils its 3D Facial Recognition System for first time in Asia (outside Japan) at Global Security Asia 05, www.nec.com.sg/bccs/News/2005/050328.htm

O'Brien, C. (2006) E-passport launched in Ireland: In the nick of time, ElectricNews.Net

Reid, D. (2006) British ePassport,
news.bbc.co.uk/2/hi/programmes/click_online/6182207.stm

Roberts, C. (2005) Biometrics, http://www.ccip.govt.nz/ccip-publications/ccip-reports/Biometrics.pdf

Sasse, M. A., Brostoff, S. and Weirich, D. (2001), Transforming the 'weakest link' – a human/computer interaction approach to usable and effective security. BT Technology Journal, - Springer

Stevens, T. (2005) The Identity Project: The Identity Cards Bill, and its potential impact on UK academic institutions, Director, Enterprise Privacy Group
http://www.jisclegal.ac.uk/events/privacy05/Presentations/Stevens_paper_privacy.doc

Wayman, J. (2000). Fundamentals of Biometric Authentication Technologies. In J. Wayman (Ed.), National Biometric Test Center Collected Works 1997-2000 (1.2 ed., pp. 1-20). San Jose.

Proceedings of the International Symposium on
Human Aspects of Information Security & Assurance (HAISA 2007)

Using Digital Systems for Deception and Influence

W. Hutchinson

Edith Cowan University, Mt Lawley, Western Australia
e-mail: w.hutchinson@ecu.edu.au

Abstract

This paper examines both the present and future uses of digital technologies to deceive and influence. Its scope is the deliberate design of processes to change the behaviour of the user by deceptive and influence techniques. The paper covers the conventional design of Web page content in the process of influence campaigns by governments, businesses, pressure groups and terrorist groups to promote their causes. It progresses to more speculative uses of deceptive methods 'newer' mobile and ubiquitous technologies. These technologies have the potential for both generic and individual targeting of those to be influenced. Their techniques used and success will depend on both the time span available which would determine whether the objective is to coerce, manipulate or convert the target(s) and what stage the persuasive process is at. The analysis proceeds from the concept of 'captology' and speculates how persuasion, influence and behavioural change can be achieved via such technologies as text messaging (or, Short Messaging Service – SMS).

Keywords

Propaganda, Influence campaigns, Persuasion, Mobile technologies, Web design, Deception.

1. Introduction and History

Since the printing press was invented technology has had a profound impact on the ability to influence large audiences. However, it was in the early 20th century that the inventions of radio and cinema supplemented newspapers and pamphlets as a means of mass influence. With the radio came a shortening of the time frames between an event and a communicative response to it. Television provided visual as well as auditory means of framing thoughts on world events. The ability to manipulate images on television and the cinema, both of which could simulate events to create a new 'reality' was quickly exploited by leaders to influence populations. These new technologies allowed a worldview divorced from physical 'reality'. A version of events not experienced by persons (or, in fact, anyone they had met) was communicated to produce a desired attitude in their audience. The task of moulding worldviews was becoming a function of technology.

The development of real time, global television based on satellite and digital technology gave a tool for influence operations anywhere in the world. In fact, the Western military and corporate worlds managed information during the First Gulf War in a way that was unprecedented by its scale (Carpenter, 1995). However, in the mid-1990s, the Internet and the newly created World Wide Web became widely available. Initially, it was widely used by unconventional groups such as pornography distributors and terrorist organisations that discovered its ability to reach large audiences (Warren and Hutchinson, 2000). In these early stages, this medium was used to 'sell' a product or idea. It was an effective method for marginalised groups to get their message out to the world. Its attractions were a low entry price and a global reach. In a sense, the Internet represented a stage in the trend from local communications and influence to a potentially global presence. At the temporal level, the time taken for a message to arrive from a reported event to the public had decreased to the point of making it almost real time.

The development of tools that could be used on the Internet such as 'chat rooms' and the development of widely available broadband services allowed the flexibility of presentation of information on computer screens made the means available for influencing others increase substantially. Recent developments of cheap mobile telephones that have become integrated into Internet computer technology have provided yet another vehicle for organisations to influence groups and individuals. This phenomenon has taken even those involved in the industry by surprise. Sir David Brown – the Chairman of Motorola - admitted that in the mid-1980 an estimate for the market for mobile telephones in the whole year of 2000 was calculated to be 900 000 worldwide (Fildes, 2006). Actually, in the year 2000 that number of mobile telephones was being sold every 19 hours. This trend has also taken those who specialise in influence by surprise as well. This was illustrated at the end of 2006 when Saddam Hussein's official and choreographed execution was superseded by a raw and more accurate version taken by someone in the execution chamber on his mobile telephone and almost immediately posted on numerous websites (Jackson and Macleod, 2007). The perception managers had been upstaged by an amateur and their version of the event discredited.

This new situation has had the paradoxical impact of being able to influence at an individual-individual level (the primitive mode of discourse, such as the Short Message Service function [SMS or Texting]) and that of an organisation being able to communicate to individuals on a global scale and vice versa. It took some years for governments to utilise the Internet for influence, the same is true for this related but new media. Each has its own strengths and means of purveying information, and thus each can influence but in different ways.

This paper will discuss the impacts of these developments and their relationships to the way populations and individuals are influenced. In this paper, the term 'influence' combines both *propaganda* and *persuasion*. Propaganda is based on sociological principles reinforcing cultural and social values and tends to be targeted at populations and thus tends to be suited to mass media. Persuasion is based on psychological principles and argument, and thus tends to be geared for individuals or small groups (Johnson-Cartee and Copeland, 2004). Deception is taken to mean the deliberate manipulation of data to produce a biased view of a situation.

The basic discussion is based on two strategies to influence. The first is to design technology to influence. The second is to develop strategies to use the new digital technologies and their functionality to influence. This paper is structured thus: section 2 covers how influence is designed into digital products, section 3 examines digital technology as a medium to influence, section 4 investigates the social impact of these developments, and section 5 speculates on the future of the digital technology-influence nexus.

2. Designed Influence

Fogg (2003) uses the term *Captology* (derived from *C*omputers *As P*ersuasive *Techn**ologies***) to encompass the deliberate designing of digital systems to persuade, that is to change attitudes and behaviour. In most cases, it is to persuade and not propagandise as the target is an individual using the system rather than a population. Fogg divides computerised persuasive systems into three components: the Tool, the Social Actor, and the Medium. Each of these perspectives of a computer system has to be considered to design an effective system. The computer as a Tool can be persuasive by increasing capability by making some desired behaviour easier, by carrying processes that motivate, or by leading the actor through a process. The computer as a Social Actor creates relationships by giving people positive feedback, providing social support and showing the user the desire behaviour. Computers as a Medium provides experience by allowing the user to create and explore cause and effect relationships, helping people rehearse behaviour (for example in simulations), and providing people with experiences that motivate. Hence, a well designed persuasive system gives increased capability, creates a relationship with the user and the desired behaviour/attitude, and further provides experience in the desired behaviour. To do this, a system needs credibility with the user, and thus must be trusted and be perceived to have the necessary expertise embedded in it.

These persuasive systems are designed to alter attitude and hence behaviour by providing a medium that is perceived to be competent and providing positive feedback. It must be added that the relationship between attitude and behaviour is a problematic one (Erwin, 2001; O'Keefe, 2002). At present, this technology is limited to fairly simple processes where the influence is to train the person in a specific skill or to warn them about undesired behaviour. Examples include complicated simulators for pilots, virtual reality systems for people to overcome phobias, and the simple feedback display of the speed of a vehicle to the driver when on the road indicating compliance to a set limit.

The deliberate design of technology to influence tends to be successful if the required end result is an uncomplicated one. The influencing of worldviews in society tends to be a more complex and dynamic problem.

3. Use of Digital Technology as a Medium to Influence

Whilst designed systems can be effective for 'personal training'; it is the purview of governments and corporations to influence populations by carrying out sophisticated influence campaigns. All methods of communications are conscripted to carry out these influence campaigns. The advent of globalised television increased the 'virtualisation' of information, and the Internet and subsequent digital technologies have furthered this process. The comment by Baurillard (1995) that the first Gulf War 'did not take place' summed up the new environment in the developed world of the mid-1990s when reality of the outside world was controlled by images determined by governments and corporations. Hence, what people perceived to have happened in such a significant event as this major war was largely an illusion created by the manipulation of the information being broadcasted by the mass media. This development of the art of 'perception management' has been promoted by other observers such as Louw (2005), Street (2001), and MacArthur (1992). The world had become virtual (or, at least, partially virtual). This process has developed since the 1990s, where computer usage and the ownership of digital devices such as mobile telephones and integrated devices such as *Blackberries* has increased so much that these devices carry a high proportion of the communicated data in this virtual world. Personalised communications such as email or SMS have meant that not only are cheap, global communications available almost universally but that these facilities has increased the virtual component of the determination of reality by individuals. Both politicians and the corporate world realise that the trend from physical information collection to second hand collection has been reinforced by an ability to change the format of the information delivered. For example, images and text were used successfully in the First World War to create hatred by using outright lies and exaggerated claims (Ponsonby, 1928). However, this information was based on knowledge of a physical reality regardless if this information was incorrect. In the contemporary world, information, except for the very local, is predominantly virtual in nature, and so, consequently, are the means of communicating this information. Thus, the context for determining reality has sources that are almost entirely derived via digital mechanisms. As one the major advantages of digital technology is its flexibility in the manipulation of data, it becomes very easy to amend data without any way of determining if it is false or not. In this way, messages about the 'real' world can be created either to deceive or influence decisions made about that world.

Whilst, it can be argued that perceptions of the real world have always been 'virtual' in nature, the difference with digital technologies is that the input to individuals' perceptions can be manufactured in very sophisticated ways to provide a dynamic and interactive 'reality' that can bear little similarity to the physical world. This is different to the influence exerted in previous ages by its ubiquitousness. Thus, a contemporary person gaining information via mobile telephone calls, SMS, emails, television and web searches is manipulated in a fundamentally different from someone in the 18th century who received information by local gossip and letters. The differences are in the number of sources and the nature of the media through which information is delivered, and, more fundamentally, how it is *created*.

4. Social Impact

The impacts covered here are not exhaustive but indicative of the changes the technology has made to the process of influence within society.

4.1 Making the influence of small groups global

The remarkable thing about the introduction and development of the Internet and its associated microcomputer and network technologies was that it provided a cheap entry for organisations of whatever size (and individuals) to communicate at a global level to a worldwide audience. So not only was the reach global in a geographic sense but, as the technology became ubiquitous, the potential audience became huge. This enabled groups that were previously very locally empowered to send their message worldwide without censorship (for example, terrorist groups now had a means to propagandise various sympathetic ethnic groups in diasporas wherever they were). Kohlmann (2006) states that as governments were protecting their networks against terrorist attacks, the terrorists were busy propagating their messages and collecting funds on the very same technology. The influence of terrorist groups could now become global as could that of other non-government agencies such as the anti-World Trade Organisation movement. Weiman (2004, 2006) points out that the Internet offers easy access, anonymity, a global audience, low cost presence, a relatively uncensored environment, ability to by-pass the formal mass media, and a presentation capability from multimedia products that can achieve a strong and influential impact. Almost all terrorist organisations have a Web presence – even the technologically averse Taliban. The sites promote their cause in the best light as any other government or commercial site would do. Each is designed to present their view of the world and to promote their agenda and, sometimes mobilise, current and potential supporters as well as public opinion.

Hoffman (2006:2) argues that the propaganda generated on these sites "…grants authority to its makers. In the first place, simply by demonstrating its ability to disseminate information that the government has banned, a guerrilla group proves that it is a viable force." Through this propaganda it can get its message through to its supporters, enemies and those that are neutral. It can influence the morale of the supporters and perhaps gain some support from those who are either indifferent or antagonistic. In some ways, some propaganda can be coercive and intimidating to those who oppose the group or are wavering in their loyalty. Hence, a virtual message can have physical or, at least, psychological impacts. More than this, it can reinforce opinions by giving the group a platform to discuss the issues (usually in a biased way) to further spread their message and its influence.

4.2 Forming communities of influence

Just as struggling extremist groups like the 'Klu Klux Klan' use their Web pages to instil a feeling of community in their supporters at a global level in the wake of the terrorist attacks of September 11th 2001 (Bostdorf, 2004), and the 'Aryan Nations' who are attempting to use their Web site to initiate an 'Aryan Jihad' (Aryan Nations, 2007), so other technologies such as chat rooms and Weblogs (blogs) enable a more personalised form of influence. These tools enable such things as the ability for lonely people to 'fall in love' with a 'virtual being', or allow a paedophile to entice children into dangerous physical situations, and although there are facilities to post 'confirming evidence' such as photographs and video, there is no way of verifying the data presented. The virtual becomes real, and influencers have the freedom to present whatever data they wish. A case of 'nothing is real'. However, in countries such as China, chat rooms have 'nannies' who are employed by website owners to monitor for any political deviation. These chat rooms are often 'hosted' by sponsors who pay to ensure that the 'right' questions are asked and, of course, the correct answers are made. Also, blogs are used artificially extol a product or governments line (Stevenson-Yang, 2006). With the obviously prejudiced reporting of the Iraq War in 2003, much hope for 'honest' reporting was put onto those who created blogs from areas of conflict such as Baghdad (Alexander, 2004). The authorities soon compensated these new sources of news by creating 'black' blogs. These were those blogs pretending to be from impartial sources but were, in fact, coming from government and/or military sources.

Whilst blogs and SMS give individuals the power to create messages that can be spread 'virally' throughout a community, they can also give 'virtual' groups the ability to influence real world events. For instance, during the Iraq War of 2003, a Christian group flooded the executive of an American television company with SMS messages and 'forced' the company to dismiss a well-respected and experienced reporter in Baghdad who was sending back reports not conducive to their way of thinking (Schechter, 2004). Whilst the same can be done with email, it seems that the personalised messaging of SMS has more impact. The 'mob' had gained a victory more effective than any physical demonstration.

4.3 Digital manipulation

Everyone has to make decisions based on the information or beliefs that are available to them. Therefore, manipulating data or views that people received can deeply affect attitudes (and conceivably) behaviour. Deception on digital devices is extremely easy to accomplish (at the least at the data output stage – making people accept the output is not as easy). In fact; the presentation of a *version of reality* can produce different results. This can be illustrated by the furore caused by the televising of the execution of Saddam Hussein. The official and silent version of the execution showed a relatively organised and 'conventional' execution. However, the Iraqi authorities, either deliberately or not, allowed video-capable, mobile telephones into the execution chamber. The grainy video taken plus sound gave a totally different version of the same event. This version of the event was available worldwide within hours creating a problem for both the Iraqi and Coalition governments in Iraq (BBC, 2007). Reality is variable as is the influence of the presentation of that 'truth'.

5. The Future

Whilst the issues described in section 4 are not exhaustive, they are illustrative of the influence that can be gained (or lost) by the use of these technologies. They have already influenced the way businesses and government are run as well as the way individuals try to influence each other and the wider world. As humans become more dependent on the use of mobile digital devices extending their natural sensory systems, the ability to manipulate the input data to human increases enormously (as does the likelihood of surveillance). Individuals and groups can be targeted with messages with ease. As the mobile devices' locations can be detected easily then the targeting of people to be influenced in a particular area in real time is possible. When connected to a personal database then the combination of possibilities is infinite. The devices that can be 'connected' the human system increase then their implications increase with them. This sensory data (visual, auditory, tactile, and olfactory) can be perceived, digitised, and then communicated to a device where it is reconverted. This is open to manipulation thereby giving an altered version of the environment that the device owner senses.

In developed and developing nations, the combination of mass media and communication networks has provided a rich, if challenging, environment for influence operations and deception. Ironically, this 'information rich' environment makes deception both more and less achievable. The ubiquity of communications makes the dissemination of data much easier. Hence, people have access to various views. However, the context with which this information is interpreted is primarily determined by the mass media that is generally owned by small cartel of interests. It is in this paradoxical world that future influencers will work. One significant impact of cheap, mobile devices is the impact on developing countries. These technologies allow developing countries to 'catch up' and to use them to effect the discrepancy of influence between the developed and underdeveloped worlds. The availability of relatively cheap, satellite based television technology as well as the more personalised Internet based technology will change the tactics of influence and deception, and probably the power differential between existing players – whether it changes the public's and individual susceptibility is problematic.

References

Alexander, A. (2004) Disruptive technology: Iraq and the Internet, in: Tell me lies: Propaganda and distortion in the attack on Iraq, ed. D.Miller, Pluto Press, London.

Aryan Nations (2007) "Decentalization and leaderless resistance", http://aryan-nations.org/index-2.htm (Accessed 25 March, 2007)

Baudrillard, J. (1995) *The Gulf War did not take place*, Power Publications, Sydney.

BBC (2007) "Iraq investigates Saddam footage", http://news.bbc.co.uk/2/hi/middle_east/6224531.stm , BBC News, 03/01/2007 (Accessed 15 Jan, 2007)

Bostdorff, D.M. (2004) "The Internet rhetoric of the Klu Klux Klan: A case study in Web site community building run amok", *Communications Studies*, Vol. 55, No. 2, pp. 340-360.

Carpenter, T.G. (1995) *The captive press: Foreign policy crises and the First Amendment*, Cato Institute, Washington DC.

Erwin, P. (2001) *Attitudes and persuasion*, Psychology Press, Hove.

Fildes, J. (2006) "Mobiles still ringing in the New Year", http://news.bbc.co.uk/go/pr/fr/-/2/hi/technology/6199293.stm (Accessed 23 Dec, 2006)

Fogg, B.J. (2003) *Persuasive technology: Using computers to change what we think and do*, Morgan Kaufmann Publishers, San Francisco.

Hoffman, B. (2006) *The use of the Internet by Islamic extremists*, Rand Corporation, Santa Monica.

Jackson, P., Macleod, O. (2007) "Mobile phone captures Iraq's cruelty", BBC News, 03/01/2007 http://news.bbc.co.uk/2/hi/middle_east/6225337.stm [Accessed 25 March, 2007]

Johnson-Cartee, Copeland, G.A (2004) *Strategic communications: Rethinking social influence persuasion, and propaganda*, Rowman and Littlefield Publishers, Oxford.

Kohlmann, E.F. (2006) "The real online terrorist threat", *Foreign Affairs*, Vol. 85, No. 5, pp. 115-120.

Louw, E. (2005) *The media and the political process*, Sage Publications, London.

MacArthur, J.R. (1992) *Second front: Censorship and propaganda in the Gulf War*, University of California Press, Berkeley

O.Keefe, D.J. (2002) *Persuasion: Theory and research*, Sage Publications, Thousand Oaks.

Ponsonby, A. (1928) *Falsehood in war*, Institute for Historical Review, Torrance, CA.

Schtechter, D. (2004) *WMD: Weapons of mass deception*, [DVD – Global Vision]

Stevenson-Yang, A. (2006) "China's online mobs: The New Red Guard?" *Far Easter Economic Review*, Vol. 169, No 8, pp. 53-57.

Street, J. (2001) *Mass media, politics and democracy*, Palgrave, Basingstoke.

Warren, M.J. Hutchinson, W.E. (2000) "Terrorism on the Web", In: *Information Systems – Research, Teaching and Practice*, eds: P. Beynon-Davies, M.D.Williams, I.Beeson. McGraw-Hill, Maidenhead.

Weimann, G. (2004) "How modern terrorism uses the Internet", www.usip.org (Accessed 19 Sep 2006)

Weimann, G. (2006) *Terror on the Internet: The new arena, the new challenges*, United States Institute of Peace Press, Washington, D.C.

Proceedings of the International Symposium on
Human Aspects of Information Security & Assurance (HAISA 2007)

Locating Risk through Modelling Critical Infrastructure Systems

G. Pye[1] and M.J Warren[2]

[1, 2]School of Information Systems, Deakin University, Geelong, Australia
Email: [1]graeme@deakin.edu.au, [2]mwarren@deakin.edu.au

Abstract

This paper introduces and discusses the research proposition of a link between the modelling of critical infrastructure system/s and risk identification and management. As a means of categorically identifying points of risk within a particular model of a critical infrastructure system/s for the purpose of solution creation and contingency development and testing in the modelling environment, prior to physical implementation. This research is at the preliminary stage of exploration and is an extension of current research into modelling critical infrastructure system/s and extends this research with regard to introducing risk perception and quantifying risk, along with establishing modelling guidelines for consistent model generation, as discussed.

Keywords

Risk management, perception, critical infrastructure, modelling.

1. Introduction

The essential services supplied to modern society by critical infrastructure systems are many and varied and traverse numerous sectors of society to reach a large number of diverse consumers. As a consequence of the high supply reliability of these systems, the delivery and availability of these services are predominately, taken for granted. For instance, when operating the light switch it is expect that the electricity will be available to energise the light globe and illuminate the room, but is there any contingency consideration given if this was not the case? For the most part, consumers expect these services to be there when needed and are not overly concerned with the threats and vulnerabilities that can put these systems at risk. Nor are they concerned with the potential inconvenience or the impact magnitude that losing any, some or all these services can potentially impose upon most facets of society's everyday function.

The consequence of society's reliance on critical infrastructure availability, technologies and the physical infrastructure supporting the delivery of their services, necessitates the existence of a level of security to protect the availability and integrity of critical infrastructure systems. To achieve this requires identifying threat issues, the proactive mitigation of known risks, identifying new risks to prepare, develop and implement appropriate contingency plans. However, due to the diverse types of critical infrastructure, its physical size and scale, the management of security and identification of risks within the systems remains a difficult task.

One way to directly address these issues is to generate a model of targeted critical infrastructure system featuring its normal operation and use the model as a means of assessing the functional integrity and security of the system. This process would enable: an in-depth and scalable system security analysis of the system model; a broadening of system understanding, and provide a valuable tool and inexpensive means of identifying points of risk within the subject critical infrastructure system/s.

Therefore, with the advent of critical infrastructure modelling, the identification of risk and the subsequent solution creation to counter the risk are potentially testable with the incorporation of the solution back into the system model. This then encourages further assessment to theorise upon the various causal factors that are likely to impact upon system availability, integrity of security and deviations from the functional norm. Furthermore, this would lead to more accurate risk identification reflecting a common point of understanding and perspective, which would enable clear communication of the risk to the public, critical infrastructure owners, operators, governments and other stakeholders regarding system threats, vulnerabilities and risks.

Initially, this paper will briefly outline critical infrastructure from an Australian perspective and its system related characteristics to establish background knowledge, before proceeding to discuss the perception of risk in relation to critical infrastructures, its context and potential magnitude, along with discussing the various types of perceived risk. Next, is discussion that describes the potential that systems modelling offers, before going on to outline some fundamental guidelines applicable to modelling critical infrastructure systems to establish a guide for consistent model development. Finally, the conclusion will address and summarise the key research points identified to this time and any future research possibilities regarding the use of systems modelling as a means to enhance risk identification within critical infrastructure systems that may prove beneficial to key stakeholders.

2. Characteristics of Critical Infrastructure

In the Australian context, as with other technology-rich western societies, critical infrastructure systems deliver essential services across many differing sectors of the nation. Typically, critical infrastructure refers to those 'physical facilities, supply chains, information technologies and communication networks which, if destroyed, degraded or rendered unavailable for an extended period of time, would significantly impact upon the social or economic well-being of the nation or affect Australia's ability to conduct national defence and ensure national security' (AGD 2004 p1).

Therefore, the loss or interruption of critical infrastructure services would impact upon the normal functionality of the banking and finance sector, transport and distribution, energy, utilities, health, food supply, communications, government services and national icons, as identified in the Australian government's national strategy (TISN 2004).

As society is ever more dependant on these services, this reliance necessitates the protection of such systems to maintain service availability, this requires a fundamental understanding of what characterises critical infrastructure systems. The principal characteristic of these critical infrastructures is that they are systems consisting of numerous sub-systems, all functioning seamlessly and cooperatively as one larger system to deliver their services. Additionally, they can also the existence with interconnections between seemingly autonomous critical infrastructure systems. The existence of these interconnections results in the formation of dependency relationships, where one critical infrastructure system can deliver or exchange services with another critical infrastructure system, which adds further complexity to the network structure of the critical infrastructure system as a whole (Pye and Warren 2006).

Therefore, critical infrastructure systems can be characterised as being complex, highly structured systems, interconnected with other highly cooperative networks to facilitate the supply of services. Scott (2005) noted this is particularly prevalent in the energy sector where the continuity of the electricity supply is essential to functionality of other critical infrastructures and their continued supply of services, particularly from the perspective of the national interest, business and social communities.

When considered from this perspective, the primary objective is maintaining infrastructure availability and the continued provision of critical infrastructure services to the community across all sectors (Pye and Warren 2005). However, the risks become apparent when considering that by their very nature critical infrastructure systems are vulnerable to damage, destruction, disruption, breakdowns, negligence, natural disasters, cyber incidents, illegal and criminal activity, vandalism and malicious damage (Pye and Warren 2006). The presumption that critical infrastructure services will always be readily available and there on demand is an expectation drawn from past experience where these services have nearly always remained available or have only been disrupted for relatively short intervals. This is particularly apparent when considering services such as electricity, information technology and telecommunications that have always maintained high levels of service availability.

The consequence of societal expectation is that critical infrastructure systems will always be available to deliver their services; therefore security of supply becomes a very important issue for owners, operators and users of critical infrastructure services. This means that they must identify their specific risk exposure at all levels, including sectors and sub-sectors of critical infrastructure such as depicted by Pye and Warren's (2005) overarching model of Australia's critical infrastructure. Hence this research asserts that the use of targeted system modelling techniques would enable improved and faster identification of risk points, security threats and areas of vulnerability within the particular system's model. Thus enabling the development and testing of contingency plans in the model environment prior to physical implementation as a means to scope the impact of critical infrastructure service loss and engender a deeper appreciation of the risks to system security and availability.

3. A Perception of Critical Infrastructure Risk

It is apparent that some organisations within Australia utilising critical infrastructure services do not wholly understand where their particular organisation or infrastructure actually fits within the larger system arrangement of the wider critical infrastructure. Nor are they particularly self-aware of their own status or fully appreciate their potential obligations to the ongoing normal function and availability of the wider critical infrastructure system and its services (Pye and Warren 2006a).

For example, in the 2004 Australian Computer Crime and Security Survey participants were asked, 'Do you consider your organisation to be part of the critical national infrastructure?' (AusCERT 2004 p.5). This question focused on the National Information Infrastructure (NII) as a subset of critical infrastructure and related directly to the 'infrastructure which comprises the electronic systems that underpin critical services such as telecommunications, transport and distribution, energy and utilities, and banking and finance' (TISN 2004a p1). What was notable about the response was that of the total respondents, 84 (35%) considered that their organisation was part of the critical NII, while 123 respondents (51%) did not and most significantly was that the remaining (equating to 14%) respondent organisations were unsure or unaware of their status with regard to their criticality and the NII.

Subsequently, the same question was again put in the 2005 Australian Computer Crime and Security Survey; here 32% of the total respondents considered their organisation to be part of the critical NII, while 52% believed their organisation as not part of the critical NII. Significantly, in the 2004 survey, 14% of respondents were not sure of their actual positioning or status concerning the NII infrastructure and this level of uncertainty had increased to 16% of respondents in the 2005 survey (AusCERT 2005).

In retrospect the increase in the number of organisations uncertain of their status in relation to NII critical infrastructure system highlights a disconcerting point that a significant number of organisations questioned in these surveys, did not necessarily appreciate or fully understand or were just not aware of their status within the NII system. This indicates a lack of risk liability awareness of these organisations within the NII critical infrastructure that could potentially and adversely impact service availability and functional security of other interconnected and dependent critical infrastructure systems (Pye & Warren 2006a).

This exemplifies a lack of circumstantial awareness and risk perception on the part of some organisations utilising a critical infrastructure system, whether this is a lack of understanding, education or awareness is unclear. Hence, this is where system modelling would clearly indicate where an organisation's own infrastructure fits within the schema of neighbouring or overall critical infrastructure system. Such modelling would enable organisations to undertake meaningful security and risk analysis to categorically determine an organisation's position, status, vulnerabilities and perhaps more importantly realise their infrastructure service availability and supply obligations to other interconnected and neighbouring critical infrastructure systems.

Therefore, this suggests that through applying systems modelling techniques, an organisation would be able to undertake further analysis to identify their own points of vulnerability within the scope of their own systems. The next step would be to extrapolate further through modelling, to see how these risks could potentially impact upon the organisation's own infrastructure and that of the wider critical infrastructure system itself. Thus, elaborating, identifying and comprehending the implications of identified risks through modelling will enable further action to categorise communicate and prioritise risk management for contingency plan development and implementation.

4. A Context of Risk

While there is an element of risk associated with any undertaking, the risk itself not only relates to the recognition of the specific threat or vulnerability, but also to determining a rating of the degree of each risk. This would involve apportioning a value or rating to each risk determining its potential to cause a deviation from normal function.

The awareness and subsequent management of risk involves identifying points of weakness within the system and determining to what extent an identified risk is acceptable and manageable. Assessing and rating the risk reflects a balance between opportunities for gains made, while minimising the potential for loss from an organisational perspective. Risk in this context is concerned with the impact and exposure to consequences of uncertainty or deviation from normal or expected function (Standards Australia 2004).

4.1 Risk and Critical Infrastructure Modelling

The modelling of a critical infrastructure system/s is an effective means of gaining an overview understanding and appreciation of system positioning and potential real-world influence within the larger critical infrastructure structure network. Of course there are other issues of system scalability, the variable dynamics within the system and supporting sub-systems along with the dependency relationships with other cooperating critical infrastructure systems; however these issues are presently outside the scope to this paper.

The primary consideration is to highlight the potential for risk identification through applying systems modelling techniques to targeted critical infrastructure system/s. The propose of this is that the modelling of critical infrastructure systems can further enhance risk detection and as a consequence, improve risk perception, appreciation and understanding across all sectors of critical infrastructure users, owners and operators to develop a common understanding of the degree of risk identified.

4.2 Degree of Risk?

The degree of risk itself incorporates a number of differing variables that when considered together can equate to a derived value of magnitude in relation to an individual risk being the possible cause of a hazardous or otherwise event occurring. Geoscience Australia (2004) applies the following risk formula to determine the degree or level of risk and likewise it can apply to critical infrastructure risk assessment where:

RISK = Hazard * Elements at Risk * Vulnerability.

This formula calculates the level of risk of an event occurring that depends on the magnitude of the hazard multiplied by identified number of elements at risk and the product of their vulnerability or susceptibility to damage or change.

This rudimentary formula provides an example of how to weight identified risk vulnerabilities within the model of a targeted critical infrastructure system and thus quantify potential risk differences within the jurisdiction of the model. Then by extrapolating this weighting value back to the actual physical infrastructure system itself, this enables risk prioritisation, investigation, analysis and communication to relevant stakeholders, together with solution development priorities to mitigate the risk. Additionally, any risk mitigation solutions implemented back into the critical infrastructure model, delivers a means of hypothesising the solution's potential effectiveness to mitigate the risk to an acceptable level.

As it stands currently, the quantifying of identified risks is an aside to this paper and will be the subject of ongoing and detailed research, but it does deliver a means of quantifying comparative risks for risk prioritisation within the model environment. However, this brief investigation does provide a starting point into its application and will assist in determining a common understanding regarding potential risk magnitude within the physical system. This would form part of the overall system analysis process as applied to the security and risk analysis of critical infrastructure system models.

4.3 Perceptions of Risk

In the context of modelling critical infrastructure and identifying points of risk, the perception of the risk itself varies depending on the perspective of those considering the risk. For instance the research of Gardner and Gould (1989) noted some common phraseology that describes technological risk from differing perspectives. For example, the phase *'speaking different languages'* referred to the different risk definitions applied by scientific community and the general public and what constitutes a *'socially acceptable'* technology. This reflects the difference in values and philosophies regarding risk as most professional risk managers, engineers, scientists and experts tend to express risk quantitatively in terms of money lost. While, the general public is more inclined to regard risk qualitatively in terms of who is impacted and the acceptability of risk from a societal perspective rather then assigning a cost that is acceptable.

In between these two broad groups is the government who must determine national policies, expenditure and resources on risk mitigation from a national perspective. Sjöberg (2001) notes that while this is part of the democratic process it is not perfect, sometimes decisions on risk policy and resource distribution means that not all stakeholders are satisfied with the outcome. Similarly from the Australian perspective, in response to the high levels of private ownership of critical infrastructure, the government initiated the Trusted Information Sharing Network (TISN) as a committee structure for managing, coordinating and sharing of restricted security information with infrastructure owners and operators. This also provides a means of managing risk in the national interest to deliver credible information (AGD 2004a), but this process has some drawbacks too.

The crux of this style of risk perception management is the gathering of credible information from a number of sources for consideration to determine a consensus viewpoint or single risk perception. However, in reality depending on one's circumstance this can potentially lead to differing interpretations and misunderstandings of the magnitude of the risks identified and communicated. In view of this situation the development of a consensus or single view of perceived risk/s is imperative to the overall management of security and risk in the critical infrastructure system/s.

Therefore, the modelling of critical infrastructure systems provides a potential avenue for determining, identifying and investigating the risks inherent in critical infrastructure systems and a means to develop a recognised point of reference for acceptable understanding and magnitude of the risk. The potential benefit to risk management and detection that modelling brings is that it enables clients to see where the risk exists within their critical infrastructure systems, the analysis of risk, its assessment and the contingency plans developed to negate the potential effects if the risk comes to fruition. This is why modelling should be an integral part of any security or risk analysis process of critical infrastructure systems because the use of models in the discipline of information systems bodes well both as a user-analyst communication tool and is a well recognised means of communicating common understandings and conceptual ideas related to real-world systems.

5. Why Modelling?

The primary aim of modelling a critical infrastructure system is to give the viewer a perspective of not only the external environment, but the internal characteristics of the system's environment and to map the targeted system boundaries to visualise its place within these surroundings. From this the modeller can begin to see and understand what influences contribute to characterising the functioning systems and its potential interactions and connections with neighbouring systems, thereby developing an appreciation of the system's status within the greater critical infrastructure schema (Pye & Warren 2006).

Maani & Cavana (2000) suggest that in order to fully comprehend the functional behaviour of any system, at any level, that modelling the system is the easiest method to generate an overview of the system and its points of connection and interactions. Modelling enables the analyst to cope with system complexity, scalability, understand the system structure, the interaction points between the system components and sub-systems, the relational influences with other neighbouring systems and theorise about potential system responses.

From this modelling perspective the system is essentially one that exhibits change and is dynamic in nature and thereby under the influence of *'cause and effect'*. With this in mind the modeller can being to manipulate the model to theorise how the actual system could potentially react to similar changes made in the physical system itself. Likewise, this principle behaviour is also a characteristic of critical infrastructure systems that also exhibit dynamic behaviour, thus enabling the analyst to model such systems to theorise and predict the potential system responses to change. Thereby enabling by extension the opportunity through *'cause and effect'* principles, to apply and model various *'what if'* scenarios. Additionally, such system modelling enhances the ability to also identify points of risk within the model that are likely to be evident within the physical system itself (Pye & Warren 2006).

Therefore, it is important to consider that the modelling process applied to critical infrastructure systems remains consistent to deliver a fair and equitable approach to modelling the target system and for the determination of security and risk points within the system. Underpinning this approach is the requirement to adopt a consistent approach to the model development thus requiring the application of fundamental guidelines with regard to the consistent development of critical infrastructure models.

6. General Fundamentals of Modelling

The overarching principle applied to critical infrastructure modelling should incorporate a keep it simple approach for the development of such system models. This is important because of the highly complex nature of critical infrastructure systems, and yet the endpoint model must also remain representative of the subject system to enable risk points within the system to become visible. To achieve this and yet remain consistent in application, the following fundamental modelling principles represent an attempt to focus on the consistent application of modelling techniques as applied to critical infrastructure systems.

The research of Pidd (1996) developed five desirable and simple principles to apply to the development of discrete computer simulations or in the use of programming language, similarly these same principles can also be adapted and utilised as guides to the development of critical infrastructure models, as follows (Pidd 1996):

1. Model Simple, Think Complicated.
   This identifies that the modeller must keep in mind that the model itself is a tool to support and extend the thinking, impressions and conceptional understanding of the physical system as a model. Therefore the avoidance of additional complexity and need for clear physical system boundaries are established for the subject system model.

2. Be Parsimonious, Start Simple and Add.
   The problem with the previous principle is identifying where the balance lies between simplicity and complexity. There is no general answer to this problem, but a solution lays in adopting a *'prototyping approach'* where the gradual development of the model starts out with simple assumptions and by only adding further complexity as it become necessary. However this does require continued refinement and revision in order to avoid adding anything unnecessary to the model.

3. Divide and Conquer, Avoid Mega-models.
   This is common advice given to those dealing with a complex problem, the aim being to breakdown the problem or in this case, decomposition the system into manageable component parts that applies the previous principle to develop the system model.

4. Do Not Fall in Love With Data.
   The model should drive the data collection, not the other way round and this requires the modeller to develop ideas for the model and its parameters from a selective perspective of what data types are collected, analysed, interpreted and implemented into the model together with a feedback testing regime to test the model developed.

5. Model Building May Feel Like Modelling Through.
   As the model is an attempt to represent part of reality or an action taken or to increase understanding, the consideration remains that the model at some point becomes the best representation it can be and continued *'muddling'* with the model can be detrimental to assumptions based on the completed model.

These modelling guides adapted from Pidd's (1996) work illustrate some key points of reference that attempt to maintain consistency when developing, analysing, and implementing models within the realm of modelling of critical infrastructure systems. This will assist the modeller in: (1) categorising and developing an understanding of the problem context for modelling: (2) deciding the model structure based on analysing the available data: (3) model realisation where the parameters of the model have been established; (4) the model assessment is the decision point at which the model is deemed acceptable, valid and usable as a model of the subject system and reflects normal functionality; and, (5) the model implementation where working with the model to gain valuable predictive data and likely responses to scenario testing.

7. Conclusion

The primary assertion of this research is that a model of a critical infrastructure system/s can provide a means to identifying and locating points of risk within the model and by extension the physical critical infrastructure system too.

This research into risk identification takes advantage of the benefits that modelling brings in establishing an overview of the subject system and its environment and presents a means of depicting a conceptual *'big picture'* view. Utilising this modelling approach lends itself to incorporation into the security analysis of critical infrastructure systems that would potentially lead to the development of a common perception and definition of risk and vulnerability, thereby narrowing the sematic gap of the identified risk/s across differing sectors of the wider critical infrastructure realm. The advantage of utilising modelling in this manner would encourage a consensus outcome of the level and exposure to the risk/s identified in the model and by association the physical critical infrastructure system itself.

Furthermore, modelling risk solutions back into the model enables further analysis and testing to determine the likely outcomes before physical implementation of the solution into the system itself. Additionally, the development of a critical infrastructure system model also provides the opportunity to apply various adverse scenarios and conditions to predict system responses to assist further in contingency plan development and testing to support the adoption of pre-emptive security measures into the physical system.

The successful enhancement of risk identification and risk perception understanding relies heavily on the comprehension and interpretation of the modelling process used to represent a particular critical infrastructure system. Therefore, the application of the general modelling guidelines outlined delivers a loose structure for the development of critical infrastructure models that will lessen the possibility of modelling and risk perception biases introduced by the modeller. Furthermore, the simple formula for quantifying risk in relation to its magnitude of hazard, the number of risks and value of the vulnerability was touched on briefly and delivers a means of prioritising risk. Additionally, this now provides a starting point for more in-depth future research into applying a value of magnitude to the risk/s and system vulnerabilities.

This paper seeks to delineate an area of future research that may prove fruitful after the initial critical infrastructure system modelling research matures. The intention is for future research to progress towards creating computer simulations of the critical infrastructure system/s modelled to further enhance the modelling, analysis process and understanding of system functionality and response. Once achieved, this will then enable analysts to closely replicate the physical system's response in a simulation and then test the system simulation with various adverse scenario tests to observe the simulated system's responses and reactions. Data and information gathered from this analysis process could then be analysed and applied to strengthen the physical critical infrastructure system's security and to mitigate risks as identified.

References

AGD Web Site (2004), "Critical Infrastructure Protection National Strategy", www.nationalsecurity.gov.au/, (Accessed 11 November 2004).

AGD Web Site (2004a), "Protecting Australia's Critical Infrastructure", www.ag.gov.au/, (Accessed 12 May 2005).

AusCERT (2004), Australian Computer Crime and Security Survey, AusCERT, Brisbane, Australia.

AusCERT (2005), Australian Computer Crime and Security Survey, AusCERT, Brisbane, Australia.

Gardner G.T. & Gould L.C. (1989), "Public Perceptions of the Risks and Benefits of Technology", *Risk Analysis*, Vol. 9, No. 2, pp. 225-242.

Geoscience Australia Web Site (2004), "What is risk?", www.ga.gov.au/urban/factsheets/risk_modelling.jsp, (Accessed 8 January 2007).

Maani K.E. & Cavana R.Y. (2000), *Systems Thinking and Modelling. Understanding Change and Complexity*, Prentice Hall, Auckland, NZ.

Pidd M. (1996), "Five Simple Principles of Modelling", in *Proceedings of the 1996 Winter Simulation Conference*, ACM, pp. 721-728.

Pye G. & Warren M.J. (2005), "Australian Commercial-Critical Infrastructure Management Protection", in *4th European Conference on Information Warfare and Security*, Academic Conference Limited (ACL), Wales, UK, pp. 249-259.

Pye G. & Warren M.J. (2006), "Conceptual Modelling: Choosing a Critical Infrastructure Modelling Methodology", in *7th Australian Information Warfare and Security Conference*, School of Computer and Information Science, Edith Cowan University, Perth, WA, pp.103-113.

Pye G. & Warren M.J. (2006a), "Security Management: Modelling Critical Infrastructure", *Journal of Information Warfare*, Vol. 5, No. 1, pp. 46-61.

Scott G. (2005), "Protecting the Nation", *AUSGEO News*, No.79.

Sjöberg L. (2001), "Political decisions and public risk perception", *Reliability Engineering and System Safety*, Vol. 72, pp.115-123.

Standards Australia (2004), *Risk Management, AS/NZS 4360:2004*, Standards Australia/Standards New Zealand, Sydney/Wellington.

TISN Web Site (2004), "Critical Infrastructure Protection National Strategy", www.tisn.gov.au/, (Accessed 10 October 2004).

TISN Web Site (2004a), "Protection of the National Information Infrastructure (NII)", www.tisn.gov.au/, (Accessed 25 May 2005).

Proceedings of the International Symposium on
Human Aspects of Information Security & Assurance (HAISA 2007)

Usable Set-up of Runtime Security Policies

A. Herzog, N. Shahmehri

Dept. of Computer and Information Science, Linköpings universitet, Sweden
e-mail: {almhe,nahsh}@ida.liu.se

Abstract

Setting up runtime security policies as required for firewalls or as envisioned by policy languages for the Semantic Web is a difficult task, especially for lay users who have little knowledge in the security domain. While technical solutions for runtime protection and advanced security policy languages abound, little effort has so far been spent on enabling users to actually use these systems to set up a security policy, and certainly not at runtime.

To start filling this gap, we give concrete and verified guidelines for designers that are faced with the task of delegating security decisions to lay users. We advocate, for example, that security policies be set up at runtime, not off-line, that the principle of least privilege be enforced and that alert windows be compact but still contain information about the consequences of a chosen action.

These guidelines have emerged from our own and others' research on usability and security. They are further strengthened through the implementation of the prototype JPerM, which follows our guidelines. JPerM is used for the runtime set-up of security policies for Java applications. Its specific design and evaluation are described in this work and serve as an illustration of the presented guidelines.

Keywords

Security policy management, access control, usability, Java, application surveillance.

1. Introduction

Setting up a security policy or security rules for a personal firewall, for application surveillance on one's computer, or for how one's web browser should interact with privacy policies of visited web sites, is a difficult task. It is technically difficult in the sense that lay users must have some grasp of technical terms, the limitations of the policy system, and policy syntax or available options. It is also difficult for users to accept the whole concept in the first place, because users can easily perceive security measures as an extra strain whose gain is not readily understood.

Still, at least one security tool for setting up security policies at runtime has succeeded: Personal firewalls are on many people's personal computers and quite a number of non-expert users have come to appreciate and master them. But firewalls are not very complex in their runtime rule syntax. They will either allow or disallow a network connection based on connection attributes—typically port and host—and the name of the local application.

Research has envisioned many advanced security policy systems and languages for end users, ranging from runtime application rules, as seen in the Java runtime environment and rules for intrusion detection systems, to policy languages for trust negotiation (Seamons et al., 2002) and advanced access control (Herrmann and Krumm, 2001). So far, no usable end-user interface has been presented for any of these advanced security controls. Thus, we are interested in studying whether users can handle more advanced security policy set-up than firewall rules and what is required from a graphical user interface for this.

The contribution of our work is consequently to present and discuss concrete guidelines for enhancing the usability and security of software that delegates security decisions to lay users and captures these user decisions as a security policy. The guidelines have emerged from pre-studies on how users want to and are capable of setting up runtime security rules (see section 2), from previous work on the usability of personal firewalls (Herzog and Shahmehri, 2007), from a usability study of a tool for off-line setting of a Java security policy (Herzog and Shahmehri, 2006) and from literature studies on usability and security. The validity of our guidelines is strengthened by a prototype implementation of a tool for setting up an access control policy for Java applications that follows these guidelines and that was received positively from users.

We chose Java and the set-up of Java security policies because Java is a language that supports runtime monitoring of security properties. But due to usability lapses (Herzog and Shahmehri, 2006) and because of alleged slowness of the Java security mechanism, which is only partially true as shown in Herzog and Shahmehri (2005), this Java feature is seldom used. Consequently, our implementation fills a need in the Java community, but by choosing Java we also arrive at an extensible test bed for user interfaces for policy languages, because many policy languages are implemented in or easily integrated into Java.

The paper is structured as follows: in the next section we report on two pre-studies, which together with our and others' work, have lead to a number of guidelines for applications that must ask their users for a security decision, and to a prototype implementation of an application monitor. The Java application monitor and permission manager JPerM is briefly presented in section 3. Section 4 presents our guidelines in the light of JPerM and in contrast to other guidelines, which are presented in general in section 5. Section 6 reports on the evaluation of JPerM. Section 7 concludes and names future work.

2. Pre-studies

Two pre-studies provided useful input about how users want to and can handle runtime security policies in the form of rules for access control to sensitive resources.

The first pre-study explored whether users were interested in application access control, what they would like to see controlled and how they want to interact with such an application. 22 students from social, technical and business programs completed a questionnaire-guided interview. The interviews dealt with the respondents' Internet activities, their security concerns, how they address them and which, if any, security-critical actions they would like to see monitored. Respondents were engaged in Internet activities like searching, browsing, downloading files, e-mailing and to a lesser degree Internet banking, purchasing items over the Internet and using chat. 10 of the participants employed IP telephony, and eight more respondents expressed that they are considering IP telephony as an Internet activity for themselves in the near future. All of the respondents had downloaded some software, most often updates and free software such as Acrobat Reader. The perceived personal risk level was considered to be low to medium, with the typical explanation that nothing much had ever happened and/or that there was no crucial data on the Internet-connected computer. 9 respondents had never had any problems with malware, 9 respondents had problems with viruses, sometimes to the extent of having to reinstall their system; 8 respondents had experienced problems, usually a slow computer, with adware or spyware. Anti-virus software was the most popular defence mechanism against malware (18 of 22); 14 respondents knew that they had a personal firewall, 8 had anti-spyware software. A common strategy of defending against malware in unknown software was also to only download from known sources or to only download known products. However, despite low risk levels and defence strategies in place, 20 respondents expressed that they would like to have application surveillance on their PC. Half or more of the respondents wanted alerts for network connections, file operations such as reading, modifying, creating, deleting, executing, and also alerts before an application starts controlling mouse, keyboard or screen and for the setting of environment or system variables. When asked to suggest an alert or elements of an alert for a security-critical action of their choice, respondents described a dialog window with the typical components of what is happening, what that means, what one should do and where one can find more information and advice. The text in the initial window should be untechnical, but details should be readily available. A number of users also described the problem of allowing an action too quickly and then having difficulties in revoking their grant and said they would like to see this addressed.

Thus, results show that people are interested in application monitoring. The positive answers may partly be a study artefact since a number of users admitted that they would not actively search for such an application but they would not mind using it if it happened to be on their computer. The less computer-literate respondents found participation in the study educational and expressed astonishment about how much could go wrong. Their new security awareness might have made them overly interested in a monitoring application.

In a second pilot study, described in detail in (Herzog, 2006), we prepared a paper prototype of an application monitor. 6 students from cognitive science, who are used to the idea of paper prototypes, were confronted with alerts from an application monitor built into a browser and observing browser plugins. There, it became clear that users had great difficulty in recognising alerts as genuine security warnings and subsequently abandoning their task because of security concerns. The security warnings interfered with the user task of (1) working with the prototype for the study and (2) following the scenario of the study which said that users should download some music files for a friend. These two-fold social settings may have made it especially difficult to accept the security warnings. In 4 of the 6 trials, users invoked a malicious application on their computer despite security warnings. However, two users did not; one of the two did not even download the malicious application.

As planned, the paper prototype evolved during the study, therefore it may be a success story for the prototype that the two users that did not install the malware were scheduled towards the end of the study (occasions 4 and 6 of 6). After user feedback, we (1) changed the wording of the alert message from very technical formulations, like "The application tries to open a socket connection to IP address 68.142.226.56:80." to "The application tries to communicate with another host on the Internet: 68.142.226.56:80.", (2) added colour coding of alerts to show the severity, and (3) refrained from showing low-severity alerts at all.

But regardless of the design of the alert message of the application monitor, the final decision to continue or to discontinue using the untrusted application is put on the user; and the user may not be inclined to distrust that application or to spend time pondering security decisions. One user made this explicit:

> "attacking the other computer' [reading aloud the alert text for an outgoing connection to the Yahoo web site] that sounds quite scary. Well, I assume that this is okay. I am only downloading a file from a page that a friend recommended. I cannot imagine that my computer is attacking another computer." [The same user when confronted with a high-risk alert and about to run the malicious application:] "This is a high-risk [action]. But I disregard this; I assume that this is perfectly okay."

Therefore, for JPerM, we made the alert texts more explicit by informing the user of the security consequences for the action and by the explanations of technical details through links.

3. Background and implementation of JPerM

We implemented JPerM, an application monitor for Java applications, to fill a need in the Java security community but also to have a test bed for testing graphical user interfaces for security alerts. In this section, we briefly present the technical background of JPerM.

The Java language contains a runtime monitor called *security manager* that intercepts potentially dangerous calls such as file operations, socket operations, setting of Java properties (Java environment variables) and access to Java-internal objects such as the security policy, Java threads, class loader creation and many more, fully described in e.g. (Gong et al., 2003). Upon interception, the security manager checks the Java security policy to determine whether the action should be allowed or not. If the action is allowed, the sensitive resource is accessed. If the action is not allowed, an exception is thrown. Usually, this results in the application terminating because it cannot proceed. For regular Java applications, the security manager is by default switched off, but for applets it is always switched on. The Java policy resides in a text file and can be edited either through a text editor or with the crude policytool, which is part of every Java distribution.

JPerM introduces a new security manager that, if it notices that a permission is not granted by the policy, invokes an alert window. JPerM also supports a logging mode, where no prompt is issued but needed permissions are collected for later review. This is, for example, useful in embedded environments where no display is associated with the Java application. JPerM is technically inspired by JSEF (Java Secure Execution Framework) (Hauswirth et al., 2000) which shows that it is technically possible to ask the user for every Java permission that the code needs. However, prompting with very technical text for every permission is not user-friendly; therefore JPerM focuses on the usability aspect of setting the policy. Thus, the focus of this article is JPerM's usability design and user interface (see fig. 1), which emerged from the guidelines presented in the following section and which were continuously evaluated through user feedback.

4. Guidelines for usable set-up of security policies

Our guidelines are specific for *applications that must ask lay users for security decisions and capture these decisions in a security policy*. The guidelines are influenced by our previously published work, the studies described in section 2, as well as more general guidelines from literature on usability and security as presented in section 6.

In the following, we discuss each guideline and describe how it is addressed in JPerM. A discussion on the influence of other work on our guidelines is shown in detail in table 1 and in general in section 6.

1. *Security must be visible without being intrusive.* If there is a useful security tool on the computer, users must be made aware of its existence. Study 1 revealed that a number of respondents did not know whether they had a firewall on their home computer. Also, our firewall evaluation showed that two firewall products do not display the firewall name in their security alert, thus leaving the user at a loss on what software is giving her/him a warning. On the other hand, study 2 showed clearly that user will quickly automate their response to alerts if there are many of them. So the frequency of warnings must be well-balanced. In JPerM, we choose the default setting to only warn for medium and high-risk actions and silently allow all highly frequent low-risk actions (but capture them in the policy).

2. *Security applications must encourage learning.* If the security software ambushes the user with technical details like IP address or port numbers without explanations of what these mean, a lay user will be discouraged, resign and set up security guided by ad-hoc strategies. Learning is rarely encouraged. Therefore we designed JPerM so that it would be easy for users to get help on the meaning of concepts. Explanatory tooltips for concepts like 'IP address' or 'HTTP protocol' and links to web pages with more information are provided.

3. *Give the user a chance to revise a hasty decision later.* Users that are busy with a primary task take security chances to get their primary task done. They may need a reminder of their suboptimal security settings and a chance to revise their settings. In the firewall evaluation, we realised that no firewall gives access to its full configuration interface from an alert window. At best, settings for the current action can be fine-tuned. JPerM contains two hooks for revising previous actions: Firstly, there is a button in the alert window that can invoke the full-fledged policy editor. Secondly, the history shows previously granted actions for this application and is meant to also allow editing in a future version.

4. *Decisions cannot be handled off-line; runtime set-up is to be preferred.* In principle, security policies can be edited off-line, for example by editing the settings of the security application after installation, and for corporate firewalls this is the opus moderandi. But lay users of security applications do not make security a primary task (unless forced), therefore it is more straightforward and usable to allow the set-up of security policies at runtime. Off-line editing must still be supported for revising decisions or for fine-tuning them. But the coarse work should be done by a runtime set-up. In fact, offline editing is a rather impossible task in application monitoring because one cannot anticipate which permissions an application will need. JPerM successfully implements runtime set-up of Java security policies and has hooks for plugging in a more usable tool for off-line policy editing than the existing Java policytool.

5. *Enforce least privilege wherever possible.* The principle of least privilege says that a subject should only receive the privileges needed to perform its requested task but not more. Least-privilege and usability may be a trade-off: It is easier to let a user set up a coarse-grained rule (e.g. "Completely trust this software?") than prompting for every needed permission. Severity classification can help to find the right balance, but the more complicated the policy, the less likely it becomes that this trade-off can be automated. While a personal firewall can assume that the lookup of a host name with the DNS server can be granted without too much risk for security, policies that contain conditions—"Application X is allowed to execute only if application Y is not currently running."—cannot be anticipated by a monitor but must be user-provided. JPerM addresses least privilege by never automatically granting permissions that contain wildcards. Such permissions must be supplied by the user by explicitly answering questions like "Allow connections to any host on port 22?". By default, JPerM remembers the permission exactly as it was required by the resource access and ignores probing attempts that check for wildcard permissions.

6. *In a security alert, the user should be informed of the severity of the event and what to do.* Study 2 made clear that users are not interested in dealing with low-risk events. If the events are not classified by severity, users do not have the energy to understand each and every alert and they resort to allowing everything in order to get their primary task done. It is advisable to set up the monitor so that warnings only appear for certain classes of events. Users also indicated that they need specific, non-technical guidance on what this event means, what it can lead to and what they should be doing. JPerM implements this by means of a clear structure in the alert: what has happened, why this is dangerous, what should be done now. The risk level is prominently illustrated by a traffic-light icon.

7. *Spend time on icons.* As Whitten (2004) and Pettersson (2005) have shown, icons are important in enhancing—and also in destroying—the understanding of security concepts. If icons are used they must be carefully tested for their understanding by users. The one prominent icon in JPerM is the traffic light for signalling the severity of an alert. It came about after realising that alert classifications in personal firewalls are not visible enough when using sliders (one personal firewall), general colour coding or texts (some firewalls) or even no classifications at all (roughly half of the tested firewalls).

8. *Know and follow general usability guidelines and test, test, and test again.* This final guideline acknowledges the importance of considering other general and specific guidelines. Our guidelines provide further focus but general guidelines will also contribute to usability. We wish to stress that the best design guideline for a specific application is to do tests. Tests can be done with paper prototypes (Snyder, 2003), which are cheap to do in terms of both time and resources and can be adapted as late as at test-time

by creating new windows and widgets as the need arises. But there must also be prototype tests with the actual application at the earliest possible stage because retrofitting usability as well as security is not possible. We show in the next section how we went about in designing and evaluating JPerM.

Guideline	Origin and motivation
1. Security must be visible without being intrusive.	Johnston et al. (2003), Nielsen (1994) and Yee (2002) propose visibility of system status as one criterion for successful HCI in security applications. Visibility contributes to the building of trust in the security application. However, users do not want to be ambushed with security alerts at all times (Sasse et al., 2003)
2. Security applications must encourage learning.	As a first step towards learning, Nielsen (1994) demands that applications use the language of the users to enhance their understanding and consequently to support the learning process. Whitten and Tygar (1999) have shown that security is difficult to understand and that concepts from educational software could and should be borrowed. Johnston et al. (2003) propose *learnability*, which we take one step further: not only should the software be learnable but also encourage the user to learn about security issues.
3. Give the user a chance to revise a hasty decision later.	Our studies in section 2 have shown that users are aware of making hasty decisions, driven by the need of getting a primary task done. While security in principle has the barn-door property (Whitten and Tygar, 1999) that the late closing of a security door may be exactly too late, because the damage is already done, this is not always or absolutely the case. But if there is no convenient way for the user to "close the door", it will remain open, and this must be avoided. This issue is also recognised as *revocability* by Yee (2002) or *easy reversal of actions* by Shneiderman and Plaisant (2004), even though true reversal may not be possible because of the barn-door property.
4. Decisions cannot be handled off-line; runtime set-up is to be preferred.	This guideline is in conflict with the guideline *support internal locus of control by making the user initiate actions, not respond to system output* by Shneiderman and Plaisant (2004) and shows clearly that not all usability guidelines can be uncritically transferred to security applications, which are typically supportive and not primary-task applications, and the user is not likely to take any actions if not prompted to do so.
5. Enforce least privilege wherever possible.	The principle of least privilege comes from Saltzer and Schroeder (1975) and is one important principle of computer security and specifically access control, which is what security policies are about. Garfinkel (2005) warns in this context of *hyperconfigurability*. Users have difficulties in managing too many options and cannot take in the consequences of their modifications. Garfinkel rather suggests "a range of well-vetted, understood and teachable policies" instead of exposing the user to fine-grained policy set-up.
6. In a security alert, the user should be informed of the severity of the event and what	Nielsen (1994) proposes that error messages should contain instructions on what to do, not only what has happened. Still, the texts must be short and focused so that they are actually read. Details and additional explanations should be accessible but not blur the main message. Yee (2002) demands *clarity* so that the effects of any actions the user may take are clear to him/her before performing the action. Also Hardee et al. (2006) state that

to do.	any decision support should contain the consequence of any action taken.
7. Spend time on icons.	Johnston et al. (2003) state that well-chosen icons can increase learnability. This is supported by Whitten (2004), who suggests icons for public-key encryption and motivates icon choices, and Pettersson (2005) who comments on the difficulty of choosing icons for privacy settings.
8. Know and follow general usability guidelines and test, test, and test again.	General usability guidelines are e.g. described by Shneiderman and Plaisant (2004) or Nielsen (1993). However, these guidelines are often so general that they can be difficult to implement for a specific case. Therefore, actual usability testing with users from the intended user segment is essential.

Table 1: Design guidelines for applications that must set a security policy, their origin and motivation

5. Evaluation of JPerM

JPerM was developed in a continuous feedback loop with users. First, we explored usability issues with a paper prototype as described in section 2. When we later had a running program, the first round of users (5 participants) consisted of students interested and educated in usability aspects. Their feedback was decisive for implementation changes for the second round of users (12 participants), where only minor changes were made.

The JPerM evaluation for both rounds of users consisted of three tasks which would expose users to the alert window of JPerM in different situations. Users were asked to set up (1) the same policy as in (Herzog and Shahmehri, 2006) in order to compare JPerM to the previously evaluated Java policytool by Sun, (2) a policy for a benign application, namely an SSH (secure shell) application, to test usability in a real application, and (3) a policy for a malicious application, in order to test whether users would recognise the maliciousness from the warnings given by JPerM. The setting for the study was that the user was at home at his computer with all three applications newly installed and JPerM running in the background. A screen recorder recorded each user session, including what happened on screen and what was said in the room.

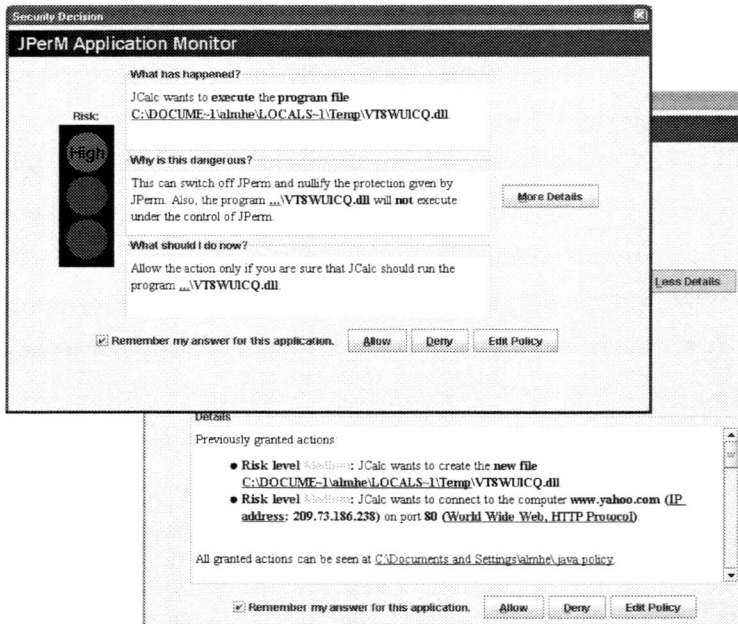

Figure 1: JPerM by the end of the study when alerting for the execution of a file. In the background, one sees the lower part of the JPerM window when the More Details-button is pressed.

In the following, we take up the most prominent findings from this evaluation:

Out of 16 trials *only two users fell for the malicious application*. One said she was assuming that the malicious application came from a reasonably trusted source such as www.download.com. The other user was busy in making the primary application work and did not take in the JPerM warnings.

Everybody understood and reacted positively to the *traffic light icon*, on the left-hand side of fig. 1, which clearly signalled the severity of the action to the users. Many users said for the medium (yellow) severity something like "This action sounds quite serious but it is only medium, so I think I will allow it.", while the high (red) severity alert caused users to sharpen their attention one more step and they would read the texts with more concentration than if it had been yet another yellow medium alert.

Many users gave *positive feedback to the clear structure of the alert* (fig. 1) which presents on top what has happened, in the middle why this is dangerous and what the consequences of allowing this action could be and on the bottom what the user should do now. No one remarked negatively on this structure.

Shortening long file names and making directories accessible through links was understood by all users. Long file names were shortened with an ellipsis instead of the path name after a first round of user comments that long file names were tiring and should appear only once. Directory exploration was introduced after having several users wonder what *other* files would reside in the directory in which a new file was about to be created.

Customised advice with e.g. the concerned file names (VT8WUICQ.dll in fig. 1) and bold lettering in every text box leads to users reading or at least parsing the text more thoroughly than when there is generic advice. The first round of users that saw generic advice complained about it being too generic, whereas it was noticeable that later users pondered more about the subsequently customised text.

It was noticeable that *only about half of the users would invoke the button for more details, follow the links or invoke policy editing.* Most users would only interact with the alert window. This is consistent with security being a secondary task that users are not willing to spend time on unless absolutely necessary. This behaviour must be anticipated by alert designers and must result in compact windows with compact information.

JPerM clearly proved to be *superior to the Java policytool* for offline policy editing. No user had problems setting up the policies for the application that we had designed for our previous study (Herzog and Shahmehri, 2006) for evaluating the offline editing of the security policy using the Sun-provided policytool. While in that study, it took 15 to 30 minutes to complete the running of that application, JPerM users would this time run the program, set up the policy while the program runs, finish the task within 3 minutes—and wonder what this was really about. The previous study users never got to the point of wondering what this truly nonsensical application was doing, as they were so busy setting up the security policy.

In general, users had a positive experience with JPerM, even though, as a security application, JPerM faces a difficult task. It wants to warn users *before* an application performs a potentially dangerous task and thus gives the user a chance to abandon the application. However, what the user *really* would need to know for his/her decision is *why* the application wants to perform this dangerous action. And this cannot be answered by an application monitor; at best, the user can take a guess by looking at the history of previously granted actions for this and other applications. We implemented this and users found it useful.

6. Related Work

Our work is positioned in the area of *usability* of *security applications*. The ISO standard 9241 defines *usability* as "the *effectiveness, efficiency*, and *satisfaction* with which specified users achieve specified goals in particular environments". That *security applications* or security features in applications differ from regular features or applications is recognised by Whitten and Tygar (1999), who note that security is typically a secondary goal, contains difficult concepts that may be unintuitive to lay users and suffers from the "barn door property", i.e. that true reversal of actions is not possible.

Figure 2 shows a number of guidelines from general usability of user interfaces (on the left-hand side of fig. 2) and guidelines for designing security features or applications (on the right-hand side of fig. 2). We position our own work as a subcategory of design guidelines for security applications, because our guidelines are specific for applications that set up a security policy through runtime user decisions.

A comparison of the guideline keywords of figure 2 shows that the guidelines overlap. Usability of security applications is strongly influenced by general usability guidelines such as those given by Nielsen (1994) and Shneiderman and Plaisant (2004). The guidelines by Johnston et al. (2003) build, for example, explicitly upon the general guidelines of Nielsen (1994) and also take up each of the points identified by the early work of Whitten and Tygar (1999). However, for the other sources, there are often a number of specific and new issues that do not appear elsewhere.

How our guidelines specifically relate to and are influenced by these existing guidelines is shown in detail in table 1. To summarise we can say that we put up specific guidelines for a specific subcategory of security applications. Our guidelines are therefore refinements of existing guidelines (our guidelines 1, 2, 3), focus specifically on the set up of runtime security policies (guidelines 4, 5) and therefore on the design of alert windows (guidelines 6, 7). Our final guideline that advocates repeated tests is surprisingly absent in other design guidelines.

Figure 2: Structured overview of guidelines for usability in security applications

Two previous systems have attempted usable access control. Zurko et al. (1999) describe Adage for letting administrators set up security policies for distributed applications. But for administrators, security is a primary task. Also, policies were edited offline. We focus on lay users that must make a security decision at runtime. Brostoff et al. (2005) describe their attempts to let lay users create role-based access control policies for their PERMIS system and show clearly how difficult this is. Their work consists of a description of their implementation and usability study but it is difficult to apply their experiences to other access control applications due to the lack of specific or general advice in the form of clearly stated guidelines or principles.

7. Conclusion and future work

While efforts for runtime control and policy languages abound, little effort has been spent on how security policies can be set up by those lay users for whom they are intended. This work has taken exploratory steps in the direction of application monitoring to explore what users want and need for a successful runtime set-up. We have presented eight specific guidelines for designers of security applications that rely on a user-provided security policy. The guidelines have been presented in comparison to previous research in the area of usability and security. The guidelines are also presented via the implementation of the application monitor JPerM, which enhances the security architecture of Java by setting up a Java security policy at runtime. Specific future work for JPerM will deal with signed code and provide a general interface for setting JPerM start-up options. A more general continuation is to see to which extent the guidelines can be applied to more advanced policy settings or policy languages

References

Brostoff, S., Sasse, M. A., Chadwick, D., Cunningham, J., Mbanaso, U., and Otenko, S. (2005). 'R-What?' Development of a role-based access control policy-writing tool for e-scientists. *Software—Practice and Experience*, 35:835–856.

Damianou, N., Dulay, N., Lupu, E., and Sloman, M. (2001). The Ponder policy specification language. In *Proceedings of the International Workshop on Policies for Distributed Systems and Networks (Policy'01)*, volume LNCS 1995, pages 18–38. Springer-Verlag.

Garfinkel, S. L. (2005). *Design Principles and Patterns for Computer Systems That Are Simultaneously Secure and Usable.* PhD thesis, Massachusetts Institute of Technology.

Gong, L., Ellison, G., and Dageforde, M. (2003). *Inside Java 2 Platform Security: Architecture, API Design, and Implementation.* Addison Wesley, 2nd edition.

Hardee, J. B., West, R., and Mayhorn, C. B. (2006). To download or not to download: an examination of computer security decision making. *interactions*, 13(3):32–37.

Hauswirth, M., Kerer, C., and Kurmanowytsch, R. (2000). A secure execution framework for Java. In *Proceedings of the 7th ACM Conference on Computer and Communications Security (CCS'00)*, pages 43–52. ACM Press.

Herrmann, P. and Krumm, H. (2001). Trust-adapted enforcement of security policies in distributed component-structured applications. In *Proceedings of the 6th IEEE Symposium on Computers and Communications*, pages 2–8. IEEE.

Herzog, A. (2006). A pilot study on setting an applet access control policy. Technical report, Linköpings universitet, Dept. of Computer and Information Science.

Herzog, A. and Shahmehri, N. (2005). Performance of the Java security manager. *Computers & Security*, 24(3):192–207.

Herzog, A. and Shahmehri, N. (2006). A usability study of security policy managment. In Fischer-Hübner, S., Rannenberg, K., and Louise Yngström, S. L., editors, *Security and Privacy in Dynamic Environments, Proceedings of the 21st International Information Security Conference (IFIP TC-11) (SEC'06)*, pages 296–306. Springer-Verlag.

Herzog, A. and Shahmehri, N. (2007). Usability and security of personal firewalls. Accepted for publication in *Proceedings of the International Information Security Conference (IFIP TC-11) (SEC'07)*. Springer-Verlag.

Johnston, J., Eloff, J. H. P., and Labuschagne, L. (2003). Security and human computer interfaces. *Computers & Security*, 22(8):675–684.

Kagal, L., Finin, T., and Joshi, A. (2003). A policy based approach to security for the semantic web. In *Proceedings of the International Semantic Web Conference (ISWC'03)*, volume LNCS2870, pages 402–418. Springer-Verlag.

Leveson, N. (1995). *Safeware: System Safety and Computers.* Addison Wesley.

Nielsen, J. (1993). *Usability Engineering*. Morgan Kaufmann Publishers.

Nielsen, J. (1994). Heuristic evaluation. In Nielsen, J. and Mack, R. L., editors (1994). *Usability Inspection Methods*. Wiley & Sons, pages 25–62.

Pettersson, J. S. (2005). HCI guidance and proposals. Deliverable D06.1.c, PRIME Project.

Saltzer, J. H. and Schroeder, M. D. (1975). The protection of information in computer systems. *Proceedings of the IEEE*, 63(9):1278–1308.

Sasse, M. A., Brostoff, S., and Weirich, D. (2003). Transforming the weakest link—a human/computer interaction approach to usable and effective security. *BT Technology Journal*, 19(3):122–131.

Seamons, K. E., Winslett, M., Yu, T., Smith, B., Child, E., Jacobson, J., Mills, H., and Yu, L. (2002). Requirements for policy languages for trust negotiation. In *Proceedings of the 3rd International Workshop on Policies for Distributed Systems and Networks (Policy'02)*, pages 68–79. IEEE.

Shneiderman, B. and Plaisant, C. (2004). *Designing the User Interface*. Addison Wesley, 4th edition.

Snyder, C. (2003). *Paper Prototyping*. Morgan Kaufmann Publishers.

Whitten, A. (2004). *Making Security Usable*. PhD thesis, School of Computer Science, Carnegie Mellon University. CMU-CS-04-135.

Whitten, A. and Tygar, J. D. (1999). Why Johnny can't encrypt: A usability evaluation of PGP 5.0. In *Proceedings of the 8th USENIX Security Symposium (Security'99)*. Usenix.

Winsborough, W. H., Seamons, K. E., and Jones, V. E. (2000). Automated trust negotiation. In *Proceedings of the DARPA Information Survivability Conference& Exposition (DISCEX'00)*, vol. 1, pages 88–102. IEEE.

Yee, K.-P. (2002). User interaction design for secure systems. In *Proceedings of the International Conference on Information and Communications Security (ICICS'02)*, pages 278–290. Springer-Verlag.

Zurko, M. E., Simon, R., and Sanfilippo, T. (1999). A user-centered, modular authorization service built on an RBAC foundation. In *Proceedings of the IEEE Symposium on Security and Privacy*, pages 57–71. IEEE.

Proceedings of the International Symposium on
Human Aspects of Information Security & Assurance (HAISA 2007)

Toward Viable Information Security Reporting Systems

F. Olav Sveen[1], J.M. Sarriegi[1], E. Rich[2], J.J. Gonzalez[3]

[1] Department of Industrial Management, Faculty of Technology, TECNUN,
University of Navarra, Paseo de Manuel Lardizábal, 13, 20.018 Donostia-San
Sebastián, Gipuzkoa, Spain
[2] Department of Information Technology Management, School of Business,
University at Albany, BA 310, Albany, NY 12222 USA
[3] Agder University College, Faculty of engineering and science, Research Cell
"Security and Quality and Organizations," Serviceboks 509, 4884 Grimstad, Norway
(and Gjøvik University College, Norwegian Information Security laboratory, 2802
Gjøvik, Norway)
Email: fosveen@tecnun.es

Abstract

Reporting and resolution of information security incidents is the basis for continuous improvement of security through learning. Incidents have varying degrees of impact, financial risk and learning opportunity for the organization. This variability naturally leads to classification of information security incidents into low and high priority for review and action. However, this classification carries with it some insidious aspects. First, high priority incidents are more costly to mitigate and as a consequence also more "uncomfortable" to report. Reporters may face reprimands, ridicule, extra workload and various other recriminations. This favors reporting of low priority incident at the expense of important high priority incidents. Incentives tied to reporting, a common policy used to stimulate reporting, may reinforce the problem. In essence, reporters face incentives and disincentives based on effects on throughput but have limited knowledge of what is important or not to the organization's security. Second, if a highly successful incident reporting policy is developed, the organization may become victim of its own success, as a growing volume of reports put increasingly higher pressure on incident handling resources. Continuously hiring more personnel is unsustainable in the long run. Developing and continuously improving automated tools for incident response promises more leverage.

Keywords

Information Security, Reporting Systems, Security Management, Human Factors, Incidents.

1. Introduction

The oil industry on the Norwegian continental shelf is moving towards Integrated Operations, a new operating paradigm (Gonzalez et al., 2005). Previously isolated offshore platforms are now connected to shore by fiber optic cable, enabling new levels of connectivity for increased decision support and operational remote control. However, increased connectivity comes with increased security needs. Computer networks from platform to shore and the Internet that were once physically separated now only have logical barriers. Remote access may be exploited by computer attackers. Protection of these operations from computer attack is clearly important to achieving operational goals.

Safety in such an environment is highly dependent upon information and communication technology. Safety reporting systems have been mandated by the Norwegian government and have been in use for many years. The Norwegian Oil Industry Association has recently published Information Security Baseline Requirements for Process Control, Safety and Support ICT Systems (OLF, 2006), where information security reporting is recommended for member organizations. Owing to the connection between safety and security in the Integrated Operations regime, it is likely that the safety and security reporting systems will have many common features; the value of a shared perspective for safety and security has been recognized (Stoneburner, 2006), but has not been widely explored. We believe that such a conceptual link is overdue.

First, we outline some of the challenges facing these systems and review some of what is currently known about information security reporting. Second, we develop a conceptual System Dynamics simulation model of an organization's information security reporting system. System Dynamics is particularly well suited to complex, socio-technical systems. It views systems as governed by information and material delays, accumulations and feedback. Given the scarcity of material on information security reporting we adapt generic experiences from safety where necessary. We build upon previous modeling on safety reporting (Rich et al., 2006) and on computer security incident response teams (Wiik et al., 2005, Wiik, 2007).

2. Recent Incident Trends, Incident Classification and Reporting

In the past few years there has been a substantial increase in information security incidents. Data published by the CERT Coordination Center show a quasi-exponential increase in the amount of incidents. By 2003 they stopped reporting since the statistics no longer gave meaningful information in assessing the scope and impact of attacks (http://www.cert.org/stats/ cert_stats.html). Data for a typical CSIRT (Computer Security Incident Response Team), the DFN-CERT, 1999-2005 show that the trend of increasing incidents continues (Wiik et al., 2005, Wiik, 2007). Organizations today face a diverse range of threats with varying impacts. To combat incidents, organizations typically employ an incident handling team, either internal or external. For example, DFN-CERT (a non-profit company) is the incident handler for the much larger DFN (Deutsche Forschungsnetz, the German Research Network).

Increasing incident volume and other considerations (see below) force handling teams to prioritize incidents according to their risk. For example DFN-CERT uses nine categories of incident priority (Wiik, 2007), the highest prioritized being attacks on DFN's network infrastructure, as this threatens the whole network. Port scans on the other hand are less important and thus classified in a lower category. Other organizations may prioritize differently. For this paper it is not necessary to know exactly how handling organizations prioritize, only that there are some incidents that are considered more important than others. Hence we will in this paper restrict ourselves to two categories, high priority and low priority incidents. Although the perceived importance of an incident may vary depending on different agents, we here refer to important incidents as those who have a high impact and financial risk to the organization as a whole.

High priority incidents carry the greatest potential for harm to the organization; learning to mitigate them reduces future loss. A plausible assumption is therefore that high priority incidents carry the greatest potential for learning, i.e. to mitigate future incidents and fix current vulnerabilities. It is thus important that high priority incidents are reported and investigated.

Perceptions of the importance of an incident by the handling team will not always be shared by the staff affected by the problem. Some attacks are highly conspicuous and cannot go unreported. An example is denial of service attacks. Other important high priority incidents, such as successful social engineering attacks, may not be reported, even if the attack was successful and staff members recognize it afterwards. They may be compelled not to report because of embarrassment or fear of recrimination from management or colleagues. This may especially be a problem if the damage or potential for damage was considerable. Such high priority attacks may also bring with them an increased workload for the reporter who has to fill out forms and participate in investigations. In the face of economic performance pressures, reporting may be omitted.

Low priority attacks carry considerably less baggage. The damage from them is less and thus staff fear of recriminations should also be less. Reporting of such incidents can also to a large extent be automated (Wiik, 2007). For example firewalls may be set to automatically report port scans.

3. What we know about Information Security Reporting

Organizations that wish to be certified in the BS-7799/ISO-17799 standard are required to implement an information security reporting scheme (Calder and Watkins, 2005). Winkler (2005) strongly advises organizations to implement a security alert system. Schneier (2000) compares the state of security reporting to the success of air safety reporting systems and finds current practices in information security reporting lacking. Gonzalez (2005) views information security reporting as a quality improvement process that is essential to reduce incidents. Ernst and Young's Global Information Security Survey (2004) report that 56% of respondents have trained users to identify and report suspicious activities. So, we know that we should have reporting systems for information security and that many organizations do have them. But, do we know if they actually work?

Wiant (2005) examined whether the presence of an official information security policy impacted incident reporting in American hospitals. He found that the presence of a written policy did not impact incident reporting. However, Wiant's study is too narrow to conclude that information security reporting does not work. There is arguably a lot more to incident reporting than just the presence of an official policy.

Wiik et al. (2004) studied the effectiveness of DFN-CERT, an external, coordinating CSIRT, and found that staff were overworked, as funding did not keep pace with growth in security incidents. The team was led into a capability trap. Working harder to cope with incidents stole resources away from development of time saving tools, leading over time to poorer incident response capabilities.

4. Safety and Information Security

In many cases safety and security is interrelated, as in eOperations. In such circumstances satisfactory safety relies on effective information security. Deliberate attacks or errors in ICT systems may cause serious accidents such as fires or explosions in production systems.

There are similarities between safety and information security reporting systems, both attempts to reduce risk by learning from incidents. We also find that similar factors affect the two. For example: Winkler (2005) outlines a series of social pressures that affect security incident reporting, e.g., bad relationship with superiors. Safety reporting is also subject to these kinds of social pressures (Johnson, 2003, Phimister et al., 2003). Furthermore, in safety, as in security, it is also common to sort incidents into high and low priority (Kjellén, 2000, Phimister et al., 2003). There are also some differences. In safety the incidents are usually unintended whereas in information security incidents are often caused by deliberate attackers.

5. Incident Reporting Causal Model

The causal structure for high and low priority incidents is essentially the same. The difference between high and low priority incidents lies in the resources assigned and the differing strengths of incentives and disincentives. To avoid repetition, the explanation of the causal model is limited to high priority incidents and the interaction between high priority and low priority incidents.

5.1 High Priority Incidents

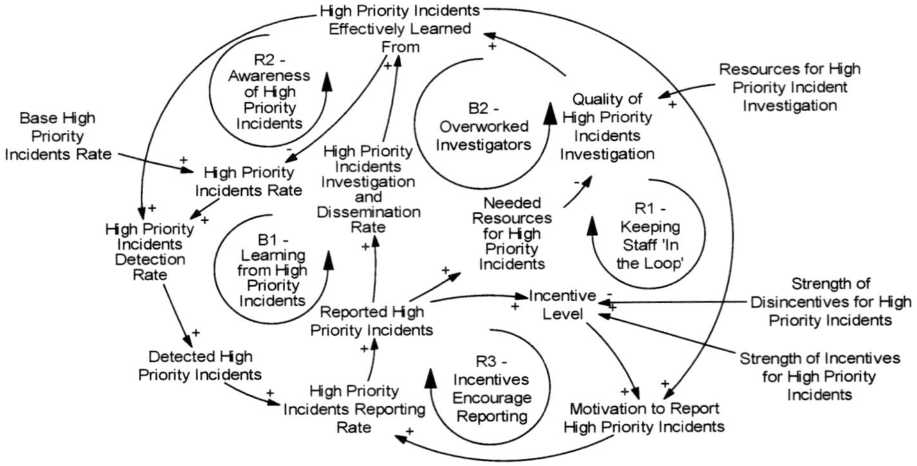

Figure 1: High Priority Incident Reporting Causal Structure

The sources of information security incidents are many. They may be software and hardware engineering errors, configuration errors or inadequate physical security which allows external attackers and malicious insiders to attack the system. Sometimes the source of a security incident may be simple mistakes. An example is the thousands of emails that are sent to wrong recipients every day. Some of those emails do contain sensitive information. To causally describe how incidents happen is beyond the scope of the model presented here. Our purpose is twofold: first, to describe how learning from incidents can prevent incident occurrence in the future, second, to describe some of the likely pitfalls an information security reporting system may run into. The source of high priority incidents is therefore modeled as an exogenous variable, *'Base High Priority Incident Rate'*.

The diagram above can be read as follows: The + and − signs at the arrow heads denote polarity. A causal link from A to B is positive if A adds to B, or if a change in A produces a change in B in the same direction. A causal link from A to B is negative if A subtracts from B, or if a change in A produces a change in B in the opposite direction (Sterman, 2000).

Reporting of incidents allows incidents to be investigated and learned from. This knowledge can be used to avoid such incidents in the future by putting into place technical and organizational countermeasures (Loop B1). We also assume that knowledge about previous incidents also improves the detection of future incidents (R2)

In System Dynamics terminology B1 is a balancing or goal seeking feedback loop. The loop attempts to balance the exogenous pressure of *'Base High Priority Incidents Rate'*. When *'High Priority Incidents Rate'* goes up more incidents are reported, investigated and lessons disseminated. Ultimately, learning from those incidents reduces *'High Priority Incidents Rate'*.

R2 is a reinforcing feedback loop. Reinforcing loops work as either virtuous or vicious circles. If there is effective learning, more incidents will be detected, leading to more learning, a virtuous circle. Vice versa, if there is little effective learning, fewer incidents will be detected, which leads to less effective learning, a vicious circle.

Once detected, the incident can be reported. But detection does not imply that the incident will be reported. As previously mentioned, Winkler (2005) writes about social pressures that affect security incident reporting. We lack extensive evidence from studies of information security reporting systems, but we know from studies of safety reporting systems that there are many forces that reduce a person's willingness to report. One factor is that staff must see the usefulness of reporting. If not, they will be less likely to report incidents in the future (R1). It is therefore important that staff always receive feedback about what is happening with their report. Johnson (2003) termed this phenomenon "Keeping staff 'in the loop'." Low quality of incident investigations may lead staff to perceive reporting as less useful. Quality of investigations is described later in the paper.

A second but equally serious factor is the many forms of disincentives that may exist. Some may be punitive in nature. For instance, medical personnel often experience reprimands or other punitive measures if they make mistakes that endanger patient safety (Anderson and Webster, 2001). Lee and Weitzel (2005) describe how punitive culture in Taiwanese airlines causes pilots to avoid reporting of potentially dangerous near-miss situations in the air.

We do not consider outright punishment as the only disincentive present in incident reporting systems. In the face of economic pressures to produce, incident reporting may be seen as unnecessarily stealing time. For example the form to be filled out may be large and complicated (Nyssen et al., 2004), or the reporter may have to participate in lengthy investigations (Phimister et al., 2003).

In the model, recriminations for high priority incidents are assumed to be twice as strong as recriminations for low priority incidents. High priority incidents are by their nature more costly to the organization than low priority incidents. For example a configuration error that allows hackers to delete crucial information from a company server may cause reprimands or other forms of punishment for the technician who made the error. Whereas an incident such as a port scan most likely will not carry with it any form of punishment at all.

Just as there may be disincentives against reporting, organizations can also choose to reward incident reports, independent of their learning value. The literature indicates that incentives directly coupled to incident reporting do encourage reporting. (However, that rewarding zero-incident targets carries risk of underreporting (Kjellén, 2000).) We assume that incentives for low priority incident reports are more effective than incentives

119

for high priority incidents. The effect of incentives for high priority incidents have been modeled at half the strength of low priority incentives. Incentives and disincentives are represented in the model by the feedback loop R3.

To learn from an incident and avoid it in the future the incident's causes must be found (Johnson, 2003, Phimister et al., 2003). This implies that incidents have to be investigated, and thus, how that process is handled becomes of importance. The investigators must have the necessary competences (Phimister et al., 2003) and there must be enough time and people to do the job properly. The quality of an investigation has been modeled in a simplified manner as a function of the resources available and the workload. If the workload becomes higher than available resources, the investigative team will push investigations through faster at the expense of quality.

Sporadic emphasis and management fear of liability may hinder success in an incident reporting system (Phimister et al., 2003). In the model, management commitment is partially represented by incentives, disincentives and resources for investigation. Management also decides policy. We will see later that different policies can have widely different long term effects.

5.2 Interaction between High and Low Priority Incidents

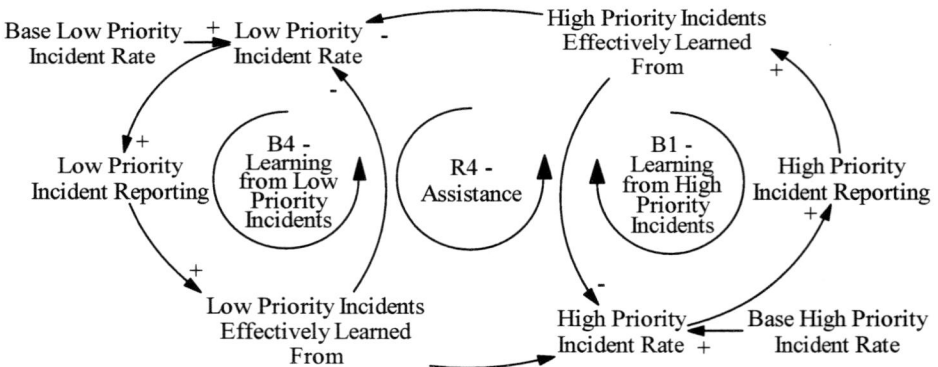

Figure 2: Interaction between high and low priority incident learning

We will now turn to describing the interactions between high and low priority incidents. We assume that lessons learned from high priority incidents will allow an organization to reduce not only high priority incidents but also low priority incidents (and vice versa). However, a crucial assumption in the model is that more can be learned from high priority incidents than from low priority incidents. In particular, learning from high priority incidents is more effective at assisting in the reduction of low priority incidents than learning from low priority incidents is in assisting with the reduction of high priority incidents (R4). Learning effects in the model have been modeled using power law learning curves (Zangwill and Kantor, 1998). For every doubling of *'Low Priority Incidents Effectively Learned From'* there is a 5% reduction in *'High Priority Incident Rate'*. A doubling of *'High Priority Incidents Effectively Learned From'* reduces *'Low Priority Incident Rate'* by 15%.

Causal loop diagrams, as seen in the previous paragraphs, are useful for describing a system's feedback structure. However, they do not say anything about the relative strength of the feedback loops, or in other words, the system's behavior over time. To investigate behavior over time we next turn to simulation.

6. Simulation Runs

6.1 Assumptions and scenarios

Although DFN-CERT represents an instance where incident handling has been outsourced, we believe that an organization with internal incident handlers would face much the same challenges in terms of the development of high and low priority incidents. We have therefore modeled *'Base High Priority Incident Rate'* and *'Base Low Priority Incident Rate'* to correspond with the trends shown in the published material on DFN-CERT (Wiik et al., 2004). This is also in agreement with the statistics that CERT has published up to 2003. Figure 3: **Exogenous Base Incident Rates** has two scales to improve readability.

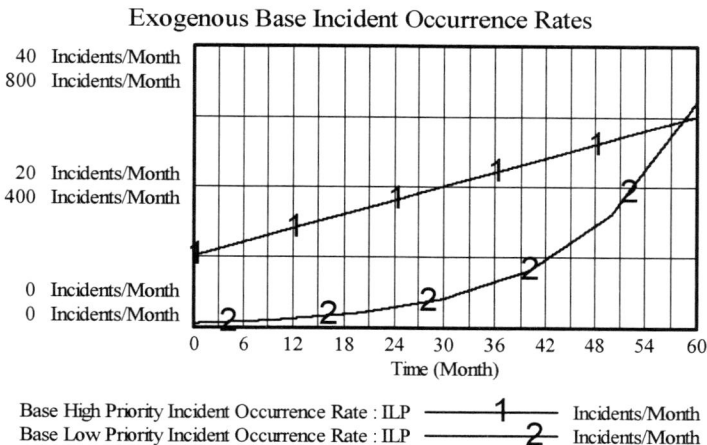

Figure 3: **Exogenous Base Incident Rates (with different scales for high and low priority incidents)**

We assume that high priority incidents take twice as long to investigate as low priority incidents. This is a conservative assumption, as low priority attacks will likely be well known and can therefore quickly be resolved. Capacity is 2.4 and 3.2 incidents / month respectively for high and low priority incidents (60-40% split in resources). Surplus resources in one category are fed into the other. Disincentives, if present, are assumed to be stronger than incentives. The incident reporting system is introduced at time zero, with no prior reporting system in existence.

We ran a series of experiments to determine different policies' impact on our conceptual system. Different combinations of disincentives, incentives and limited resources were run.
Figure 4: **Table of Policies** shows an overview of the policy experiments.

Scenario	*Low Priority Incentives*	*High Priority Incentives*	*Low Priority Disincentives*	*High Priority Disincentives*	*Limited Resources*
1: ILP	X				
2: ILP LR	X				X
3: ILP DIHP LR	X			X	X
4: IHP DILP LR		X	X		X

Figure 4: Table of Policies

6.2 Incentives and Disincentives under Unlimited Resources

Scenario **1: ILP** assumes that incentives are only effective for low priority incidents. Unlimited incident handling resources lead to an improvement in incident rates compared to base incident occurrence rates. High priority incidents are stabilized with only a slight increase at the end of the simulation. Low priority incidents, although still growing significantly, are about 100 at the end of the simulation period, much less than the maximum base rate of 650.

6.3 Effect of Limited Resources

When limited resources are added to the **ILP** scenario a different behavior emerges (scenario **2: ILP LR**). High priority incident rate initially improves, but as increasing low priority reports put higher strains on incident handling teams, the system runs out of resources. Initial gains are reversed.

3: ILP DIHP LR adds strong recriminative culture around reporting of high priority incidents. Predictably, the simulation shows little gain in high priority incident rate and low priority incident rate. The situation is significantly worse compared to **2: ILP LR**. There are two effects that cause this result. First, there is an initial decrease in the rate of high priority incidents. But high priority incident reporting drops when staff experience disincentives and, as a result, learning slows down. Second, the absence of disincentives and presence of incentives triggers a flood of low priority incident reports – to the detriment of reporting of high priority incidents. The system has surplus resources for high priority incidents and these resources are fed into low priority incidents. However, the surplus resources are not enough to compensate for the increase in reported low priority incidents. The quality of investigation of low priority incidents falls, causing a further drop in learning from incidents.

Graph for High Priority Incident Occurrence Rate

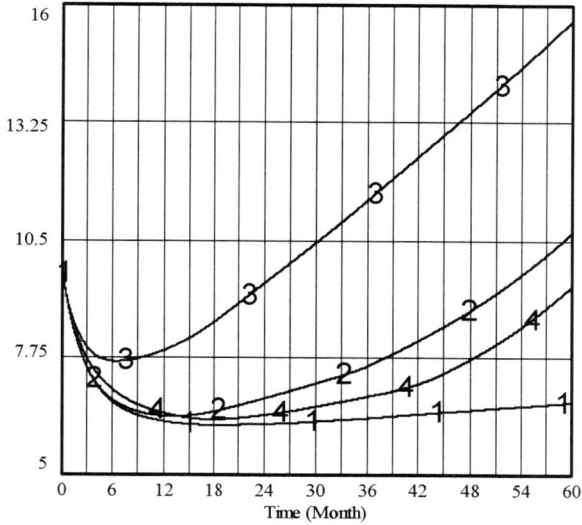

Graph for Low Priority Incident Occurrence Rate

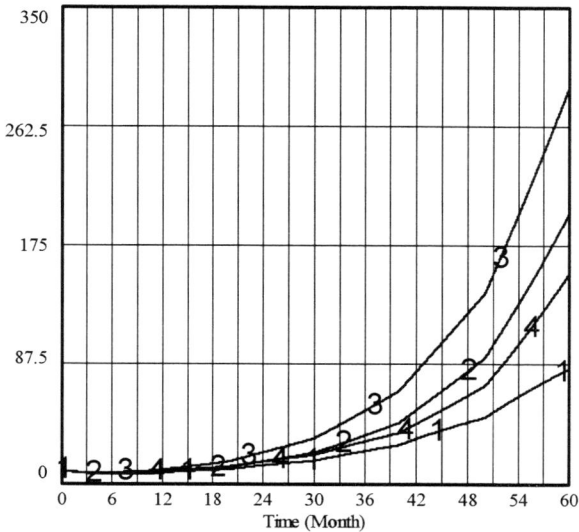

Graph for High Priority Incident Reporting Rate

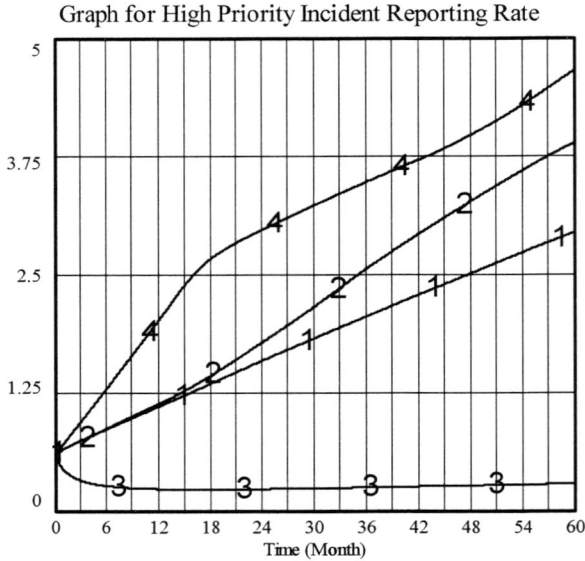

Graph for Low Priority Incident Reporting Rate

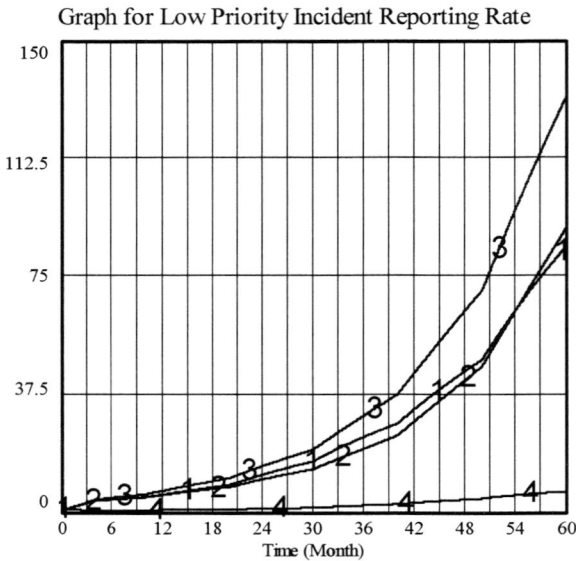

Low Priority Incident Reporting Rate : ILP	Incidents/Month
Low Priority Incident Reporting Rate : ILP LR	Incidents/Month
Low Priority Incident Reporting Rate : ILP DIHP LR	Incidents/Month
Low Priority Incident Reporting Rate : IHP DILP LR	Incidents/Month

Figure 5: Low and High Priority Incident Occurrence and Reporting Rates

Discouraging low priority incident reports (**4: IHP DILP LR**) improves the situation significantly. The compounded effects of low priority incentives and high priority disincentives are removed. Although the initial gains are slightly lower than in **2: ILP LR**, the occurrence of both kinds of incidents drops below that of **2: ILP LR**. As low priority incident reports are discouraged, the system's resources last longer. However, this highly successful policy leads to a significant increase in high priority incident reports, straining the system's resources. High priority reports are also more labor intensive. The system eventually reaches the resource bottle neck. The problem is only postponed.

6.4 Victim of Own Success

In both the **ILP LR** and **IHP DILP LR** scenarios the system becomes a victim of its own success. The growth in incident reports overwhelms the investigative resources available. The first solution that springs to mind is to hire more people. However, it is unlikely that such a policy would be economically viable, given the exponential growth in low priority incidents. More leverage could be obtained by developing tools to handle low priority incidents. Their high frequency and relative low sophistication make them good candidates for automatic procedures.

7. Observations and Future Work

The introduction of critical and complex ICT infrastructure into critical infrastructure, such as oil and gas production, elevates the need to manage computer incidents to the best practice in safety management. This paper begins an examination of the challenges of incident management by looking at how incident reporting policies and incident handling efforts interact to produce successful or unsuccessful outcomes. We draw heavily from the experience of industrial safety reporting systems to structure the analysis.

Successful security incident handling requires effective reporting, mitigation, and learning. Within the organization, however, these activities are not always seen as beneficial to those tasked with reporting. The relative impact of reporting incentives and disincentives will affect their frequency, reliability, and learning value. When incident reporting is discouraged because of fear of recriminations or pressure to appear secure, the decision to notify the incident handlers rests in the hands of the reporters. These staff may have only a limited understanding of the effects of the incident on the organization's security. In contrast, a high volume of low-impact reports, stimulated by incentives, pushes the evaluation for review and mitigation onto the incident handling team. If the incident handling team becomes overwhelmed with reports of limited value, their effectiveness will drop, reducing their ability to identify areas for operational change and improvements for security.

Where then shall the problem detection burden be placed? An effective security policy in a setting of limited resources encourages reporting of high priority incidents and discourages reporting of low priority incidents. The ability to differentiate high priority incidents from low can be cultivated in reporting teams, but such policies may not integrate with other social and economic demands. If this differentiating ability is not cultivated, and unimportant incidents flood the reporting process, incident handling teams must triage, focusing resources on the important and time-sensitive problems that are presented to them, or become overwhelmed and lose their effectiveness as an agent for learning and future protection. On the other hand, discouraging reporting reduces the effects of reporting on staff and on the reporting teams, but may mask hidden vulnerabilities. A collective view of the tradeoff between security and operational costs is needed to ensure appropriate management. This view may be stimulated by common risk analysis and goal-setting, though transfer of lessons among organizational units takes time to reach convergence (Martinez-Moyano et al., 2007).

While the parallels between safety reporting and computer incident reporting are clear, there are critical differences that must be considered in future work. Safety systems strive for high reliability (Cooke and Rohleder, 2006), but they do not face exponential growth in low priority incidents that have been observed in computer security incidents. From the incident reporter's perspective, a safety incident may have very visible and immediate risk of personal injury, where a computer incident's effects may be far removed from the immediate worksite. Finally, the continued growth of sophisticated and innovative attacks on computer systems, driven in part by the speed of change in the ICT environment, creates new opportunities for failure with each generation of technology. It may well not be possible to provide staff the knowledge needed to keep up with these changes, increasing our dependence on technology to separate high priority from low priority problems.

References

Anderson, D.J. & Webster, C.S. (2001) A system approach to the reduction of medication error on the hospital ward. *Journal of Advanced Nursing*, 35, 34-41.

Calder, A. & Watkins, S. (2005) *IT Governance*, London and Philadelphia, Kogan Page.

Cooke, D.L. & Rohleder, T.R. (2006) Learning from incidents: From normal accidents to high reliability. *System Dynamics Review*, 22.

EYGM (2004) Global Information Security Survey. Ernst & Young.

Gonzalez, J.J. (2005) *Towards a Cyber Security Reporting System - A Quality Improvement Process*, Berlin Heidelberg, Springer Verlag.

Gonzalez, J.J., Qian, Y., Sveen, F.O. & Rich, E. (2005) Helping Prevent Information Security Risks in the Transition to Integrated Operations. *Telektronikk*, 101, 29-37.

Johnson, C. (2003) *Failure in Safety Critical Systems: A Handbook of Incident and Accident Reporting*, Glasgow University Press.

Kjellen,U. (2000) *Prevention of Accidents Through Experience Feedback*, London and New York, Taylor & Francis.

Lee, P.I. & Weitzel, T.R. (2005) Air carrier safety and culture: An investigation of Taiwan's adaptation to western incident reporting programs. *Journal of Air Transportation*, 10.

Martinez-Moyano, I.J., Rich, E., Conrad, S., Andersen, D.F. & Stewart, T.R. (2007) A Behavioral Theory of Insider-Threat Risks: A System Dynamics Approach. *ACM Transactions on Modeling and Computer Simulation*, (forthcoming).

Nyssen, A. S., Aunac, S., Faymonville, M. E. & Lutte, I. (2004) Reporting systems in healthcare from a case-by-case experience to a general framework: An example in anaesthesia. *European Journal of Anaesthesiology*, 757-765.

OLF (2006) OLF Guideline No. 104:
Information Security Baseline Requirements for Process Control, Safety and Support ICT Systems. Norwegian Oil Industry Association.

Phimister, J.R., Oktem,m U., Kleindorfer, P.R. & Kunruether, H. (2003) Near-miss incident management in the chemical process industry. *Risk Analysis*, 23, 445-459.

Rich, E., Sveen, F. O. & Jager, M. (2006) Overcoming Organizational Challenges to Secure Knowledge Management. *Secure Knowledge Management Workshop.* New York, US.

Schneier, B. (2000) *Secrets and Lies*, Wiley Computer Publishing.

Sterman, J. D. (2000) *Business Dynamics: Systems Thinking and Modeling for a Complex World*, Irwin McGraw-Hill.

Stoneburner, G. (2006) Toward a unified security/safety model. *IEEE Computer*, 96-97.

Wiant, T. L. (2005) Information Security Policy's Impact on Reporting Security Incidents. *Computers & Security*, 24, 448-459.

Wiik, J. (2007) Dynamics of incident response effectiveness – A system dynamics approach. Bergen, University of Bergen.

Wiik, J., Gonzalez, J. J. & Kossakowski, K.-P. (2005) Limits to effectiveness of Computer Security Incident Response Teams (CSIRTs). *Twenty Third International Conference of the System Dynamics Society.* Boston, MA, The System Dynamics Society.

Winkler, I. (2005) *Spies Among Us*.

Zangwill, W. I. & Kantor, P. B. (1998) Towards a Theory of Continuous Improvement and the Learning Curve. *Management Science*, 44, 910-920.

Proceedings of the International Symposium on
Human Aspects of Information Security & Assurance (HAISA 2007)

On the Imbalance of the Security Problem Space and its Expected Consequences

K. Beznosov[1] and O. Beznosova[2]

[1]Electrical and Computer Engineering, University of British Columbia, Vancouver,
Canada
[2]Political Science, University of British Columbia, Vancouver, Canada
email: [1]beznosov@ece.ubc.ca [2]olga@beznosov.net

Abstract

This paper considers the attacker-defender game in the field of computer security as
a three-dimensional phenomenon. The decomposition of the problem space into
technological, human, and social factors enabled us to analyze the concentration of
public research efforts by defenders. Our analysis suggests that over 94% of the
public research in computer security has been concentrated on technological
advances. Yet attackers seem to employ more and more human and social factors in
their attacks. As the arms race in computer security progresses, social factors may
become or already are increasingly important. The side that capitalizes on them
sooner may gain the competitive advantage. Drawing on recent results in the
organizational theory, sociology, and political science, we discuss avenues for
investigating the social dimension by the defenders.

Keywords

Computer Security, Social Factors, Organizational Factors.

1. Introduction

Computer security is a complex subject whose interdisciplinary nature is clearly
delineated by Anderson (2001). To generalize the famous quote by Needham and
Lampson about cryptography, we believe that people who think their security
problem can be solved with only technology do not understand the problem and do
not understand the technology. But how much attention is paid by both attackers and
defenders to aspects of computer security that are not technological? If these other
aspects are not being explored, what are the implications?

This paper reports on the results of our analysis of the computer security problem
space and suggests the areas with highest potential for making progress in the
attacker-defender game. To analyze the problem space, we qualitatively decomposed
the major activities in computer security on the basis of technological, human, and

social (THS) factors, then estimated the proportions of these activities in research on science and engineering world-wide as well as the attention to them paid by the press.

We use the term "activity" instead of "area" or "functionality" (or similar terms) to highlight our focus on offensive (e.g., social engineering, phishing) and defensive (e.g., cryptography, intrusion detection, information assurance, access control) practices, as well as those aspects of computer security that can be employed by either side (e.g., economics and politics of security).

Our simple, but hopefully symptomatic, estimation of world-wide research activities related to several major areas of computer security indicates that over 94% of these activities have so far concentrated on the technological dimension (e.g., cryptography, access control, intrusion detection, malware). Activities focused on the human and social aspects of the security problem account for less than 6% in total. Although the way we estimated the volumes is unlikely to sustain any criticism from statisticians, we do believe the results are representative.

These results, for one, underscore the popular notion that in the last forty years, progress in computer security has been mostly due to technological advances. The results of our queries on Google News Archives—which indicate that 'public' opinion rates social and human dimensions of security significantly higher than the share of the corresponding public research—point at least to the mismatch between the public concerns and the focus of the researchers. Drawing on recent results from other disciplines, we believe that as the computer security arms race progresses, social factors may become increasingly important. In fact, the next big spiral in this arms race may very well be due to advances in the social dimension. Arguably, potential advantages of the social dimension have already been exploited by attackers, as demonstrated by numerous cases of social engineering (Mitnick, et al. 2002, Gordon 1995). It is not clear who, attackers or defenders, will take the lead. The other side will have to catch up.

The rest of the paper is organized as follows. Section 2 describes our analysis of the computer security problem space and discusses the expected consequences of the identified imbalance. Section 3 discusses social dimensions of computer security and considers the application of some methods and results from social sciences to it. Section 4 discusses avenues for future research. Section 5 concludes the paper.

2. The Imbalance of the Security Problem Space

While the dominant role of the technology in the research on computer security can be easily established by, for example, browsing through the proceedings of major professional and research conferences devoted to security, we wanted to validate popular beliefs about the bias towards technology, using a more systematic approach. This section describes a simple study we performed, the results collected, and our interpretation of the results.

2.1 Methods

To gain an understanding of which aspects (technological, human, or social) of the computer security have been the focus of the research community, we first selected representative activities of the attacker-defender game. We then mapped each activity into THS basis. Due to the space limitation of this paper, we do not discuss the method and results of our mapping in detail. Finally, we used Web of Science[1] and Engineering Village's Compendex[2], and Inspec[3] citation databases to estimate the relative volume of publications on each selected activity in the science and engineering communities. The rest of this section describes the activity selection and steps of our analysis.

The set of selected computer security activities is listed in the left-most column of Table 1. This list is not intended to be comprehensive, and some of the selected activities do overlap. For instance, cryptography is directly employed in some access control solutions, and information assurance does rely on access control and cryptography. However, since the purpose of this analysis was to uncover global trends, signs of which have accumulated in the scientific and engineering publications, we believe that the selected activities are representative of the major focus areas. After selecting the activities, we performed the mapping.

Our premise in mapping was that most computer security activities—performed by either attackers or defenders of computer systems—can be viewed as consisting of components related to either technological, human, or social aspects, and therefore can be broken down on the THS basis[1]. By technological we refer to all aspects of computer security that involve purely technological solutions. We use the term human aspects to refer to such factors as human psychology, physiology, and cognition at the individual level. By social aspects we refer to those factors that are due to interactions among more than one person in social or formal organizations and within wider social context. Using our judgement, we mapped the selected activities on the THS basis. Figure 1 graphically depicts the results of our mapping.

[1]Web of Science (2007) is a citation database of approximately 8,700 research journals.
[2]Compendex is a bibliographic database of engineering research that contains over nine million references and abstracts from 1969 to present taken from over 5,000 engineering journals, conferences and technical reports.
[3]Inspec is a bibliographic database that contains over eight million bibliographic records taken from 3,500 scientific and technical journals and 1,500 conference proceedings. Approximately 330,000 new records are added to the database annually.

Activity	Engineering Village search query	Relative weight (%)		
		Google News Arch-s	Web of Science	Eng. Village
Technology-centric cumulative		**58.3**	**94.2**	**95.6**
Cryptography	Cryptography OR cryptographic OR encryption OR decryption	30.5	90.2	79.1
Malware	Malware OR "computer worm" OR "computer virus"	14.4	1.6	1.9
Information assurance	Computer AND ("security assurance" OR "information assurance") NOT financial NOT social	0.7	0.2	1.2
Intrusion detection	Intrusion AND detection AND computer AND security	3.9	1.5	5.5
Access control	("access control" OR authorization) AND computer AND security	8.7	1.0	8.0
Human-centric cumulative		**30.4**	**2.3**	**2.3**
Usable security	Security AND (usability OR usable OR HCI)	17.6	1.9	1.8
Phishing	Phishing	12.6	0.3	0.4
Shoulder surfing	"shoulder surfing"	0.2	0.04	0.03
Social-centric cumulative		**6.0**	**3.2**	**2.1**
Social engineering	"social engineering"	5.3	2.3	0.2
Politics and security	(politics OR bill OR legislation OR regulation) and ("information security" OR "computer security")	4.3	0.2	1.0
Economies of security	(economies AND ("information security" OR "computer security")) OR "security economies"	0.5	0.1	0.2
Organizational and social	(security AND "human factor") OR "security awareness" OR "security training" OR "security culture" AND (computer OR information)	1.2	0.6	0.7
Total for individual types of activity		**100**	**100**	**100**

Table 1: Search queries and the results for representative keywords

In order to estimate the relative weight of each activity in the public research community, we determined the percentage of indexed publications related to each activity, according to the number of entries returned by the search engines of Web of Science (2007) and Engineering Village (2007) in response to our queries. As the query syntax for all three data sources was similar, the second column of Table 1 lists only Engineering Village version of the search queries for each activity. To be safe, we aimed to construct queries that were liberal (i.e., returned more rather than fewer results) for activities with significant social and human aspects, and conservative for technology-centric activities, according to the mapping described in the next section.

To avoid double-counting of those publications that were returned for more than one query in the same THS group, we also obtained statistics on each of these three groups by making a single query that comprised all queries in the group. We were unable to do so for Google News Archives due to the limitations on the search string length. The queries limited our search to public content written in the English language only. Since we were concerned with the relative (rather than absolute) volume of each activity, it is an open question whether this limitation biased the results.

2.2 Results

The percentage of scientific or engineering publications related to each type of activity found through Web of Science and Engineering Village (rounded to tenths of percentile) are listed in the two right-most columns of Table 1. Figure 1 presents each activity mapped on the THS basis.

When we grouped activities into technology-centric (cryptography, access control, intrusion detection, information assurance, and malware), human-centric (security usability, phishing, and shoulder surfing), and social-centric (economics of security, social engineering, politics of security, as well as organizational and social factors), the first group consistently accounted for over 94% of indexed publications in scientific and engineering outlets, the human-centric and the social-centric groups enjoyed no more than 2-3% each.

For comparison, the table also shows statistics of these categories' popularity in the Google News Archives search engine, which likely correlates with the degree of recent press coverage. Table 1 reveals the divergence between the results of the queries from 'popular' discussions on Google News Archives and those in the research community. While in the latter, human and social-centric cumulative scores were just 2-3 per cent each, in the former it was significantly higher - 6% and 30% of queries returned references to the social and human dimension of security respectively.

[1]We use the term basis in this paper by analogy with the *vector space basis*, which is a list of vectors $(v_1, v_2, \ldots, v_n)$ in vector space V such that for any $v \in V$ it can be represented as a composition of the vector space basis: $v = a_1v_1 + a_2v_2 + \cdots + a_nv_n$. The *dimension* of V is n.

2.3 Discussion

The results of our analysis indicate that the focus of public research related to computer security has been overwhelmingly focused on technological aspects, leaving human and social dimensions mostly uncharted. This imbalance between technology-centric and human/social centric activities can be interpreted in a number of ways. Computer security (including information security) has from its beginnings been a technology-focused game played by attacker(s) against defenders(s). One can argue, therefore, that the current focus on technology is normal and will continue on both sides in the foreseeable future. Our view is different.

We believe that the attackers have become increasingly aware of the importance of human and social aspects in the attacker-defender game. It is indirectly confirmed by Fathi, Microsoft's vice president for the Windows core operating system, who stated that "most users encounter PC security issues because they fall for social engineering tactics . . . " (Hines 2007). The testimony before the U.S. Congress by arguably "the world's most famous hacker" Kevin Mitnick—who then said "I was so successful in that [social engineering] line of attack that I rarely had to resort to a technical attack" (The Associated Press 2000)—confirms that it is often easier for the attackers to exploit human and social weaknesses of the defenses than to defeat the technological countermeasures. For research in computer security to sustain the arms race, it ought to explore the social dimension of the problem space.

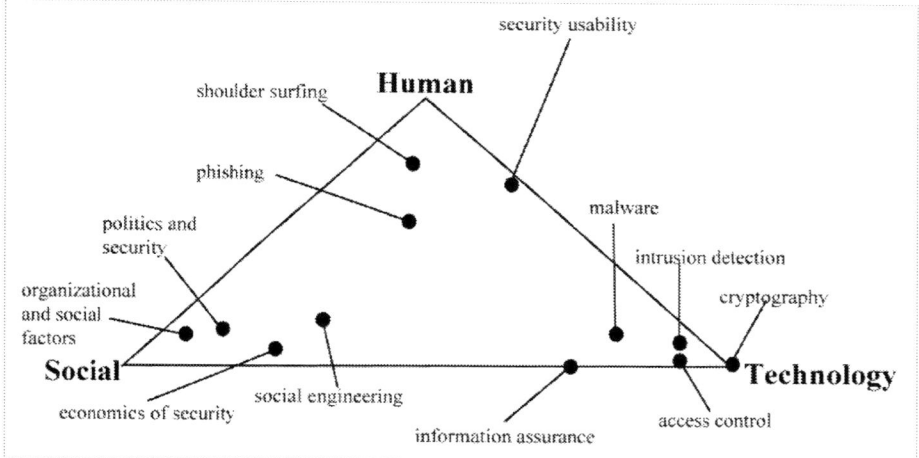

Figure 1: Activities mapped on the THS basis.

3. Social Dimension

We define social aspects of security as those that are exclusively due to interactions among more than one human actor on either side of the attacker-defender game. Of course, the boundaries of such categories can sometimes be fuzzy. Some may be relatively easy to classify, e.g., economics of security qualify as social dimension and usability of security controls as human aspect of the problem space. Other phenomena, for example social engineering, may be more difficult to label. While the success or failure of a particular social engineering attack depends on actions of a particular human being, these actions are determined by a larger context of habitual and widely accepted organizational practices and societal norms, which emerged together with the development of interfaces and software. Therefore, to disarm a social engineering attacker this context could be altered through training or awareness campaigns. Hence, the solution might have been located on the social plane of the problem space.

We suggest that taking into account social and organizational matters may be important for computer security research in order to advance in the attacker-defender game. The examples below illustrate that when attacks take social factors into account, the magnitude and scale of their impact may be increased manifold, leaving the other side to cope with it. Consequently, when organizational and social factors are left unattended in certain situations, the outcomes may be quite disastrous.

Intuitively, it seems that in the attacker-defender game, social factors may bring competitive advantage to the side that employs them first. The following examples cited by Denning (2001, p. 257) provide a number of illustrations of how exactly social factors may bring to the table what was not predicted and planned for by the defenders.

In 1999 protests were set up to coincide with a meeting of the G8 in Cologne, Germany. A group called J18 coordinated the protests through a web site inviting people to plan individual actions focusing on disrupting financial centres, banking districts, and multinational corporate power bases. Hackers from Indonesia, Israel, Germany, and Canada simultaneously attacked the computers of at least 20 companies, including the Stock Exchange and Barclays. More than 10,000 attacks were launched over a five-hour period (Ungoed-Thomas & Sheehan 1999).

On June 15, 1999, the Electronic Disturbance Theater organized an act of Electronic Civil Disobedience to stop the war in Mexico. The suggested action was for people using computers to simply point their web browsers to a specific URL at a particular time. By directing web browsers toward the Zapatista FloodNet URL during this time period, people joined a virtual sit-in. Their individual computers began sending re-load commands over and over again for the duration of the time they were connected to FloodNet. The results of the June 18 Electronic Disturbance Theater virtual sit-in were that the Zapatista FloodNet URL received a total of 18,615 unique requests from people's computers in 46 different countries. The repeated re-load command of the individual user - multiplied by the thousand engaged - clogged the Internet pathways leading to the targeted web site. In this case on June 18, FloodNet was directing these multiple re-load browser commands to the Mexican Embassy in the UK. The global Zapatista FloodNet action was the first that the Electronic Disturbance Theater called for in 1999. The group began in the spring of 1998 and launched a series of FloodNet actions directed primarily against web sites of the Mexican government, but action targets also included the White House, the Frankfurt Stock Exchange, the Pentagon (Wray 1999).

Individuals acting alone or in small groups have used network flooding tools to disable internet servers. During the Kosovo conflict, Belgrade hackers conducted such attacks against NATO servers. Bombarding NATO's web server with ping commands, they caused line saturation of the targeted servers (Allison 1999).

To be sure, attackers can exploit social aspects of security without human buy-in and active participation. The best examples are flooding and spamming attacks that use botnets – collections of compromised end-user PCs remotely controlled by attackers. However, we argue that the social dimension is crucial even in botnets. The recent trend among attackers is to create botnets by implanting malware on victim's computers using "drive-by download" attacks – which rely on the combination of vulnerabilities in web browsers and social engineering tricks, according to Viega (2007) the Chief Security Architect of a major antivirus and computer security company McAfee. He predicts these attacks to become more and more cost effective, as the average level of user security knowledge declines due to the growth of the broadband Internet penetration, which is expected to exceed 50% among US households in 2007 (ParksAssociates 2007).

As the above discussion suggests, social organization of the attackers allowed them to achieve the results not possible otherwise, shifting the balance in favor of the protesters and away from the defenders of the computer systems. A number of social science disciplines, including organizational theory, sociology, and political science, developed theories that enhance our understanding and management of social aspects of conflictual and competitive situations. In the remaining part of the section, we suggest to broaden the scope of research to involve organizational behavior and structure as well as social capital aspects that are currently not high on computer security research agenda.

Organizational processes and behavior. Probably one of the most influential schools of organizational thought, referred to as the decision-making or behavioral school, was developed by Simon and March in 1950s. The school focuses on the connection between bounded rationality and behavioral structure, demonstrating that because individuals and organizations are limited in knowledge and computational abilities, they have to rely upon habits, routines, and other forms of programmed behavior in making decisions. The critical point to understand about organizations is that structure arises out of cognitive limitations. Allison's (1971) one of the most influential books in modern politics, analyses the Cuban missile crisis to demonstrate how certain international security events can be understood differently based on the model employed. One of Allison's models, the organizational process model, is built around Simon-March tradition, which emphasizes bounded rationality and routine behavior of the major organizations involved in the crisis: the State department, the Soviets, the military, etc. (Moe 1991).

Organizational structure. Another area of research concerns structural characteristics of organizations and is quite often employed in the study of terrorism and organized crime. For example, Arquilla, et al. (1999) conducted a study of the impact of ongoing information evolution and networks on terrorist capabilities, and how this development may be associated with a move away from emphasis on traditional, episodic efforts at coercion to a new view of error as a form of protracted warfare. They suggest the term *netwar* to refer to:

> "... an emerging mode of conflict and crime at societal levels, in which the protagonists use network forms of organization and related doctrines, strategies, and technologies attuned to the information age. These protagonists are likely to consist of dispersed small groups who communicate, coordinate, and conduct their campaigns in an internetted manner, without a precise central command. Thus, information age *netwar* differs from modes of conflict and crime in which the protagonists prefer formal, standalone, hierarchical organizations, doctrines, and strategies, as in past efforts."
>
> (Arquilla et al. 1999, p. 47)

Critical here is the attention to a change in organizational forms along with strategies and tactics that terrorists (or other attackers for that matter) use, and the implications this change has for those who design protection measures. According to Arquilla & Ronfeldt (2001), organizational purposes affect the suitability and effectiveness of various types of social structures. For example, Arquilla and Ronfeldt illustrate how different organizational structures—a chain network, a "star" or hub network, and an all-connected network—can aid organizations in achieving certain objectives, such as information sharing, communications, cooperation, as well as their defensive and offensive potential. In a computer security attacker-defender game, security administrators may find themselves in a disadvantaged position if they are not prepared to deal with changing organizational forms and tactics of the attackers' teams.

Considering the context and environment in which the game takes place is imperative for determining the actors' chances of success. For example, research on business organizations (Saetre 1996, Boudreau, et al. 1998) and criminal networks (Williams 2001) demonstrates that in the globalizing world, the constraints, rigidities, and inefficiencies of hierarchical organizational structures rendered them inadequate and forced the competing organizations to restructure. It was shown that actors could gain competitive advantages in this changing environment through what was sometimes called "agile networks" (Saetre 1996) or "virtual organizations" (Boudreau et al. 1998). To accommodate environmental constraints and take advantage of opportunities, considerable emphasis in these organizations is placed on flexible internal communication networks, strategic connections, the ability to respond rapidly to external opportunities and challenges, rapid information processing, and quick decision making (Lewin & Stephens 1993, Saetre 1996).

Culture, norms, social capital: While the right organizational routines and structure may be necessary for gaining competitive advantage, they may not be sufficient. Researchers and practitioners alike increasingly recognize that social capital, which includes both structural and attitudinal components of social organization, is critical for effective functioning of organizations and for gaining competitive advantage. It has been demonstrated by research in sociology (Coleman 1990), conflict studies (Colletta & Cullen 2000) and business (Saetre 1996, Handy 1995) that organizations with higher levels of trust, horizontal cooperation, and loyalty show better performance and efficiency than those that are deficient in these factors.

As this brief overview of the literature suggests, under the conditions of conflict and competition, achievements in the technological dimension of the THS basis only may not necessarily give attackers or defenders sufficient advantage to stay on top of the game. The intervening factor may well be the interaction between the social and organizational structures of the actors, the actors' goals, and the broader environmental context, which could be responsible for the success or failure of actors' strategies. What this discussion suggests for computer security research, is that studying social dimensions of information security problem space will allow the computer security community to better understand existing problems and design more effective solutions for some of them.

4. Suggestions for Further Research

Drawing on the discussion in the previous sections, we suggest a number of areas for further research: organizational processes, behaviors, and structures, as well as organizational culture, and societal norms.

One potentially fruitful research agenda concerns the relationship between organizational processes and behavior and the effectiveness of security defenses. For example, one could study decision making processes and operational routines within organizations to better understand how they influence security posture of the organizations. In particular, taking into account business goals of the defenders, the ways in which security-related decisions are made and carried out, and the structure of formal and informal cooperative relationships within defender's organization, what kinds of processes meet defender's objectives best?

Another interesting direction is the exploration of the relationship between organizational structures and security. As mentioned above, there is a wide variety of organizational structures, from hierarchies to flexible task-specific networks. For example, Botta, et al. (2007) find that the IT security job is distributed across multiple employees, often affiliated with different organizational units or groups within a unit and responsible for different aspects of security, typically with single coordinator, who is not necessarily higher on the organization ladder than the other group members. Comparing security postures and effectiveness of security programs within organizations, one could determine what kinds of organizational structures are more effective for defending against which security threats.

If to further this direction, the relationship and interaction between attackers' and defenders' organizational structures could be investigated. Is it possible to study models of attackers' organizations, and determine the relationship between attacker's organizational structure and the effectiveness of their attacks? What kinds of countermeasures can be employed by defenders to effectively oppose the attackers, given the organizational structure of the two?

As discussed in the previous section, organizational culture, norms, and social capital might play an important role in the effectiveness of security measures. While Knapp, et al. (2006) find positive correlation between top management support and security culture as well as security policy enforcement, further investigation is needed to establish the causal relationship between organizational cultures, norms, and social capital and the effectiveness of organizational security strategies and programs.

Social aspects of security do not stop at the doorstep of specific organizations. End user behaviors intertwine inextricably with the overall level of individual security. However, as more and more users connect to Internet through high-speed channels, the network effect results in the exponentially increasing impact of personal security behavior of individual users on others. Even worse, the higher penetration of broadband Internet connections in the households of modern societies also results in the lowering average level of personal security "hygiene". It is thus useful to look at wider societal aspects of security promotion mechanisms, such as education, awareness building, and policy. For example, what kind of mechanisms would be effective to increase awareness about security risks, and personal security hygiene? Such a study can benefit greatly by borrowing from other disciplines. Some of the examples could be the development of societal norms and policies pertaining to recycling, seat belt use, as well as drinking and smoking.

5. Conclusion

The bulk of the published research in the computer security has so far been in the technological dimension. The human and social aspects are currently largely neglected in computer security research. As the arms race in computer security progresses, social factors may become or already are increasingly important. The side that exploits these factors sooner may gain competitive advantage, since by employing different organizational structures and processes and adapting better to the wider social context, either side can gain sufficient advantages even when lacking in technological capabilities.

The next big spiral in the computer security arms race may very well be due to advances in the social dimension. It is not clear who, attackers or defenders, will be first to fully exploit this area. The other side might end up in catch-up mode, as the modern history of social engineering, phishing, and terrorism illustrates.

Acknowledgments

The authors would like to thank anonymous reviewers for their constructive and helpful comments, Lee Iverson for feedback on an earlier version of this paper, and Craig Wilson for improving the readability of this paper.

References

Allison, G.T. (1971). The Essence of Decision: Explaining the Cuban Missile Crisis. Little, Brown, Boston, MA, USA.

Allison, R. (1999). 'Belgrade Hackers Bombard MoD Website in 'First' Internet War'. PA News.R. J. Anderson (2001). Security Engineering: A Guide to Building Dependable Distributed Systems. Wiley.

Arquilla, J. & Ronfeldt, D. (2001). 'The Advent of Netwar (Revisited)'. In J. Arquilla & D. Ronfeldt (eds.), Networks and Netwars: The Future of Terror, Crime, and Militancy, pp. 61–97. Rand Corporation.

Arquilla, J. (1999). 'Networks, Netwar, and Information-Age Terrorism'. In I. O. Lesser, B. Hoffman, J. Arquilla, D. Ronfeldt, M. Zanini, & B. M. Jenkins (eds.), Countering the New Terrorism. Rand Corporation, Santa Monica, CA.

Botta, D., et al. (2007). 'Studying IT Security Professionals: Research Design and Lessons Learned'. position paper for the CHI Workshop on Security User Studies: Methodologies and Best Practices.

Boudreau, M.C., et al. (1998). 'Going Global: Using Information Technology to Advance the Competitiveness of the Virtual Transnational Organization'. Academy of Management Executive 12(4):120–128.

Coleman, J. (1990). Foundations of Social Theory. Harvard University Press, Cambridge, MA.

Colletta, N.J. & Cullen, M.L. (2000). Violent Conflict and Transformation of Social Capital: Lessons from Cambodia, Rwnada, Guatemala and Somalia. World Bank, Washington DC.

Denning, D. (2001). 'Activism, Hacktivism, and Cyberterrorism: the Internet As a Tool for Influencing Foreign Policy'. In Networks and Netwars: The Future of Terror, Crime, and Militancy, pp. 239–288. Rand Corporation.

Engineering Village (2007). 'Engineering Village'. http://www.engineeringvillage2.org/.

Gordon, S. (1995). 'Social Engineering: Techniques and Prevention'. In in Proceedings of the 12 World Conference on Computer Security, Audit and Control, pp. 445–451, Westminster, London, U.K. Oxford, U.K.: Elsevier.

Handy, C. (1995). 'Trust and the virtual organization'. Harvard Business Review 73(3):40–50.

Hines, M. (2007). 'Vista Aims to Stop Hackers' Social Engineering Ploys'. http://www.eweek.com/article2/0,1895,2084631,00.asp.

Knapp, K.J., et al. (2006). 'Information security: management's effect on culture and policy'. Information Management & Computer Security 14(1):24–36.

Lewin, A.Y. & Stephens, C.U. (1993). 'Epilogue: Designing Postindustrial Organizations: Combining Theory and Practice'. In G. P. Huber & W. H. Glicks (eds.), Organizational Change and Redesign, pp. 393–410. Oxford University Press, New York.

Mitnick, K.D., et al. (2002). The Art of Deception: Controlling the Human Element of Security. John Wiley & Sons.

Moe, T. (1991). 'Politics and the Theory of Organization'. Journal of Law, Economics, and Organization 7. Parks Associates (2007). 'U.S. Residential Broadband Penetration to Exceed 50% in 2007'. http://www.parksassociates.com/press/press releases/2007/dig lifestyles1.html.

Saetre, A.S. (1996). 'The Agile Network: A Model of Organizing for Optimal Responsiveness and Efficiency'. presented at The Fift National Agility Conference.

The Associated Press (2000). 'Noted Hacker Speaks Before Senate Panel'. http://partners.nytimes.com/library/tech/00/03/biztech/articles/02hack.html.

Ungoed-Thomas, J. & Sheehan, M. (1999). 'Riot Organisers Prepare to Launch Cyber War on City'. Sunday Times.

Viega, J. (2007). 'Malware in the Real World'. In The 14th Annual Network & Distributed System Security Symposium, Invited Talk, San Diego, CA. Internet Society.
Web of Science (2007). 'Web of Science Web Site'. http://www.isiknowledge.com.

Williams, P. (2001). 'Transnational Criminal Networks'. In J. Arquilla & D. Ronfeldt (eds.), Networks and Netwars: The Future of Terror, Crime, and Militancy, pp. 61–97. Rand Corporation.

Wray, S. (1999). 'June 18: The Virtual and the Real Action On the Internet and In Austin, Texas / Zapatista Floodnet and Reclaim the Streets'.

Proceedings of the International Symposium on
Human Aspects of Information Security & Assurance (HAISA 2007)

Empirical vs. Non-Empirical Work in Information Systems Security: A Review and Analysis of Published Articles 1995-2005

J.M. Stanton

Syracuse University School of Information Studies
jmstanto@syr.edu

Abstract

Information Systems Security is generally recognized as a small subfield of the larger field of Information Systems. A literature analysis of articles published in the field of Information Systems Security in the years 1995-2005 is presented. Results from the analysis suggested showed that the mix of article content in this subfield favored articles without data. This finding, along with other related findings suggests that the field is in a relatively early state with respect to scientific maturity. Comprehensive literature review articles published in high impact Information Systems journals and a journal dedicated to the subfield may help ISS to progress into a more scientifically mature phase.

Keywords

Information systems security, Empirical research, Literature review.

1. Introduction

Empirical research provides the substantive basis for advances in social science. In the field of Information Systems (IS), a variety of authors have reviewed the state of empirical literature in the field with an eye towards identifying paradigms, trends, and patterns that help to understand the direction and future needs for research. Benbasat and Zmud (Benbasat and Zmud, 1999) commented that the field's "continuing emphasis on performing rigorous research has paid off," with respect to the quality of published research. Claver, Gonzalez, and Llopis (2000) reviewed 16 years of research in Information Systems and found that as the field matured there was an "increase in the number of empirical articles over theoretical ones," and that "the most frequent of the empirical studies is the field study, followed by the case study." Interestingly, their data also showed a gradual decline in the amount of research on information security between 1981 (5.5% of articles in IS) and 1989 (0.4% of articles in IS), after which the percentage began to climb. Vessey (2002) reviewed the diversity of IS research between 1995 and 1999. She found that most studies used a hypothetico-deductive approach, although the reference disciplines used by the researchers were highly variable. Looking across the past two or three decades, then, the IS field has adopted a range of the available methodological approaches from the social sciences and employed them in the service of conducting and publishing more and more rigorous research.

What is true for the field as a whole, however, is not necessarily true of every subfield. In the subfield of Information Systems Security (ISS), which began to flourish only with the onset of the widespread use of the Internet in the early 1990s, the use of empirical methods to explore security-related phenomena may not reflect the same trends as in the larger field of IS. In particular Kotulic and Clark (2004) have commented that conducting security research, particularly in organizational contexts provides unique challenges because of the sensitivity of the subject matter. To use an analogy, organized studies of public health occurred no later than the early 1800s (e.g., John Snow's studies of drinking water and cholera in London), but the first large scale public health studies of sexuality did not begin until at least a century later (e.g., the infamous Tuskeegee syphilis study). Information security breaches are a matter that most organizations are highly reluctant to discuss, particularly with outsiders such as academic researchers whose primary intention is to publish their findings. Nonetheless, as the analogy shows, difficult, sensitive, and private behaviors are subject to scientific study, given sufficient creativity and persistence by researchers.

Thus, the purpose of this paper is to examine the extent to which researchers in Information Systems Security (ISS) have begun to conduct the rigorous empirical research that marks a more mature field or subfield. Alternatively, if a majority of the research is non-empirical – theory and conceptual development, or editorial expressions of opinion and analysis – then it may be possible to conclude that the ISS subfield is still in a relatively immature state. This paper does not attempt to make a value judgment on the significance or contribution of particular pieces of research – whether conceptual or empirical – but rather tries to ascertain the state of literature in ISS to provide an informative picture that can guide future research.

2. Background

In the *Structure of Scientific Revolutions*, Kuhn (1970) describes three phases of development in which research activity occurs. The pre-scientific phase is marked by a lack of consensus on theory and methods, the normal phase includes the production of a substantial amount of research under conditions of consensus about theories and methods, and the transition phase includes various crises in which the theories and methods of the current paradigms of normal science are shown to produce results incommensurable with current assumptions. Physics has passed through several such periods including the shift from Newtonian physics to the ideas of relativity introduced by Einstein. Psychology has also witnessed several paradigm shifts including the rise and fall of Skinnerian behaviorism.

Of primary relevance to this paper, the pre-scientific period in a field includes multiple divergent attempts to develop conceptual frameworks that will serve as the basis of future empirical research and theory development. Note that Kuhn did not intend the term pre-scientific as pejorative toward the skills and knowledge of researchers and academics active in a newly emerging field, but rather as a gross categorization of the level of consensus in the community about what to study and how to study it. While empirical research does occur during the pre-scientific period, its prevalence relative to non-empirical work is likely to be low. Likewise, among the non-empirical work, there is likely to be a wide variety of writings, including material intended to advance a particular theoretical perspective, material that editorializes for or against the importance of a particular problem, and material that seeks to persuade researchers of the superiority of a particular viewpoint or perspective.

The goal of the literature analysis presented below was to examine whether the patterns of publication in the subfield of ISS over the last decade (1995-2005) fit Kuhn's notion of a field in its pre-scientific phase. These patterns would primarily appear on the basis of examining the topic matter of the literature over time and most importantly the evidentiary mix appearing in the literature. Literature may contain the author's opinions, analysis of previously published literature or archival materials, evidence from simulations or generated data, evidence from laboratory settings, or evidence from in vivo (field) settings. Some articles may contain more than one type of evidence. A preponderance of articles containing archival, simulated, laboratory, or field data, collected and analyzed in the context of a particular theoretical paradigm, would be indicative of a normal science phase. A preponderance of articles containing authorial opinions and/or analysis of previous literature, suggesting pre-consensus attempts at conceptual and theoretical development, would be indicative of a pre-scientific phase. To this end, a rough hierarchy of article types appears in Table 1.

In addition to examining the types of articles over time, it may be fruitful to check a few other sources of information. For example, citation rates of articles can help to indicate the extent to which a research area is consolidating itself around a particular perspective or framework. In addition, to assess the notion that information security research was difficult at first because of the sensitivity issues, but has become easier over time, it may be useful to examine the evolution of sample sizes over time. A pattern of increasing sample sizes may indicate a move from conceptual articles toward empirical articles.

Type	Mix of Evidence
Editorial	Primarily authorial opinion, possibly supplemented by basic discussion of previous literature or anecdotal practitioner material. Example article: Darragh and Darragh (2001).
Developmental	Systematic analysis of previous literature focused on development of conceptual or theoretical frameworks. Possible limited use of small-N techniques such as case studies to support development. Example article: Gonzalez and Sawicka (2002).
Pragmatic	Studies involving the use of small-N techniques, simulations, design exercises, and other evidence collected and analyzed without use of an orthodox theoretical and measurement context. Example article: Schwartz and Zalewski (1999).
Empirical	Data-based studies that collect and analyze data within the context of an accepted conceptual or theoretical framework. Laboratory, field, or archival data studies that try to confirm, modify, or extend existing frameworks. Example: Straub and Welke (1998).

Table 1: Research Articles and Evidence Types

3. Method

3.1 Article Selection

Publications from peer reviewed journal articles and archival, published conference proceedings (e.g., by the Association for Computing Machinery) were included in the data set. Publications were located through searches in major databases containing Information Systems (IS) research, such as ABI Inform, Google Scholar, EBSCO Business Source Elite, and Emerald Fulltext. In all searches, the quoted phrase "information security" was used to separate articles on this topic from articles on related topics such as privacy. Because "information security" also provides results from engineering and computer science – including articles on primarily technical topics such as cryptographic algorithms – a variety of additional search terms were used to qualify these searches. Additional search terms included user, organization, organizational, behavior, and human.

Articles were rejected from inclusion if they were not peer reviewed, if they did not contain at least one reference, if the topic matter was technical and did not contain an organizational or human component, or if the topic matter pertained to teaching or curriculum development for the college classroom (as opposed to organizational training and development topics, which were included). Because the analysis for this paper also included consideration of citation rates, it was necessary not to choose articles published very recently. A minimum publication delay of one year allowed inclusion of articles from 2005 and earlier. An arbitrarily chosen study period of eleven years included the middle and late 1990s – a period of major growth in research and publication on ISS topics. Thus, articles were included only if their publication date was between 1995-2005.

3.2 Article Coding

Article characteristics were coded by the author through the application of a coding rubric. A code was assigned designating each article as editorial, developmental, pragmatic, or empirical. Differentiating between editorial/developmental versus pragmatic/empirical was straightforward as the collection of data was evident or absent in each article. The distinction between editorial and developmental was made on the basis of whether the author presented a framework or other theoretical structure, as well as on whether the stated purpose of the article was to guide future research. The distinction between pragmatic and empirical was made on the basis of the presence or absence of theoretical discussion, statement of hypotheses, and/or use of established or systematically developed measures or research protocols. In the great majority of cases the code designations were not controversial.

Number of years since publication was coded as 2007 minus publication year. For convenience, citation counts were collected from Google Scholar and were not corrected for self citation[1]. Number of citations was corrected to take into account years since publication in order to avoid an unfair advantage for older articles. For developmental, pragmatic, or empirical articles containing data, the sample size was coded based on reading the method sections of the articles and summing all of the "cases" reported across all data collections in the article at the finest level of analysis. Thus a case study in which a company was analyzed at a general level from unstructured observations was counted as N=1, whereas another study in which 10 individuals were separately interviewed within a single company was counted as N=10. Articles without data were coded as N=0. Because sample size was very highly positively skewed, we used the base 10 log of sample size in our analyses. We also recoded sample size as a binary indicator of whether the article had data or not.

4. Results

Using the article selection criteria described above, we located 496 articles that qualified as peer reviewed literature on Information Systems Security (ISS). From this large set we randomly sampled n=98 articles for coding by choosing every fifth article from the compiled list. Some articles appeared both in the form of a conference proceedings paper and a journal article, and in these cases we only considered the latter of these. The mean time of publication was 2002 and the modal year was 2005, suggesting that a greater amount of literature was published later half of the study period.

---

[1]Google Scholar citation figures are known to contain inaccuracies, including self citations, but nonetheless provide information over a much broader set of publication outlets than ISI Web of Science

The modal article type was a developmental article that focused on reviewing existing literature and/or developing a theoretical or conceptual framework for later use; 36.7% of articles were of this type. The next most common type of article was an editorial article; 29.5% of articles consisted of an author's opinion and/or analysis of an issue in ISS. Pragmatic articles with small-N data collection and no reference to theory accounted for 9.2% of the articles. Empirical articles containing more substantial data sets and using theoretical or conceptual frameworks accounted for 24.5% of the articles. Using these percentages the most important contrast to notice is that empirical articles comprised about one third of the literature whereas non-empirical articles comprised the remaining two thirds. The average sample size across all articles was N=50, but this is a somewhat deceptive figure: The average sample size counting only articles that had data collections was N=145.

On average, articles in the data set were cited 9.3 times. This measure was highly skewed, however, as the modal number of citations was zero. About 18% of the articles had no citations at all, whereas an additional 17% had just one citation).The most highly cited article was Straub and Welke (1998) – an empirical article – which had 95 citations. The time-corrected citations measure was somewhat less skewed: about 1.8 citations per year. Note that citations were counted up to the present and corrected for the span of time from publication year to the present. Thus an article published in 2005 that had a total of two citations would have a time-corrected value of one citation per year.

A small set of correlations highlights key patterns in these data. The point-biserial correlation between years since publication and whether or not the article was data-based was not statistically significant, suggesting no evidence of a trend toward more empirical articles as the research advanced through time. Likewise the correlation between years since publication and article type was also not significant, an absence of evidence that more empirical and pragmatic articles might be appearing more frequently in recent years. The correlation between years since publication and the (base 10 log) sample size was not statistically significant, indicating no evidence of researchers collecting more data for recent articles as opposed to older articles. The correlation between citation rate and (base 10 log) sample size was also not statistically significant, indicating a lack of evidence that researchers cited articles with more data more frequently. The correlation between citation rate and article type was $r=.36$, $p<.001$, indicating that articles that contained data were substantially more highly cited than articles that did not. Further clarification of this evidence came from comparing the citation rates of articles with data versus those without: Articles with data were cited at a rate of 2.1 citations per year, whereas those without data were cited at 1.64 per year.

5. Discussion

The preponderance of editorial/opinion and conceptual review type articles in the Information Systems Security (ISS) literature – relative to the occurrence of articles with data – suggests that ISS is still in the earliest stages of development as a subfield of Information Systems. Articles with data constituted slightly less than one third of all published studies in ISS, whereas the remaining two thirds were non-data-based. Contrast this with Claver et al.'s (2000) review of research in the Information Systems field, which showed 68.7% of articles as empirical while only 31.3% were theoretical. The proportions are essentially reversed in ISS. Additionally, over the 11 year study period there was no indication that empirical articles were becoming more common over time. Likewise, there was no indication that sample sizes were increasing over time, lending continuing support to Kotulic and Clark's (2004) proposition that collecting organizational data on a sensitive topic such as information security continues to provide an important barrier to the conduct of empirical ISS research.

Kuhn (1970) characterizes this earliest stage of scientific development as a period in which researchers struggle to find common ground on matters of theory and method. With this perspective, it is comforting to note that theoretical and conceptual development articles far outnumbered those of the editorial variety, at least by a small margin. It is likely that because of the very large practitioner population in the information security world, editorial and opinion articles will remain popular as they provide a conduit for researchers and others to express ideas in non-academic language that can be considered by practitioners. Nonetheless, it is the developmental and empirical articles that will ultimately advance the research area, so the preponderance of developmental articles at this stage is an encouraging indication that researchers are trying to create a dialog about theories and methods within the community.

The citation analysis provides additional evidence concerning this issue. The pattern of citations was highly positively skewed, with an average of 9.3 citations per article but fully 36% of the articles with one or zero citations. No comparative benchmark is needed to know that an article with no citations is not particularly influential on subsequent research, but comparisons with top information systems journals show that the mean citations per year of 1.8 is comparable with the citation rates for articles in information systems journals (e.g., MISQ: 1.96 citations per article per year, see Katerattanakul et al., 2003).

This evidence suggests a possible paradox in ISS research. On the one hand the proportion of empirical articles is low: Researchers are productively generating constructs, frameworks, and models, but the number of data-based articles testing out all of these ideas is small. On the other hand, the most influential articles in ISS (e.g., Straub and Welke) are cited at rates comparable with other areas of information systems, suggesting accumulation of research results over time that is similar to the mainstream. One possible resolution of this paradox lies in comparing citation rates of articles with and without data. Those ISS articles with data are cited comparably to other areas of information systems, whereas those without are cited at much lower rates. Another way of saying this is that ISS researchers are paying substantial attention to each others' data, but less attention to proposed constructs, frameworks, and models. This finding suggests an important need for a journal whose editorial policies will support the production of articles addressing the development of scholarly consensus on appropriate models and theories to guide future ISS research. A special issue of an existing high impact journal would provide one fruitful venue for such articles.

All of the issues described above suggest the need for one or more journals dedicated to the subfield of ISS. Although a multitude of journals currently exist with "computer security" or "information security" in the title, few among these focus exclusively on theories, methods, and empirical research for ISS. As the data from this study show, a journal whose editorial policies encourage the publications of ISS studies containing data, and that help the ISS scholarly community reach consensus on appropriate models and theories will push the subfield of ISS forward into the next phase of scientific maturity.

References

Acquisti, A. & Grossklags, J. (2003) Losses, gains, and hyperbolic discounting: An experimental approach to information security attitudes and behavior. *2nd Annual Workshop on Economics and Information Security-WEIS*, 3.

Adams, A. (1999) The Implications of Users' Multimedia Privacy Perceptions on Communication and Information Privacy Policies. *Proceedings of Telecommunications Policy Research Conference.*

Alner, M. (2001) The effects of outsourcing on information security. *Information systems security,* 10, 35-43.

Atkinson, W. (2005) Integrating Risk Management & Security. *Risk Management,* 52, 32.

Backhouse, J., Hsu, C., Tseng, J. C. & Baptista, J. (2005) A question of trust. *Association for Computing Machinery. Communications of the ACM,* 48, 87.

Belsis, P., Kokolakis, S. & Kiountouzis, E. (2005) Information systems security from a knowledge management perspective. *Information Management & Computer Security,* 13, 189.

Benbasat, I. & Zmud, R. W. (1999) Empirical Research in Information Systems: The Practice of Relevance. *MIS Quarterly,* 23, 3-16.

Beulen, E. & Streng, R. J. (2002) The Impact of Online Mobile Office Applications on the Effectiveness and Efficiency of Mobile Workers' Behavior: A Field Experiment in the IT Services Sector. *Proceedings of ICIS,* 629–640.

Blatchford, C. (1998) Information security, business, and the Internet. *Information systems security,* 7, 44-53.

Boukhonine, S., Krotov, V. & Rupert, B. (2005) Future Security Approaches and Biometrics. *Communications of the Association for Information Systems,* 16, 1.

Braithwaite, T. (2001) Executives need to know: The arguments to include in a benefits justification for increased cyber security spending. *Information systems security,* 10, 35-48.

Brostoff, S. & Sasse, M. A. (2001) Safe and sound: a safety-critical approach to security. *Proceedings of the New Security Paradigms Workshop, Cloudcroft, NM*, 41-50.

Brusil, P. & Hale, J. (2005) The Shifting Sands of Security Management. *Journal of Network and Systems Management*, 13, 241.

Campbell, K. (2003) The economic cost of publicly announced information security breaches: empirical evidence from the stock market. *Journal of Computer Security*, 11, 431-448.

Chellappa, R. K. & Pavlou, P. A. (2002) Perceived information security, financial liability and consumer trust in electronic commerce transactions. *Logistics Information Management*, 15, 358-68.

Chen, Y. S., Chong, P. P. & Zhang, B. (2004) Cyber security management and e-government. *Electronic Government, an International Journal*, 1, 316-327.

Claver, E., Gonzalez, R. & Llopis, J. (2000) An analysis of research in information systems (1981-1997). *Information & Management*, 37, 181-195.

Darragh, D. M. & Darragh, S. M. (2001) On the 6 th day: A nonprofessional's view of information systems security. *Information systems security*, 10.

Dhillon, G. (2001) Challenges in Managing Information Security in the New Millennium. *Information Security Management: Global Challenges in the New Millennium.*

Dhillon, G. & Backhouse, J. (2000) Technical opinion: Information system security management in the new millennium. *Communications of the ACM*, 43, 125-128.

Dhillon, G. & Backhouse, E, J. (2001) Current directions in IS security research: towards socio-organizational perspectives. *Information Systems Journal*, 11, 127-153.

Doherty, N. F. & Fulford, H. (2005) Do Information Security Policies Reduce the Incidence of Security Breaches: An Exploratory Analysis. *Information Resources Management Journal*, 18, 21.

Dynes, S., Brechbuhl, H. & Johnson, M. E. (2005) Information Security in the Extended Enterprise: Some Initial Results From a Field Study of an Industrial Firm. *Workshop on the Economics of Information Security.*

Ezingeard, J.-N., McFadzean, E. & Birchall, D. (2005) A MODEL OF INFORMATION ASSURANCE BENEFITS. *Information Systems Management*, 22, 20.

Foote, P. & Neudenberger, T. (2005) Beyond Sarbanes--Oxley compliance. *Computers & Security*, 24, 516.

Furnell, S. M., Gaunt, P. N., Holben, R. F., Sanders, P. W., Stockel, C. T. & Warren, M. J. (1996) Assessing staff attitudes towards information security in a European healthcare establishment. *Med Inform (Lond)*, 21, 105-12.

Furnell, S. M., Gennatou, M. & Dowland, P. S. (2002) A prototype tool for information security awareness and training. *Logistics Information Management*, 15, 352-357.

Gallor, E. & Ghose, A. (2003) The Economic Consequences of Sharing Security Information. *2nd Workshop on Economics and Information Security*, 29-30.

Gonzalez, J. J. & Sawicka, A. (2002) A Framework for Human Factors in Information Security. *WSEAS International Conference on Information Security, Rio de Janeiro.*

Gonzalez, J. J. & Sawicka, A. (2003) The Role of Learning and Risk Perception in Compliance. *Proceedings of the 21st International Conference of the System Dynamics Society, New York.*

Gordon, L. A., Loeb, M. P. & Lucyshyn, W. (2002) An economics perspective on the sharing of information related to security breaches: Concepts and empirical evidence. *The First Workshop on Economics and Information Security.*

Gupta, A. & Hammond, R. (2005) Information systems security issues and decisions for small businesses: An empirical examination. *Information Management & Computer Security,* 13, 297.

Hansche, S. (2001a) Designing a security awareness program: Part I. *Information systems security,* 9, 14-22.

Hansche, S. (2001b) Information system security training: Making it happen, part 2. *Information systems security,* 10, 51-70.

Hazari, S. (2005) Perceptions of End-Users on the Requirements in Personal Firewall Software: An Exploratory Study. *Journal of Organizational and End User Computing,* 17, 47.

Holzinger, A. (2000) Information security management and assurance a call to action for corporate governance. *Information systems security,* 9, 32-39.

Hone, K. & Eloff, J. H. P. (2002) Information security policy-what do international information security standards say? *Computers and Security,* 21, 402-409.

James, H. L. (1996) Managing information systems security: a soft approach. *Proceedings of the Information Systems Conference of New Zealand,* 10-20.

Kankanhalli, A., Teo, H. H., Tan, B. C. Y. & Wei, K. K. (2003) An Integrative Study of Information Systems Security Effectiveness. *International Journal of Information Management,* 23, 139-154.

Karart, C. M., Karat, J. & Brodie, C. (2005a) Why HCI research in privacy and security is critical now. *International Journal of Human-Computer Studies,* 63, 1-4.

Karat, J., Karat, C. M., Brodie, C. & Feng, J. (2005b) Privacy in information technology: Designing to enable privacy policy management in organizations. *International Journal of Human-Computer Studies,* 63, 153-174.

Katerattankakul, P., Han, B. & Hong, S. (2003) Objective quality ranking of computing journals. *Communications of the ACM* 46, 111-114.

Keller, S., Powell, A., Horstmann, B., Predmore, C. & Crawford, M. (2005). Information Securirty Threats and Practices in Small Businesses. *Information Systems Management,* 22, 7.

Khalfan, A. M. (2004) Information security considerations in IS/IT outsourcing projects: a descriptive case study of two sectors. *International Journal of Information Management*, 24, 29-42.

Kim, E. B. (2005) Information Security Awareness Status of Full Time Employees. *The Business Review, Cambridge*, 3, 219.

Kokolakis, S. A. (2000) The use of business process modelling in information systems security analysis and design SA Kokolakis, AJ Demopoulos, EA Kiountouzis The Authors. *Information Management & Computer Security*, 8, 107-116.

Kotulic, A. G. & Clark, J. G. (2004) Why there aren't more information security research studies. *Information and Management*, 41, 597-607.

Krause, M. & Brown, L. (1996) Information security in the healthcare industry. *Information Systems Security*, 5, 32-40.

Krishnan, R., Peters, J., Padman, R. & Kaplan, D. (2005) On Data Reliability Assessment in Accounting Information Systems. *Information Systems Research*, 16, 307.

Kuhn, T. S. (1970) *The Structure of Scientific Revolutions*, Chicago, University of Chicago Press.

Kunreuther, H. & Heal, G. (2003) Interdependent Security. *Journal of Risk and Uncertainty*, 26, 231-249.

Leach, J. (2003) Improving user security behaviour. *Computers and Security*, 22, 685-692.

Lee, S. M., Lee, S. G. & Yoo, S. (2004) An integrative model of computer abuse based on social control and general deterrence theories. *Information and Management*, 41, 707-718.

Liu, L., Yu, E. & Mylopoulos, J. (2003) Security and Privacy Requirements Analysis within a Social Setting. *Proc. of RE'03*, 151–161.

Ma, Q. & Pearson, J. M. (2005) ISO 17799: "Best Practices" in Information Security Management? *Communications of the Association for Information Systems*, 15, 1.

Miyazaki, A. D. & Fernandez, A. (2000) Internet Privacy and Security: An Examination of Online Retailer Disclosures. *Journal of Public Policy & Marketing*, 19, 54-61.

Murray, W. H. (1998) Enterprise security architecture. *Information systems security*, 6, 43-54.

Nagaratnam, N., Nadalin, A., Hondo, M., McIntosh, M. & Austel, P. (2005) Business-driven application security: From modeling to managing secure applications. *IBM Systems Journal*, 44, 847.

Nyanchama, M. (2005) Information Security Management Enterprise Vulnerability Management and Its Role in Information Security Management. *INFORMATION SYSTEMS SECURITY*, 14, 29.

O'Rourke, M. (2005) Data Secured? Taking on Cyber-Thievery. *Risk Management*, 52, 18.

O'Brien, D. G. & Yasnoff, W. A. (1999) Privacy, confidentiality, and security in information systems of state health agencies. *American Journal of Preventive Medicine,* 16, 351-358.

Paliotta, A. R. (2001) Beyond the Maginot-line mentality: A total-process view of information security risk management. Based on COSO principles and supplemented by other control models and the author's experience. *Information systems security,* 10, 21-50.

Palmer, M. E., Robinson, C., Patilla, J. C. & Moser, E. P. (2001) Information security policy framework: Best practices for security policy in the E-commerce age. *Information systems security,* 10, 13-27.

Peltier, T. R. (1998) Information classification. *Information systems security,* 7, 31-43.

Pernul, G. (1995) Information Systems Security: Scope, State-of-the-art, and Evaluation of Techniques. *International Journal of Information Management,* 15, 165-180.

Pollitt, D. (2005) Energis trains employees and customers in IT security. *Human Resource Management International Digest,* 13, 25.

Poore, R. (2000) Valuing information assets for security risk management. *Information systems security,* 9, 17-23.

Riley, R. A. J. & Kleist, V. F. (2005) The biometric technologies business case: a systematic approach. *Information Management & Computer Security,* 13, 89.

Rindfleisch, T. C. (1997) Privacy, information technology, and health care. *Communications of the ACM,* 40, 92-100.

Ryan, J. J. C. H. & Ryan, D. J. (2005) Proportional Hazards in Information Security. *Risk Analysis,* 25, 141.

Saffady, W. (2005) Risk Analysis and Control: Vital to Records Protection. *Information Management Journal,* 39, 62.

Saint-Germain, R. (2005) Information Security Management Best Practice Based on ISO/IEC 17799. *Information Management Journal,* 39, 60.

Schlarman, S. (2002) The case for a security information system. *Information systems security,* 11, 44-50.

Schultz, E. E. (2002) A framework for understanding and predicting insider attacks. *Computers & Security,* 21, 526-531.

Schwartz, A. P. & Zalewski, M. A. (1999) Assuring data security integrity at ford motor company. *Information systems security,* 8, 18-26.

Shaw, E. D., Ruby, K. G. & Post, J. M. (1998) *Insider Threats to Critical Information Systems. Technical Report #2; ,* Washington. DC, Political Psychology Associates.

Siponen, M. T. (2001) On the Role of Human Mortality in Information System Security: From the Problems of Descriptivism to Non-Descriptive Foundations. *Information Resources Management Journal.*

Siponen, M. T. (2005) An analysis of the traditional IS security approaches: implications for research and practice. *European Journal of Information Systems,* 14, 303.

Spurling, P. (1995) Promoting security awareness and commitment. *Information Management & Computer Security,* 3, 20-26.

Stacey, T. R. (1996) Information security program maturity grid. *Information Systems Security,* 5, 22-33.

Stanton, J. M., Stam, K. R., Guzman, I. & Caledra, C. (2003) Examining the linkage between organizational commitment and information security. *Systems, Man and Cybernetics, 2003. IEEE International Conference on,* 3.

Stanton, J. M., Stam, K. R., Mastrangelo, P. & Jolton, J. (2005) Analysis of end user security behaviors. *Computers and Security,* 24, 124-33.

Stewart, A. (2005) Information security technologies as a commodity input. *Information Management & Computer Security,* 13, 5.

Straub, D. W. & Welke, R. J. (1998) Coping with Systems Risk: Security Planning Models for Management Decision Making. *MIS Quarterly,* 22, 441-469.

Sullivan, W. E. & Ngwenyama, O.K. (2005) How are Public Sector Organisations Managing IS Outsourcing Risks? An Analysis of Outsourcing Guidelines from Three Jurisdictions. *The Journal of Computer Information Systems,* 45, 73.

Summers, W. C. & Bosworth, E. (2004) Password policy: the good, the bad, and the ugly. *Proceedings of the winter international symposium on Information and communication technologies,* 1-6.

Tassabehji, R. & Vakola, M. (2005) Business email. *Association for Computing Machinery. Communications of the ACM,* 48, 64.

Thompson, E. D. & Kaarst-Brown, M. L. (2005) Sensitive information: A review and research agenda. *Journal of the American Society for Information Science and Technology,* 56, 245.

Thomson, K.-L. & Von Solms, R. (2005) Information security obedience: a definition. *Computers & Security,* 24, 69.

Toval, A., Nicolas, J., Moros, B. & Garcia, F. (2002) Requirements Reuse for Improving Information Systems Security: A Practitioner's Approach. *Requirements Engineering,* 6, 205-219.

Trim, P. R. J. (2005) Managing computer security issues: preventing and limiting future threats and disasters. *Disaster Prevention and Management,* 14, 493.

Trompeter, C. M. & Eloff, J. H. P. (2001) A Framework for the Implementation of Socio-ethical Controls in Information Security. *Computers and Security,* 20, 384-391.

Tryfonas, T. (2001) Embedding security practices in contemporary information systems development approaches T. Tryfonas, E. Kiountouzis, A. Poulymenakou The Authors. *Information Management & Computer Security,* 9, 183-197.

Turner, C. W., Zavod, M. & Yurcik, W. (2001) Factors that Affect the Perception of Security and Privacy of E-Commerce Web Sites. *Intl. Conf. on E-Commerce Research (ICECR,* 2, 628-636.

Vera-Munoz, S. C. (2005) Corporate Governance Reforms: Redefined Expectations of Audit Committee Responsibilities and Effectiveness. *Journal of Business Ethics,* 62, 115.

Vessey, I. (2002) Research in Information Systems: An Empirical Study of Diversity in the Discipline and Its Journals. *Journal of Management Information Systems,* 19, 129-174.

Von Solms, B. (2001) Corporate Governance and Information Security. *Computers and Security,* 20, 215-218.

Von Solms, B. & Von Solms, R. (2005) From information security to...business security? *Computers & Security,* 24, 271.

Von Solms, S. H. (2005) Information Security Governance - Compliance management vs. operational management. *Computers & Security,* 24, 443.

Vroom, C. & Von Solms, R. (2004) Towards information security behavioural compliance. *Computers & Security,* 23, 191-198.

Wen, H. J. & Tarn, J. M. (2001) Privacy and security in E-healthcare information management. *Information systems security,* 10, 19-34.

Winkler, I. S. & Dealy, B. (1995) Information Security Technology?... Don't Rely on It: A Case Study in Social Engineering. *5 thUNIX Security Symposium, June,* 5-7.

Yan, J. (2000) *The Memorability and Security of Passwords: Some Empirical Results,* University of Cambridge, Computer Laboratory.

Appendix A: Articles Included in Data Analysis

(Acquisti and Grossklags, 2003)
(Adams, 1999)
(Alner, 2001)
(Atkinson, 2005)
(Backhouse et al., 2005)
(Belsis et al., 2005)
(Beulen and Streng, 2002)
(Blatchford, 1998)
(Braithwaite, 2001)
(Brostoff and Sasse, 2001)
(Brusil and Hale, 2005)
(Campbell, 2003)
(Chellappa and Pavlou, 2002)
(Chen et al., 2004)
(Darragh and Darragh, 2001)
(Dhillon, 2001)
(Dhillon and Backhouse, 2000)
(Dhillon and Backhouse, 2001)
(Doherty and Fulford, 2005)
(Dynes et al., 2005)

(Miyazaki and Fernandez, 2000)
(Murray, 1998)
(Nagaratnam et al., 2005)
(Nyanchama, 2005)
(O'Brien and Yasnoff, 1999)
(O'Rourke, 2005)
(Paliotta, 2001)
(Palmer et al., 2001)
(Peltier, 1998)
(Pernul, 1995)
(Pollitt, 2005)
(Poore, 2000)
(Riley and Kleist, 2005)
(Rindfleisch, 1997)
(Ryan and Ryan, 2005)
(Saffady, 2005)
(Saint-Germain, 2005)
(Schlarman, 2002)
(Schultz, 2002)
(Schwartz and Zalewski, 1999)

(Ezingeard et al., 2005)
(Foote and Neudenberger, 2005)
(Furnell et al., 1996)
(Furnell et al., 2002)
(Gal-Or and Ghose, 2003)
(Gonzalez and Sawicka, 2002)
(Gonzalez and Sawicka, 2003)
(Gordon et al., 2002)
(Gupta and Hammond, 2005)
(Hansche, 2001a)
(Hansche, 2001b)
(Hazari, 2005)
(Holzinger, 2000)
(Hone and Eloff, 2002)
(James, 1996)
(Khalfan, 2004)
(Kankanhalli et al., 2003)
(Karat et al., 2005a)
(Karat et al., 2005b)
(Keller et al., 2005)
(Kim, 2005)
(Kokolakis, 2000)
(Kotulic and Clark, 2004)
(Krause and Brown, 1996)
(Krishnan et al., 2005)
(Kunreuther and Heal, 2003)
(Leach, 2003)
(Lee et al., 2004)
(Liu et al., 2003)
(Ma and Pearson, 2005)

(Boukhonine et al., 2005)
(Shaw et al., 1998)
(Siponen, 2001)
(Siponen, 2005)
(Spurling, 1995)
(Stacey, 1996)
(Stanton et al., 2003)
(Stanton et al., 2005)
(Stewart, 2005)
(Straub and Welke, 1998)
(Sullivan and Ngwenyama, 2005)
(Summers and Bosworth, 2004)
(Tassabehji and Vakola, 2005)
(Thompson and Kaarst-Brown, 2005)
(Thomson and von Solms, 2005)
(Toval et al., 2002)
(Trim, 2005)
(Trompeter and Eloff, 2001)
(Tryfonas, 2001)
(Turner et al., 2001)
(Vera-Muñoz, 2005)
(von Solms, 2001)
(von Solms, 2005)
(von Solms and von Solms, 2005)
(Vroom and von Solms, 2004)
(Wen and Tarn, 2001)
(Winkler and Dealy, 1995)
(Yan, 2000)

Proceedings of the International Symposium on
Human Aspects of Information Security & Assurance (HAISA 2007)

User Perception of the Security & Privacy Concerns of RFID Technology

F. Li[1], N.L. Clarke[1] and C. Bolan[2]

[1] Network Research Group, School of Computing, Communications & Electronics,
University of Plymouth, Plymouth, UK
[2] School of Computer and Information Science, Edith Cowan University, Perth,
Western Australia

Abstract

The adoption of wireless technologies has undergone unprecedented growth, beginning with cellular devices and now including Wi-Fi and Bluetooth. A relative newcomer to this domain is RFID, a shortwave communications technology capable of tagging almost any physical item. Unfortunately, as with all wireless technologies, RFID based technologies face a range of security and privacy threats. Indeed, many RFID systems completely lack any security or data protection provision whatsoever. This paper presents a survey into the end user perception towards security and privacy of RFID technologies in order to establish the level of understanding and concern towards its adoption. Noticeably, users are very responsive towards the use of wireless technologies and RFID in particular, however, only to the point at which their privacy is not negatively affected. 93% of respondents considered their privacy to be important. The survey established users do have a some appreciation of security and privacy but encouragingly are also aware of limitations in this respect and are eager to learn more.

Keywords

Mobile, Wireless, Security, RFID, Privacy.

1. Introduction

The dramatic uptake of wireless technology has provided a platform for the ubiquitous access to telecommunication and data networks, now central to the modern lifestyle. According to Cellular Online (2006) there are now over 2 billion mobile phone users and more than 130,000 publicly available WiFi hotspots in 130 countries, and these numbers are increasing daily. As with any growth in technology there is a need to balance the enthusiastic uptake with due concern towards security and privacy issues. This is evidenced by the multiple published vulnerabilities of WLANs, Bluetooth and other wireless technologies (Bolan, 2005; Wong, 2005).

Radio frequency identification (RFID) technology stems back to Faradays' discovery that light and radio waves were both forms of electromagnetic energy. The first concrete step towards the modern conception of RFIDs was made by Harry Stockman in his 1948 paper Communication by means of reflected power (Stockman, 1948), although it was not until 1973 that the first direct patent on passive RFID tags was lodged in America by ComServ (Cardullo, 2005). For the present RFID systems remain too expensive to completely penetrate all possible markets, with typical transponders costing around US$0.50 – US$1.00 (Sarma *et al.*, 2002). However, with mass production coupled with an open standard, supporters aim to bring the price down to around US$0.05 – US$0.10 which would see RFID integration into almost every facet of life. This has prompted predictions such as Boone (2004) who estimates that over 1.3 billion dollars will be spent on RFID integration in 2008.

As RFID technology is a member of the wireless family, it will inherit many commonly known wireless security and privacy threats currently linked to its wireless cousins. Beyond this, new attacks and threats are being discovered such as cloning, spoofing and kill attacks (Young, 2006; Bolan, 2006a). When such concerns are coupled with warnings that by 2016 Britain will increase the level of tracking to unknown levels, and the monitoring of individual consumer behaviour will emerge as an unavoidable facet of daily life, a worrying trend emerges (Ford, 2006). While it is likely that this dystopian image of the future is overly alarmist, as with all advancements in modern life, it is better for the public to have a clear idea of the security and privacy implications before product saturation becomes irreversible. Before a reasoned discussion may take place it is important to gauge the current level of awareness and fears surrounding the technology, and how these levels may impact on RFID's uptake and acceptance.

This paper presents the findings of a survey conducted to assess the level of public awareness regarding the security and privacy aspects of RFID technology. Section 2 presents background information on the problem of privacy and security of RFID technology. Section 3 describes the aim and methodology of the study, whilst section 4 presents the key results. Section 5 puts the results into context and provides a discussion on the implications of its findings. The conclusions are presented in the final section.

2. Security and Privacy Concerns of RFID

While RFID tags are typically silicon-based microchips, functionality beyond simple identification-upon-request may be achieved through the inclusion of integrated sensors, read/write storage, encryption and access control (Weis *et al.*, 2003). The downside to such operations is the increased production cost of the RFID tag away from the ideal market penetration cost, thus RFID security is often focused on reader security ignoring the obvious avenue of attack due to tag limitations (Choi et al., 2005).

Added to this is the debate as to whether the adoption of some RFID security measures is against the original vision of the technology. Knospe & Pohl (2004) argue that, as the primary purpose of RFID technology is as a cheap automated identification, it is unreasonable to expect that standard security mechanisms be implemented, due to the complexity and constraints of the resource. Ranasinghe et al. (2004) use this as a basis to propose that RFID security be implemented at the data processing subsystem and thus leave RFID tags merely for identification. However, others argue that security is possible without affecting tag cost or the original vision for the technology (Engberg et al., 2004).

Irrespective of these arguments, no single security or encryption standard for tags or readers has been adopted and thus many systems remain insecure (Weis, 2003; Henrici & Müller, 2004). Noting such issues, Hennig et al. (2004) voice the following concerns:

- *"Worldwide unique IDs enable tracking"* – the adoption of unique Electronic Product Code (EPC) tags will allow anyone who carries at least one of these tags to be tracked worldwide.
- *"Unnoticed remote reading without line-of-sight"* – the very nature of RFID technology allows RFID tags to be read without line-of-sight or any overt suggestion that they are being engaged. Such features make unauthorised access more likely.
- *"Small hidden tags and readers"* – As tag sizes decrease the ease with which it becomes possible to install hidden tags and readers increases.
- *"Tracking and profiling through sporadic surveillance"* – with a sufficient spread of strategically placed RFID readers it is possible to track and profile without the need for continual activation. Also, through the use of natural bottlenecks such as doorways it is further possible to ensure an individual passes within range of a reader.

3. Research Methodology

Although RFID systems have existed for some time it is only recently, with advancements in technology, the demand for RFID-based technology has begun to thrive. Organisations are utilising RFID technology for a variety of purposes with inventory control being one of the most popular. To date, many of the applications of the technology have been developed for business use, with few real large scale consumer RFID products. As such, it is suggested that public awareness of RFID technology is fairly low. Some people might be using the technology but unaware of its inner workings and classification as a RFID product – for instance, remote central locking devices for cars, the Oyster card, anti-theft devices in supermarkets and biometric passports. Nevertheless, as the popularity of RFID technology increases it is inevitable that consumers will begin to interact and directly utilise RFID technology. However, the nature of RFID introduces a number of additional concerns regarding the security and privacy of individual's information. As such, a survey was conducted to provide some preliminary insight into consumer's awareness of RFID, its possible applications, and the threats posed by the technology. The purpose of the survey was to assess the degree to which consumers would accept the benefits/additional services provided by RFID when facing threats to the privacy of their information.

Compared to other wireless technologies, such as cellular, Wi-Fi and Bluetooth, RFID is relatively unknown technology. Therefore, in order to maximise the usefulness of the survey findings and to provide a context/point of comparison, the survey asked a series of questions regarding the general topic of wireless technology, in addition to specific questions regarding RFID technology and its applications. This assisted in judging whether respondents were more or less concerned about security and privacy when compared to other more familiar wireless technologies. In addition, to ensure the survey received informed opinions from respondents, the survey included a paragraph of text describing RFID technology and how it can be used.

The survey comprised of four sections:

- Demographic questions to establish an understanding of the respondent population
- General security questions to gauge the level of awareness of security across wireless technologies
- General privacy questions to understand the privacy concerns of respondents regarding wireless technologies
- Specific RFID questions to assess the degree to which respondents are concerned over the use of the technology

4. Survey Findings

A total of 365 completed surveys were received. An analysis of the demographic questions reveals a fairly even gender split, with 54% male respondents compared to 44% female. The age of respondents, however, was found to be skewed heavily (77%) towards the 18-30 age group. There is also a notable bias in the level of education, with 96% of respondents declaring a university level education. Although both the age and education are clearly not representative of the general population, it is felt this bias would only serve to provide a more informed opinion. Prior surveys have demonstrated the 18-30 age group as having amongst the highest market penetration of mobile devices (Competitive Commission, 2003).

4.1 Awareness of Wireless Security

Prior to assessing the level of concern about wireless technologies it is prudent to establish the degree of awareness that exists within the respondent population. Figure 1 illustrates a breakdown of the principal consumer wireless technologies. The table clearly shows a lack of awareness of RFID technologies with only a third of respondents registering a positive awareness. Respondents were very aware of all other wireless technologies, receiving well over three quarters of the response, with the slight exception of the newer 3G telephony networks. It is interesting to note however, that 77% respondents stated they were aware of GSM/GPRS. Given the market penetration in Europe and the respondent population, the number of respondents actually using a GSM/GPRS mobile phone is likely to be greater than this, perhaps highlighting a lack of awareness of the underlying technology.

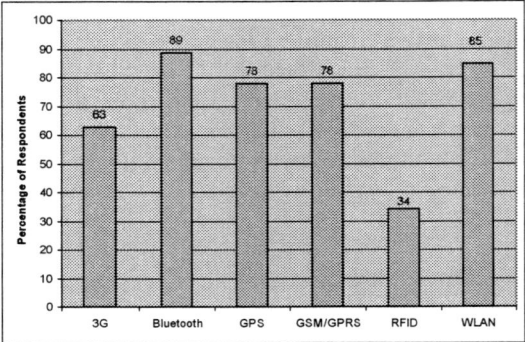

Figure 1: Respondent Awareness of Wireless Technologies

Respondents' use of the technology would also be a useful indicator as to the practical experience and subsequent relevance of responses they provide. Table 1 provides a breakdown of the usage of wireless technologies. The most frequently utilised technologies include WLAN and GSM/GPRS, although similarly to the earlier question, the percentage of the latter is surprisingly low. All wireless technologies have some level of usage from respondents, with RFID being the least utilised technology. Interestingly, although respondents were made aware of what RFID technology is with example applications, 34% of respondents were unsure if they used the technology. This lack of understanding regarding what technology they are utilising could have a significant impact upon the user, as they would either not understand, or misunderstand, what the security and privacy threats against the technology are.

	Very often (daily) (%)	Often (few times a week) (%)	Not very often (few times in two weeks) (%)	Few times a month (%)	Do not use it (%)	Do not know (%)
3G	11	5	5	10	62	7
Bluetooth	12	14	10	22	39	3
GSM/GPRS	30	13	6	12	30	9
GPS	8	6	6	16	57	7
RFID	3	3	4	7	49	34
WLAN	46	11	5	7	24	8

Table 1: Frequency of Usage of Wireless Technologies

Given the medium of communication, wireless systems exhibit additional security threats when compared to more traditional wired networks. War driving in particular is one well known example of such misuse. The perception of how secure a technology is will be essential to the successful widespread adoption of a technology. When asked how secure they consider wireless technologies to be, the largest proportion of respondents indicated "secure" – which if technically true and not a misconception is a reassuring statistic. It is however, also worth noting that over 55% of respondents indicated they felt wireless technologies to be only a little secure or not secure at all. Figure 2 presents theses findings and illustrates a skew towards feelings less secure overall.

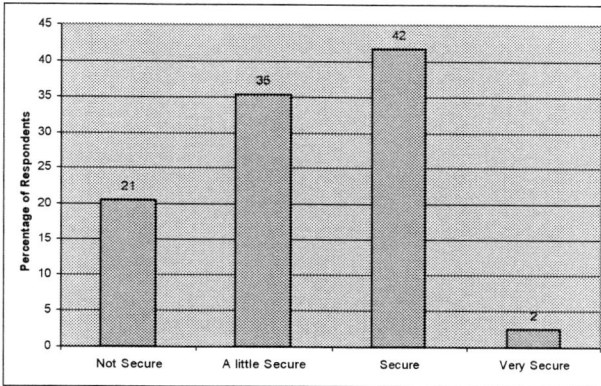

Figure 2: User Perception of the Security Wireless Technologies

Upon analysing respondents' use of security controls, it certainly seems that a good majority of users are aware of the typical countermeasures. As illustrated in Table 2, 79%, 78%, 72% of respondents use Antivirus, Firewalls and password authentication respectively on their laptop. Notably, the use of such controls is less on other types of mobile device, however, given the level of threat to date against these technologies (when compared to their laptop/desktop counterparts) and the maturity of the controls that exist for these platforms, it is not unexpected.

	Mobile phone (%)	PDA (%)	Wireless Laptop (%)
Antivirus software	7	25	79
Biometrics	2	8	7
Firewall	6	25	78
Password/PIN	45	56	72
Switch off when not using it	32	35	68

Table 2: Security Controls Implemented

Switching the device off when not in use has the potential to prevent exposure to a wide variety of threats, particularly if the threat is utilising Bluetooth. Typically, with the exception of laptops which have an obvious power consumption problem, the majority of respondents do not switch off their device when not in use. Interestingly, when asked specifically with regards to Bluetooth, a larger proportion of respondents (58%) did state they switched it off when not it use. It is unclear whether this is due to respondents' security awareness of for example Bluejacking, Bluesnarfing and Bluebugging, or perhaps simply through a lack of use of Bluetooth, or just to conserve power.

When asking respondents to rate their security awareness, the largest group of respondents chose the middle ground (40%). In fact, an analysis of the findings illustrated in Figure 3, show a fairly Gaussian distribution, with a very slight left skew towards poor. On average, respondents do feel they have a level of security awareness, which is reinforced when analysing the security controls they have put in place. It is worth pointing out, 32% of respondents felt they have a 'poor' or 'very poor' level of security awareness.

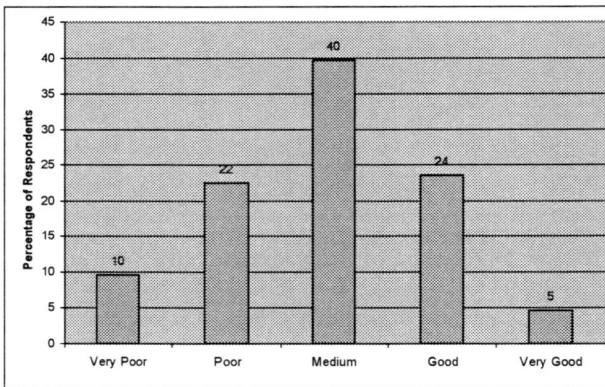

Figure 3: Respondents' Level of Security Awareness

Even though 68% of the respondent population felt they had 'medium' to 'very good' awareness of security for their devices, an overwhelming 86% stated that they would benefit from learning more about security. This figure shows how much more work needs to be undertaken in successfully educating the public regarding not only the security threats but also the implications of the technology they utilise.

4.2 Wireless Privacy Concerns

Personal privacy is becoming an increasingly important concern. As our use of technology continues to expand, the amount of personal information we have increases. The nature of the information can vary from direct sources such as corporate files, personal expense records, contact lists, personal and business messages, to more indirect sources or side-channel information, such as a person's location both past and present, frequency of use and shopping habits. Each of the different wireless technologies has its own unique properties and threat vectors.

However, what is clear from the respondents' perspective is their privacy is an important consideration. 93% felt their privacy to be at least important or greater, with the largest group of 41% selecting 'extremely important' as the most appropriate category.

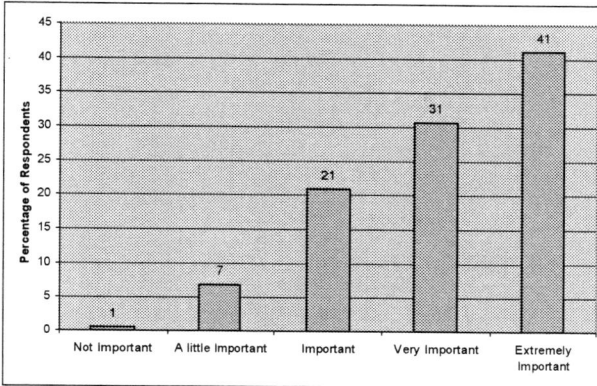

Figure 4: The Important of Privacy to Respondents

Respondents were particularly concerned (75%) about the possibility of being tracked via wireless technologies. Upon being presented with a list of wireless technologies that could possibly be used in tracking, only 5% of respondents felt none of the technologies could be used for tracking, as illustrated in Figure 5. Obviously, the degree to which these technologies can be utilised for tracking is somewhat dependent upon the technical capabilities of the adversary, with some technologies (such as WLAN) being far simpler to monitor than others (such as GSM/GPRS). Nevertheless, the perception and awareness of the respondents is on the whole quite high, with 4 of the 6 technologies listed eliciting a response of over 50%. A pattern again can be seen with the newer 3G and RFID technologies both receiving less attention. Although it is unlikely to have a direct impact currently given the fairly low penetration of the technology, both these technologies inherently offer a finer level of tracking through location-based services of 3G and inventory control of RFID than other wireless technologies traditionally have (with the exception of GPS of course). These services will provide an opportunity for an unprecedented level of personal tracking.

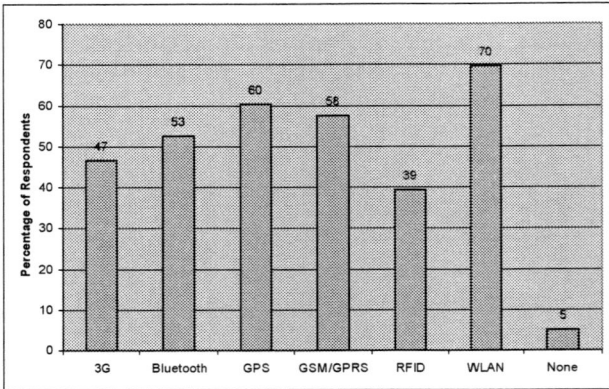

Figure 5: Respondent Perception of Tracking Technologies

Although respondents are clearly concerned about privacy and have some awareness of one key threat to privacy, tracking, it is clear that this knowledge and awareness is certainly not uniform across the respondent population. In fact, upon analysing the results from the level of privacy awareness the majority of respondents only feel they have a 'medium' level of awareness, with an overall skew towards a poor level (as illustrated in Figure 6).

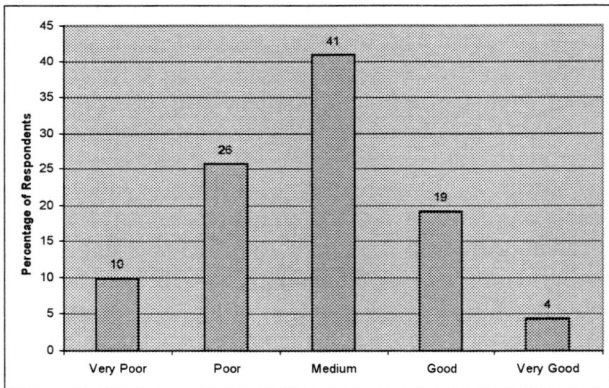

Figure 6: Respondents' Level of Privacy Awareness

4.3 Applications of RFID

In order to establish the degree of threat people might be open to, it is useful to understand the level to which they would be willing to use various types of RFID application. Respondents were asked to indicate what services they used from a prescribed list and which they would be willing to use with RFID based technology. The list of services/applications was compiled based upon their current applicability to RFID. As Figure 7 illustrates, respondents use a wide range of the services, with only inventory control resulting in a low percentage. This is expected, as the use of inventory control is not something that has particularly been adopted by consumers and resides as more of a business service. However, with the increasing widespread use of RFID, inventory control applications such as fridges understanding when the milk needs replacing or whether the butter has run out will become far more commonplace. This concept is not lost on the respondents with more positive responses towards its future use than current. That said, however, the overall response towards utilising these services when based upon RFID technology was not overly supportive, with the library system receiving the highest proportion of respondents (46%). It is unfortunately unclear why this is the case. It could be a result of the lack of understanding of how RFID technology can be applied, or moreover, perhaps a clear understanding and fear of using the technology because of potential security and privacy concerns. It is clear, however, that should these services look for widespread deployment, significant education and awareness training will be required before the technology becomes more acceptable to the general public.

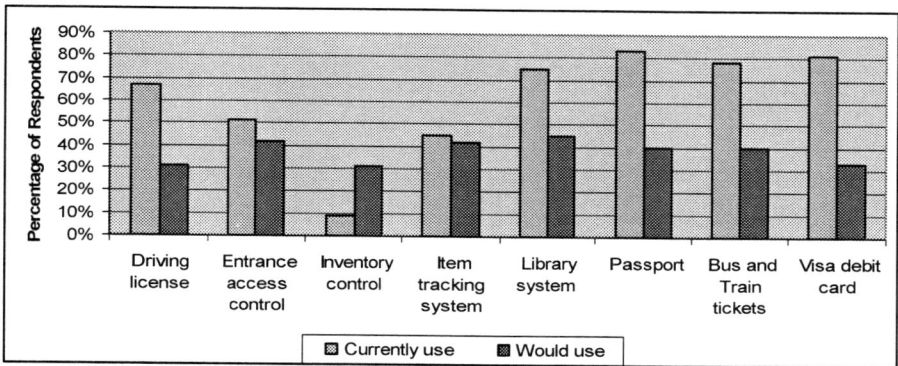

Figure 7: Services Respondents Currently Utilise and Would Utilise with RFID

The respondents were also given a couple of specific examples of how RFID technology could be implemented in the future. The examples given were the tagging of clothes, so that a washing machine could identify if an item of clothing was in avertedly included in the wash (e.g. a black sock in a white wash), and the tagging of food, for automated notification or ordering of food. As illustrated, in Table 3, respondents have conversely responded more positively towards these types of service, with over 60% in favour of tagged clothes and just over 50% in favour of tagged food. When compared to previous response (illustrated in Figure 7), this suggests perhaps that their responses were more based upon a lack of understanding of how the technology would be used.

	Yes	No
Tagged Clothes	64	36
Tagged Food	53	47

Table 3: Popularity of Future Applications of RFID

4.4 Privacy Versus Service

Given the specific concerns raised by RFID technology it was decided to establish the level to which people preferred the use of an application or service over the potential loss of privacy. Respondents were asked to comment on the same applications scenarios (tagged clothes and tagged food), but this time with respect to the level of privacy concern they would feel. The idea of other people knowing what is contained in your fridge appears to be a concern for respondents (59%). Respondents were a less concerned with people knowing what brand of clothing they wear, however, interestingly a large proportion of respondents didn't know if they are concerned, suggesting perhaps a lack of understanding towards the impact of such an application.

	Yes	No	Don't Know
Tagged Clothes	36	23	41
Tagged Food	59	22	19

Table 4: Privacy Concerns of Future RFID Applications

When comparing the results from Tables 3 and 4 it certainly presents a mixed distribution of responses. Tagged clothes are a more popular service with smaller concerns over privacy than tagged food. This mixed response illustrates that not all RFID based applications will necessarily receive the same level of acceptance, and a careful analysis of what the service will provide and how it will effect individuals (in terms of the information is provides to third parties) is imperative.

Further analysis also shows that a reasonable percentage of the respondents are neither interested in using these services and are concerned about the privacy aspects that might result from them. Businesses wishing to implement such services must be aware of these concerns and provide truly effective mechanisms for ensuring personal privacy. Recent literature has demonstrated simply killing the tags is completely ineffective (Bolan, 2006b).

The respondents were finally asked to assess what their preference was towards personal privacy versus the use of personalised services – based on the assumption that personal privacy could not be achieved if RFID based personalised services were in use. As illustrated in Table 5, two thirds of the respondent population chose personal privacy over personalised services. This reinforces the importance of ensuring RFID technology can provide a sufficient level of security and privacy before looking to implement personalised services.

	% of Respondents
Personal Privacy	67
Personalised Services	33

Table 5: Respondents' Preference between Privacy and Services

5. Discussion

The results have demonstrated that respondents are broadly aware of wireless technologies and well over half of them use one or more wireless technologies on a fairly regular basis. Although, respondents' knowledge of RFID technology lagged behind other consumer popular technologies, their prior experience and knowledge of wireless technologies will enable them to comment usefully on their perception of security and privacy for wireless and RFID technologies.

It would appear that respondents generally perceive wireless technologies to be secure, with a large proportion of them using more traditional security controls such as anti-virus, firewalls and authentication. However, even given this perception and usage, users' perceived level of security awareness is only average, with 86% stating they would benefit from learning more about security. It is interesting to note their acknowledgment of a lack of awareness and willingness to learn more about security. This is certainly a positive attribute, as a lack of awareness and education would make the deployment of any potentially harmful technology extremely difficult.

This understanding of how important security is to them is also reflected in how important they perceive their privacy to be. Overwhelmingly, respondents felt their privacy to be extremely important. However, as with security, respondents did not feel they have a good level of privacy awareness. With increasing wireless devices and services it is important that users perceive they are in control of their technology and have a good understanding of the possible threats when using it.

The popularity of possible RFID applications certainly suggests RFID technology has the potential to be as successful as many of the popular consumer wireless technologies. Indeed, recent years have already seen a number of larger consumer based application being successfully deployed. However, respondents have clearly indicated a preference towards privacy of their information over more useful or convenient applications. With 98% of respondents considering privacy to be at least an important consideration, it is imperative that RFID technology is embedded with security and privacy at all levels: the tag, the reader and backend systems.

6. Conclusions

It can be concluded from the survey that the most important considerations to users of wireless technology are security and privacy. Although wireless technologies have become successful independently of these to date, with the increasing popularity of these technologies, and increasing functionality and amount of information, it will only take a serious breach against personal information to make users aware of the real dangers to them and for them to subsequently refrain from using it.

The pervasiveness of RFID technology, and real lack of any degree of security, raises a question about its appropriateness as a consumer technology. Although it has been suggested by some authors (Kumar, 2003; Floerkemeier, Schneider &

Langheinrich, 2004) that the security and privacy concerns with RFID systems may be, in part, addressed through the creation of suitable policy and through organisational and legislative policies, it is unlikely that such measures will assuage concerns or deter an attacker. It is also notable that policy based approaches, including governmental and self regulation, have failed to prevent privacy or security concerns over other similar technologies. As such, Ranasinghe *et al.* (2004a, p.4) notes that all that RFID policy can really focus on is who may collect information, how it may be used, and ultimately who has ownership.

It is clear that, like many systems, in order to provide an effective and secure RFID system, a multi-facetted approach to security is required. Policies and legislation alone will not be a solution, but rather a series of measures including policy, legislation, technical controls and user education will be essential to ensure all stakeholders benefit from adopting the technology, not simply those looking to deploy it.

References

Bolan, C. (2005). Radio Frequency Identification - A Review of Low Cost Tag Security Proposals. *Proceedings of the 3rd Australian Computer, Network & Information Forensics Conference*. Perth, Western Australia: School of Computer and Information Science, Edith Cowan University.

Bolan, C. (2006a). *Strategies for the Blocking of RFID Tags*. Paper presented at the Sixth International Network Conference, Plymouth, UK.

Bolan, C. (2006b). *The Lazerus Effect: Ressurecting Killed RFID Tags*. Paper presented at the 4th Australian Information Security and Management Conference, Perth, Western Australia.

Boone, C. (2004), "RFID: The Next Big Thing?",
http://www.ftc.gov/bcp/workshops/rfid/boone.pdf, (Accessed 14 November 2006)

Cardullo, M. (2005). Genesis of the Versatile RFID Tag. *RFID Journal, 2*(1).
Cellular Online (2006), "Stats Snapshot", http://www.cellular.co.za/stats/stats-main.htm, (Accessed 09 November 2006)

Choi, E. Y., Lee, S. M., & Lee, D. H. (2005). Efficient RFID Authentication protocol for Ubiquitous Computing Environment. In T. Enokido, L. Yan, B. Xiao, D. Kim, Y. Dai & L. Yang (Eds.), *International Workshop on Security in Ubiquitous Computing Systems - SECUBIQ2005* (Vol. 3823, pp. 945-954). Nagasaki, Japan: Springer-Verlag.

Competition Commission. (2003). "Vodafone, Orange and T-Mobile. Reports on references under section 13 of the Telecommunications Act 1984 on the charges made by Vodafone, O2, Orange and T-Mobile for terminating calls from fixed and mobile networks". Competition Commission. http://wwwcompetition-commission.org.uk/rep_pub/reports/2003/475mobilephones.htm

Engberg, S. J., Harning, M. B., & Damsgaard-Jensen, C. (2004). Zero-knowledge Device Authentication: Privacy & Security Enhanced RFID preserving Business Value and Consumer

Convenience. *Proceedings of the Conference on Privacy, Security and Trust - PST*. New Brunswick, Canada

Floerkemeier, C., Schneider, R., & Langheinrich, M. (2004). Scanning with a Purpose - Supporting the Fair Information Principles in RFID Protocols. *Proceedings of the International Symposium on Ubiquitous Computing Systems - UCS*. Tokyo, Japan: Springer-Verlag.

Ford, R. (2006), "By 2016, they'll be able to watch you everywhere", http://www.timesonline.co.uk/article/0,,2-2433304_1,00.html, (Accessed 03 November 2006)

Hennig, J. E., Ladkin, P. B., & Sieker, B. (2004). *Privacy Enhancing Technology Concepts for RFID Technology Scrutinised* (No. RVS-RR-04-02). Bielefeld, Germany: University of Bielefeld.

Henrici, D., & Müller, P. (2004). Tackling Security and Privacy Issues in Radio Frequency Identification Devices. In A. Ferscha & F. Mattern (Eds.), *Pervasive Computing* (Vol. 3001, pp. 219-224). Vienna, Austria: Springer-Verlag.

Knospe, H., & Pohl, H. (2004). RFID Security. *Information Security, 9*(4), 39-50.

Kumar, R. (2003). Interaction of RFID Technology and Public Policy. *Proceedings of the RFID Privacy Workshop*. Cambridge, Massachusetts

Ranasinghe, D., Engels, D., & Cole, P. (2004). Security and Privacy: Modest Proposals for Low-Cost RFID Systems. In *Auto-ID Labs Research Workshop*. Zurich, Switzerland.

Sarma, S. E., Weis, S. A., & Engels, D. W. (2002). RFID Systems and Security and Privacy Implications. In *Workshop on Cryptographic Hardware and Embedded Systems* (Vol. 2523, pp. 454-470).

Stockman, H. (1948). Communication by Means of Reflected Power. *Proceedings of the IRE*, 1196-1204.

Weis, S. (2003). *Security and Privacy in Radio-Frequency Identification Devices*. Unpublished Masters, Massachusetts Institute of Technology (MIT), Massachusetts, USA.

Weis, S. A., Sarma, S. E., Rivest, R. L., & Engels, D. W. (2003). Security and Privacy Aspects of Low-Cost Radio Frequency Identification Systems. In D. Hutter, G. Muller, W. Stephan & M. Ullmann (Eds.), *International Conference on Security in Pervasive Computing - SPC 2003* (Vol. 2802, pp. 454-469). Boppard, Germany: Springer-Verlag.

Wong, L.W. (2005). Potential Bluetooth Vulnerabilities in Smartphones, In Proceedings of the 3rd Australian Information Security Management Conference, Edith Cowan University, Perth, Western Australia, pp.123-132.

Young, T. (2006), "Biometric passports cracked", http://www.computing.co.uk/computing/news/2161836/kacers-crack-biometric, (Accessed 15 August 2006)

Author Index